Europe at *Walking* Pace

Ben & Betty Whitwell

Third Age Press

ISBN 1 898576 13 0

Third Age Press Ltd, 1998
Third Age Press, 6 Parkside Gardens
London SW19 5EY
Managing Editor Dianne Norton

© Ben & Betty Whitwell

All rights reserved. This book is sold subject to the condition that it shall not, by way of trade or otherwise, be lent, re-sold, hired out or otherwise circulated without the publisher's prior consent in any form of binding or cover other than that in which it is published and without a similar condition including this condition being imposed on the subsequent purchaser.

Layout design by Dianne Norton
Printed and bound in Great Britain
by Intype

EUROPE AT *WALKING* PACE

BEN & BETTY WHITWELL

EDITED BY DIANNE NORTON

THIRD AGE PRESS

London 1998

Contents

[A map of each walk is given at the end of the chapters]

Introduction   7

The Jura in May, just emerging from winter   16
    Walk 1. Fesches-le-Châtel to Nyon ~15 days

The Alps - vertical landscapes and snow blocked passes   28
    Walk 2. Montgenèvre to St. Sauveur de Tinée ~14 days

Nice and the pre-Alps: suddenly summer   46
    Walk 3. Nice to La Palud sur Verdon ~ 9 days

Provence in the heat of July   58
    Walk 4. La Palud sur Verdon to St. Rémy de Provence ~18 days

The Rhône and Cevennes   74
    Walk 5. St. Rémy de Provence to Le Vigan ~ 13 days

Crosscountry to Carcassonne   87
    Walk 6. Le Vigan to Carcassonne ~11 days

Les Corbiéres and Les Fenouillèdes through the vineyards   100
    Walk 7. Carcassonne to Perpignan ~ 8 days

The Pyrenees and into Spain   114
    Walk 8. Perpignan to Monistrol ~15 days

Down the East Coast of Spain   131

Calpe Interlude   143

Gran Recorrido 7 through Alicante and Murcia Provinces   148
    Walk 9. Elda to Caravaca ~ 6 days

Granada and the Alpujarras   158
    Walk 10. Granada to Almeria ~ 6 days

Sunseed and Almeria   170

The Coast of Portugal   183

Santiago and the first part of the French Pilgrim Route   196
    Walk 11. Santiago to Burgos ~ 20 days

Pilgrim Route — Part Two   216
    Walk 12. Burgos to St. Jean Pied de Port ~14 days

France ~ again   232

... England, after all   243
    Walk 13. Downham Market to Caistor, Lincs ~7 days

Afterwords   252
    Photograph of the Ben & Betty Whitwell   253

Index of place names   254

More about Third Age Press   259

Par les soirs bleus d'été, j'irai dans les sentiers,
Picoté par les blés, fouler l'herbe menue;
Reveur, j'en sentira la fraîcheur à mes pieds,
Je laisserai le vent baigner ma tête nue.

Je ne parlerai pas, je ne penserai rien;
Mais l'amour infini me montera dans l'âme,
Et j'irai loin, bien loin, comme un bohémien,
Pas la nature, - heureux comme avec une femme.

Artur Rimbaud

In the blue evenings of summer, I will wander along the footpaths,
Pricked by ears of wheat, treading on the close-cropped grass,
Feeling its freshness under my feet, as I dream,
With the wind's caress soothing my bare head.

I will not speak, I'll think of nothing,
But an infinite love will fill my soul,
And I will go far, far away, like a vagabond,
In step with nature, - happy as with a woman.

INTRODUCTION

We are both over 60. What on earth possessed us to set off walking round Europe? Perhaps because we were footloose types from childhood. One of Betty's early memories is of setting off from home with her younger sister Pauline in tow, deliberately to try and get lost. As for me, so keen was I to tramp the Welsh hills with my father, that when I had no suitable footwear, much to his horror I donned my Wellington boots. There were those who thought our venture was the ultimate self-indulgence, but for some, we put ourselves beyond the pale for preferring to do something different and odd, in which they could see no value; others were full of admiration or envy.

Family and friends were generally encouraging, if in some cases rather puzzled by our obvious zest. We benefited greatly from their active help and support and particularly from their letters, received on our travels. Anyone who is away for as long as we were, will realise just how important these letters are. The idea of this book started out as a thank you to them, but then we realised that others, who were planning for holidays or retirement, would be interested too.

We have been married 31 years, have six children and eight grandchildren. When our children were growing up, we began to tackle some of the splendid long distance footpaths in England and Wales, as we could find the time, long weekends or annual holidays. In this way, we walked most of the Pennine Way, the Pembrokeshire Coastal Path, the South Downs Way, the Wolds Way, the Viking Way, Offa's Dyke and all of the South West Coast Path. For a start we relied on bed and breakfast accommodation, but after a while it became obvious that we would need a tent if we were going to walk continuously on some of these paths. This was a major step, not least financially, as it meant also investing in other lightweight gear; sleeping mats, bags and cooking equipment, and then backpacks big enough to carry it all. Then we would find that our precious bit of annual holiday was often bedevilled by bad weather on these UK paths.

So it was that we began to explore the French footpath network. We chose the Grand Randonnée (G.R.)10, west to east along the

Pyrenees, a magnificent walk which we again completed in annual holidays from work. In a succession of annual leaves we covered part of the G.R.5, which runs from Hoek van Holland to Nice. It was on our return from walking the wonderful stint over the elegantly rounded tops of the Vosges, that we took stock. We felt frustrated and envious when we met up with long term wanderers, such as a lone American, who we had met that summer, walking the whole of the G.R.5. We promised ourselves that one day we would take off like him. So when I retired early from my job as an archaeologist, we decided to go for it.

Planning for our journey

A key factor in making our plans for a long walk financially viable, was letting our house. We were fortunate in getting some ideal tenants, Andrew and Paula, who really valued what we had to offer — a cottage with an organic vegetable and fruit garden, which had been Betty's pride and joy. They also took on her wholefood business which she had operated from the house for some years, and our cats and chickens as well. Our weekly retirement income when added to the rent from letting the house, came to about three quarters of the amount that we had spent each week when walking during our holidays. We realised that we would have to keep strictly to a budget which amounted to £300 a week, or around £42 a day. Without the expenses of house and car at home, this budget had to cover, not only daily food and lodging for the two of us, but occasional expenses like replacement clothes, maps and guides, phonecard and public transport. Once on our travels, we carefully kept a daily note of all outgoings and averaged it over the week, to make sure that we kept in budget. Each time we had to get used to a new currency, the first thing we did was to establish the exchange rate, take a low figure to allow for fluctuations, and work out our daily quota.

The first part of our route planning was easy, since we wanted to complete the G.R.5 to Nice. Thereafter our plan was to walk westward and southward to the Pyrenees, with the idea of crossing them and moving south through Spain to have warmer weather through the winter. After that, we had only a few objectives on our itinerary; to join Betty's sister Pauline and her husband Peter, at Calpe for

Christmas and the New Year; to work at the Sunseed Desert Project, near Almeria in southern Spain; to follow the pilgrim route from Santiago de Compostela back into France; and if possible to visit old friends in France on the way back. It seemed to be tempting providence to plan in too much detail, until we saw how we fared.

We wrote to the Ramblers' Association and their Information Officer sent some useful articles and the address of the Long Distance Walkers Association (LDWA). The reply from the LDWA started, 'I do not like receiving letters like yours, they make me extremely envious. . .', and concluded with the useful advice to check our boots for scorpions and to watch out for snakes at all times. For our route from Nice to the Pyrenees, we received helpful suggestions from the Fédération Française de la Randonnée Pédestre (FFRP), giving us a detailed route plan such as the AA provide for motorists, but on a succession of long distance footpaths which would bring us to the Pyrenees. They also enclosed a catalogue of the published topoguides which covered most of our route. Such is the efficiency of the French service to walkers.

From England, we wrote to Tourist Information Offices along the route, for details of accommodation, and bought what topoguides and maps we could obtain for France. We didn't have a great deal of success with Spain but we did at least obtain from Madrid the 'state of the art' summary of the Spanish long distance footpath network, entitled *Gran Recorrido*. Although this lacked detail it was useful because it allowed us to plan in outline. Portugal remained a complete blank in our planning until we got there. In practice for all the countries, the Michelin 1:400,000 scale motoring maps were useful for initial planning, back-up *en route*, and to provide the wider picture. In France, we used the Series Verte 1:100,000 scale, which have the GR footpaths marked on them. In Spain for Catalonia only, there is good, recently-surveyed 1:50,000 cover with GR footpaths marked. For the rest of Spain, the Army 1:50,000 scale maps provide general cover but without the G.R. footpaths marked. It is not advisable to rely on these alone to find the way, and the same goes for Portugal. In France, there is also total coverage of the country at 1:25,000 scale, and in Spain partial coverage. Though this is the ideal scale of map for the walker, the weight and cost of the large numbers required when planning a walk of any length, make this series impracticable.

We both attended language classes, Betty to improve her very rusty French and I to start from scratch learning some Spanish. From childhood exchanges with a French family, I retained enough French to get by for everyday transactions. It made an enormous difference to the enjoyment of our travels to be able to communicate in and understand a bit of the languages involved.

Equipment

There are plenty of books which detail the sort of equipment that is needed for a walking holiday. We are not attempting that here. Basically we managed with the same amount of gear for long term, as for a three week annual holiday. One of the main differences in walking over a long period is that you have to settle for what is available along the route for replacements. When walking for just two or three weeks you can usually take with you everything you will require. A few items of equipment only are worth a special mention here.

The 80% wool, 20% nylon socks which Betty knitted by far outlasted all proprietary brands and were also the most comfortable to walk in. Both of us are fortunate in having 'good feet', but even so we look after them, using combinations of one or two pairs of inner soles and one or two pairs of socks. If you don't find ways of keeping your feet happy, then the whole enterprise is a non-starter.

For many years we have both walked in the cheap Spanish boots, marketed in England as 'Spanish fell boots', and in Spain simply known as 'work boots', *calzados de trabajo*. Their great advantages are that they are cheap, light and instantly comfortable. Betty had never been able to walk in the expensive, rigid boots that are favoured for walking, in spite of valiant efforts at breaking them in. Four pairs of these work boots lasted her for the whole journey. For my part, two pairs of Spanish boots lasted me to Tarascon, about 12 weeks. Then one pair of KSB boots passed on to me by Peter, lasted the rest of the time, around 50 weeks. But it has to be said that their natural life was extended by many weeks by repairs to the soles with slices of motor tyre attached with super glue.

The only other equipment which need specific mention here are our Globetrotter stoves - we carried one each. The cylindrical pan which, with its twin, doubled as a neat and sturdy container for the stove, was just the right size to boil enough water for two cups of tea or coffee. Reading about our walking you will realise just how vital these Globetrotters were to our survival. Whenever bushed, lost or waiting, out came a Globetrotter for a brew up. And the day always started with tea wherever we were and whatever the weather conditions. An efficient windshield is essential. Apart from brewing vital cups of tea, the 'trotters' must have saved us hundreds of pounds, since while in France, they cooked us nearly all our meals. In Spain and Portugal by contrast, we could more frequently afford to eat our main meal out, whilst still self-catering for breakfast and picnic lunches. The 190g cylinders of gas were widely available in all three countries.

The French topoguides are comprehensive lightweight guides, with page-size maps of the path opposite a written account of the route. They also give the distance between each landmark and spot heights along the way. The guides indicate where you will find shops, accommodation, camp sites and public transport. For stretches not covered by these topoguides, we bought the French Series Verte maps. What maps and topoguides we were able to buy in England, we parcelled up in numbered lots, to be sent out to our *poste restante* pick up points along the way. Where it worked smoothly, we re-used the envelope of the latest batch received, to send back those we had finished with.

For Spain, though the *Gran Recorrido* book gave details of the topoguides and maps for different routes, none of them were available in England. Once in Spain we found that the topoguides were often out of print or simply just not stocked by local bookshops. We tried following the 1:50,000 scale military maps, but apart from not having the waymarked footpaths on them, they were frequently very out of date. Most of those that we used had been published during Franco's regime and not revised since. Rumour has it that these maps had been deliberately kept short on detail, in order to make life difficult for any potential enemy into whose hands they might fall!

On the trail

The waymarked footpath network of France covers many thousands of kilometres over the whole country. The waymarking takes the form of bands of red and white paint, strategically placed on trees, rocks, buildings or posts. As far as possible, you walk on actual earth paths, farm tracks, old droveways or mule tracks, though occasionally, perforce, tarmac roads connect one section of path with another. The red and white two-way marking is generally excellent, though it usually fades out in towns and villages. The organisation of this footpath network has taken 50 years to build up. Though Spain is a long way behind, recreational walking is fast becoming popular, and the Camino de Santiago, the Picos de Europa, the Gredos and the Pyrenees, are justly very popular. European money has gone into rebuilding a viable walking route for the Camino in the last ten years. Maybe the next ten years will see the Portuguese starting to turn their attention to re-establishing walking routes. There, the old pilgrim footways have often disappeared under tarmac, only quite recently. So, obviously, the making again of footpaths is not going to be a high priority for quite a time.

By trial and error and experience, we established that 20 kilometres a day was a comfortable distance that we could keep up, if required, day after day. It was essential to know what was realistic, when we were planning our stints. Once we were on the trail, we were constantly on the lookout for up-dated information on camp sites and *gîtes d'étape*, since these were amongst the cheapest options for an overnight stay. As members of the International Hostellers, we made use of Youth Hostels in all three countries. On the pilgrim route in northern Spain cheap accommodation was provided in *refugios* at intervals along the way.

It was a particularly important part of our strategy for keeping healthy and living cheaply, that where possible we cooked for ourselves. We kept our basic travelling pantry stocked with emergency stores which could come in if there were no shops. This consisted of, olive oil, quick-cook pasta and/or rice, pasta sauce, parmesan cheese, a packet of dehydrated soup, teabags, coffee, sugar, powdered milk and a bottle of salad dressing. In the hotter temperatures it is impossible to carry butter. We carried the European Union form E111 by which you can recoup the cost of some medical care. Fortunately we never had to use it.

Keeping in touch

Letters from family and friends were a vital part of our support system. We collected our mail from pre-arranged *poste restante* addresses along our route. Generally this worked well, but there were occasions when we probably confused people by changing our schedule. Usually mail was kept for a maximum of 14 days and then returned to sender. The odd mishap did occur, for instance a pair of Betty's boots disappeared without trace within the French postal system. The Spanish system of *la lista de los correos* worked in the same way. From our side we tried to keep up a steady flow of cards and letters, and the occasional up-dated progress bulletin. We also phoned our daughter Becky roughly once a week.

How to use this book

Parts of our journey could be followed as shorter walks, complete in themselves. These are described in a day by day itinerary with a sketch map, table of distances and other useful information. In a journey as long of ours there are bound to be some parts we couldn't really recommend as continuous walks but they all had their particular interest, and we have tried to convey this as a series of snapshots in the chapters about the east coast of Spain, Portugal and returning through France. Interludes in our travelling, relating to Calpe and the Sunseed Project are there to give a more in depth look at aspects of life in Spain.

Thanks

We need to say a special 'thank you' to daughters, Becky and Susie for help on the home front; Becky with mail, bank account and being our lifeline at the end of a phone; Susie with the rent. Between them they dealt efficiently with any repairs or maintenance needed at home. They really made the whole venture possible. Pauline and Peter gave their support and encouragement throughout, with a regular supply of letters. They were also extremely patient with us during the writing up phase, when we shared a flat in Spain. Our tenants, Andrew and Paula, temporarily stationary wanderers themselves, egged us on and to prove they meant it, paid the rent with great regularity! Our friends, Peg and Geoff Bruton, who live in Spain, very efficiently fielded our mail whilst we perambulated Spain and Portugal.

Andrew McCloy personally, whilst employed as Information Officer of the Ramblers' Association, helped us in the planning stage and encouragement when it came to seeking a publisher. Roger Perrier of the Fédération Française de la Randonée Pédestre gave us advice on routes and sent out topoguides; both he and the President of the FFRP sent us extremely welcome letters of support. Whilst in Spain, we owe Tomás Vega Fernández, of the Mountaineering Club of Murcia University, our thanks for his courtesy and help in supplying us with unpublished information, which allowed us to walk a beautiful section of the GR7 in the mountains of Murcia. Geoffrey Williams, of the Ramblers Association (Wales), was a prompt and helpful correspondent, particularly in promoting the elusive European Ramblers Association, an idea whose time has definitely come, since one of their stated aims is to provide information for those who are planning long-distance walks in Europe. However, we personally failed to get any response from them.

Throughout our travels, we had a particular respect and gratitude for the anonymous help received from countless tourist information offices, *mairies* and *ajuntamientos* in sorting out our way ahead and lodgings. Without the unsung work of the waymarkers from local walking groups, particularly in France, the great national network of footpaths would often have been a closed book to us.

Getting the text on to a word processor was made possible with the help of our son Phil, who selected a suitable portable lap-top and printer for us. His expertise and tuition guided the work to a successful conclusion, without too much tearing out of hair. (We understand now why he keeps his short!). We are grateful to elder son Jon's help with the cover design. When we ran into an operating impasse in Spain, we had invaluable help from Jack and Anita Bremner, and then from Duncan Allan, headmaster of the Sierra Bernia International School.

Useful information, addresses and bibliography

Ramblers Association
1 - 5 Wandsworth Rd
London SW8 2XX

Fédération Française de la Randonnée Pédestre
14 Rue Riquet, F-75019 Paris, France

Federación Española de Montaña y Escalada
Alberto Aguilera 3-4
E-28015, Spain

Clube de Actividades Ar Libre
Centro Associativo du Calhau Tartue Florestal de Monsant
Lisboa 1,600, Portugal

European Ramblers Association,
Walter Sittig (Sec.)
Wilhelmshoher Allee 157 - 159
D-34121 Kassel, Germany

Stanfords, 12 - 14 Long Acre
Covent Garden
London WC2P 9LP (For maps and walking books).

Jarvis Books, 57 Smedley St East Matlock, Derbyshire DE4 3FQ (Catalogue of walking books available)

La Tienda Verde, Maudes
23 & 38, 28003 Madrid,
Spain (for Spanish maps and guides)

International Hostellers Association, 8 St Stephens Hill, St Albans, Herts. AL1 2DY

Euro-Lines and National Express Offices at Victoria Coach Station, London (for cheap international travel)

Rough Guides to France, Spain and Portugal

Trekking in Spain, Lonely Planet Guide Books

Guía de Estaciones Verdes by RENFE. *Book of walks* available from train stations throughout Spain.

Walking Europe from Top to Bottom by Margolis and Harmon: Sierra Club Travel Guide (good for equipment etc.)

Sunflower Books: several titles for areas of France, Spain & Portugal, with local walks from fixed bases.

THE JURA IN MAY
~ JUST EMERGING FROM WINTER

Our first objective was to complete the Grande Randonnée 5 (G.R.5), the long distance footpath from Hoek van Holland to Nice starting at Belfort in the broad valley between the Vosges and the Jura, at the western edge of the fertile plain of the river Rhine. The Vosges are rounded sandstone tops, the Jura, by contrast, are a rugged limestone range, which give their name to a whole geological era, the Jurassic. We were to meet up with many different limestone landscapes in our 15 months' journey.

The Jura mountains were our training ground for the months to come, where we got acclimatised to living our lives outdoors. In these beautiful and quite remote mountains, with their high, flowered meadows and wooded slopes, winter lasts for eight months, is harsh, and had only recently given way to spring as we set off, so we were cold and wet at times. If it had not been for our impatience to get going, we could have done with delaying our start for another three or four weeks. But even then, in these mountains there is no guarantee that the weather would have been any better. Also we were conscious that if we delayed too long, we would probably be running into bad weather as we crossed the Pyrenees later in the year.

This was it! Time to go. No more waiting and wondering. No more time to let the doubts creep in. No more waking up at night thinking, 'My god, what are we doing, swapping our comfortable, stay-at-home life for a roaming outdoor life and the complete unknown.' We packed our backpacks, walked out of the door and across the churchyard, caught a bus to Hull and another to the ferry and were sailing out of the Humber estuary towards Zeebrugge, as evening fell. The most difficult step had finally been taken and all the worries about last minute problems, exchanged for a wonderful feeling of excitement and anticipation for what lay ahead. The following day we travelled by train across Belgium and France to Belfort to be greeted by pouring rain. All our resolutions to search out the cheapest forms of accommodation were cast aside as we dived into the nearest hotel.

Table of Distances

1. Fesches-le-Châtel - Vandoncourt	8.5km
2. Vandoncourt - St. Hippolyte	26.0km
3. St. Hippolyte - Fessevillers	19.0km
4. Fessevillers - La Côtote	22 0km
5. La Côtote - Villers-le-Lac	23.0km
6. Villers-le-Lac	(rest day)
7. Villers-le-Lac - Vieux Chateleu	17.0km
8. Vieux Chateleu - Montbenoît	13.0km
9. Montbenoît - Pontarlier	22.0km
10. Pontarlier	(rest day)
11. Pontarlier - Malbuisson	16.0km
12. Malbuisson - Mouthe	31.0km
13. Mouthe - Chapelle-des Bois	20.0km
14. Chapelle-des-Bois - Le Bief de la Chaille	25.5km
15. Le Bief de la Chaille - Nyon (train)	24.0km

Day 1: Fesches-le-Châtel — Vandoncourt

We had deliberately planned a short stint of only eight and a half kilometres for our first day, to ease ourselves gently into what was to be our long term way of life. So we bought some bread and cheese and discovered that we could take a bus at 11.15am to Fesches-le-Châtel to pick up our footpath. It was around midday as we set off in cool windy weather. We stopped to eat in the woods, using some huge felled beech logs as our table. In the stillness we listened to the wonderful birdsong and realised with a surge of happiness that our long walk really had begun.

At Vandoncourt, wondering where the *gîte* was, we were hailed from a phone box by Thea, a Dutch woman who was staying at the *gîte* and led us there. By advertising, she had managed to get a series of walking companions to accompany her on the G.R.5. One had just returned, she was due to meet the next one on the following day.

Thea was fascinated by all the details of our organisation, and thereby gave us several phrases which stayed with us throughout our travels. She called the notebooks, which Betty used, one for details of accommodation, another for our expenditure, our 'leetle books'. Like us, she too was travelling 'low budget'. Her aim to reach Nice in four weeks impressed us, as we had allowed double that time.

Day 2: Vandoncourt — St. Hippolyte

Thea went to St. Hippolyte by road to meet her companion. We set off on the footpath in bright sunshine, but as we walked on, it clouded over and started to rain. Pouring rain drove us to picnic in a disused barn where we waited in vain for the rain to stop, and eventually continued, through lovely valleys, wooded with mature beeches, to Villers Blamont, and along the crest which, here, forms the border between France and Switzerland. It was hard going as the path was, by now, very slippery but we walked doggedly on to Chamesol — there was nowhere to shelter, and to stop was to be instantly cold.

We downed black coffees and cognacs at the village café. Enough was enough, and we phoned for a taxi to take us the remaining seven kilometres to St. Hippolyte. As we had left England with lingering coughs, this cautious but expensive step didn't cause much heart-searching. At St. Hippolyte we met up with Thea with her Dutch walking companion, Henni. So, blowing our budget wide open, we stayed at the Hotel des Terrasse and all had dinner together, overlooking the river Doubs, pronounced 'Doo', as the young waitress told us. This had been a fairly inauspicious start to our travels but we did not for a moment have any second thoughts and were greatly encouraged by the good company of our two Dutch friends, who were as hooked on the trail as we were.

Day 3: St. Hippolyte — Fessevillers

It was good walking, high up along the Doubs valley to Soule Cernay where we crossed the river. We climbed up to 800m then down to Courtefontaine where we had a draughty picnic lunch in a magnificent stone-built village wash-house, roofed over and with benches all round the sides. Though disused now, this must have been a focal point in the village once, where the women would gather and make a social event of their washing. But on a day like this one, sunny but with a cold wind, it was no place to linger too long. We pressed on through woods and meadows, filled with a profusion of wild flowers, such as you rarely now see in England — dark blue salvias, side by side with the paler blue of forget-me-nots, yellow bedstraws, buttercups and pansies, pink campions and ragged robin, white stitchwort and many more, amongst the lush grasses of the meadows.

When we arrived at Fessevillers, it seemed too early to stop and I was all for pressing on another 7km to Goumois but Betty was for stopping and her good sense prevailed. Now that we were retired, there was no need to cram in as much mileage as possible. We could please ourselves and take our time. We were first in to the *gîte* and lit a fire in the large open fireplace. Next came Thea and Henni, who made a beeline for the fire, and others followed. Milk was available from the farm, wine and beer from the *auberge* and cheese, yoghurt and eggs from the *fromagerie*. Everyone took turns to cook their supper on the one gas ring available and sit on benches round the big wooden table near the fire to eat. Replete and warmed, we made our way to sleep in the dormitories.

Day 4: Fessevillers — La Côtote Refuge
A magic walk through dewy meadows, where our tracks were picked out in the low early light, crossing a carpet of spiders' webs, brought us down to Goumois to meet the river Doubs again. Sometimes the

path hugged the river bank, and sometimes it wound high above. Past the ruined mill, Moulin de la Carbonière, right on the riverside, we came to the so-called Echelles de la Mort, a metal ladder fixed in the vertical rock. This formed a variant of the G.R.5, which we were happy to avoid. From there, we followed the road steeply up to the refuge at La Côtote. On this final, rather knackering stint, we were overtaken by a Citröen van which hooted at us, and in the back we could see Thea and Henni waving madly. Though somewhat sickened to see that they had hitched a lift, while we were still toiling up the hill, we waved back.

When we arrived at the refuge half an hour later, Henni came out to greet us, waving teabags. It was a gesture at the same time welcoming and absurd, which we often laughed about later. Henni was deceptive. She appeared at first sight to be always nervous, somewhat scatty and rather ill at ease on the trail. But she had been walking years before with her sons on Mont Blanc and now she wanted to go there again. It was she who had insisted on climbing the vertical Echelles de la Mort, which we had avoided. Her hidden stores of energy and nerve were constantly surprising.

There was a large party of French staying at the refuge, who were setting about preparations for their evening meal with the usual national enthusiasm for food. They started their meal with a great plate of oysters each, some of the party having brought them from Brittany that day. This was followed by several courses, and the wine flowed. Beside this feast, our country omelette and bread seemed paltry. But we quickly forgave them for eating so well, when Thea managed to cajole one of the men into selling us a bottle of wine from their more than adequate stocks. If Thea had persisted in her shameless advances we would probably have been **given** several bottles. This small, lean, 60+ woman with her bright red hair, certainly had a way with her.

Day 5: La Côtote — Villers-le-Lac
Going steeply down a little country lane, we met the river once again opposite Blaufond on the Swiss side, and wended our way along the wooded bank, again with limestone cliffs to either side of the river.

My back was not behaving itself that afternoon, when the uneven stony surface of the path tended to jar it. I was spurred to a slightly less than snail-like pace by the news that there was half an hour to go till the last ferry from Sant du Doubs left for Villers-le-Lac. This information was passed on to us by two French children, who sped by me when called by their parents up ahead, *'Allez, venez vites'*. Betty set the pace and with the aid of a trusty hazel staff gathered along the way, I managed to gather a bit of speed, knowing that the alternative, to a supreme if knackering effort at this point, was another seven kilometres of walking. The boat trip was sheer bliss. The densely wooded banks glided peacefully by, smoothly and effortlessly.

The *gîte* at Villers was open but empty. As is the trusting tradition, we installed ourselves and went in search of some food. We half expected that Thea and Henni would be there but we were on our own, apart from a visit for the rent from the friendly *guardienne*. Sadly, we never met up with our Dutch friends again.

Day 6: Villers-le-Lac

This was a rest day, which started with a proper breakfast of bowls of hot chocolate, croissants and lots of orange juice. We got all our dirty clothes washed by hand and were able to dry them in the *gîte* garden, as it was a perfect sunny day — the best yet. Writing up our journal and post cards to the family took up most of the day. Betty toted up our accounts, and our daily outgoings were about 280ff (about £40) a day, averaged over seven days, so we were well within our budget ceiling of 300ff. In the evening we walked down into the town and phoned our daughter Becky, to check that all was well and report on our progress so far.

Day 7: Villers-le-Lac — Vieux Chateleu

We climbed from 750m to 1200m to reach the Côte du Maix Musy, a ridge along the Franco-Swiss border. The path up was via a succession of plateaux with meadows and woods to either side. Flowers at this higher altitude were noticeably different, with abundant pale blue violets and yellow oxslips as well as cowslips. We also saw both trumpet and smaller star gentians, the former dark, the latter a bright, lighter blue. There was just one small field full of them, then no more. A rare treat. Reaching the auberge at Vieux Chateleu by 4.30pm, we decided not to stop, in retrospect a mistake. After finding the *gîte* at Grand Mont closed, we ended by wearily retracing our steps there. We were able to camp free outside the auberge, in which we were pathetically grateful to be able to eat fondu and salad. This was a pleasant end to a long day, as it was about 8.30pm when we got pitched up. The auberge was one of the huge, wide buildings, with low-pitched roof and wide overhang, which are characteristic of the Jura. As dusk fell and we were settling down for the night, we heard howling and baying from the edge of the forest on the opposite side of the road. Betty fancied it might be wolves, but we were really too tired to worry.

Day 8: Vieux Chateleu — Montbenoît

It was a beautiful dawn with tiers of mountains outlined by the early sun and in the morning light we could see that the noise we had heard the night before, came from pens housing husky dogs, which all started wagging their tails, when we emerged from our tent. So much for the wild creatures of the night. Unwashed and unbreakfasted, we were off to an early but bad start, soon losing the way for lack of markers around Mont Chateleu. Though we should have been avoiding its summit by a long way to the west, we ended up after two hours wandering, having breakfast near its top! Fortified, we soon found the route. The path took us steeply down through woods to Les Gras.

After walking through open meadowland and woods, we reached Monbenoît by 3.0pm, well ready for an early halt. We'd had difficulty following the path that day, even when we had relocated the markers, because many of the field gates were very firmly wired or chained up. This meant that we had either to struggle over them with our packs on, or still more cumbersome, take them off and pass them over. The man and his English wife at the Tourist Office explained that the cattle had just been let out from their winter quarters and were, not surprisingly, full of *joie de vivre* and inclined to burst open the gates if they were not very firmly secured. We were directed to the *gîte d'étape* at La Grosse Grange, — a huge rambling medieval building by the river Doubs, probably the main grange or farm for the monastery there, which was founded in the 12th century. It was much warmer outside than in this enormous stone building, so full of character and so lacking in comfort. The showers were like dungeons, with only a trickle of tepid water. In this month of May, the Jurassiens had just finished with eight months of winter, so it probably felt wonderful to be out in the sunshine, after being snowed up for ages.

Day 9: Monbenoît — Pontarlier
Armed with fresh bread bought from the bakery, we set off walking along the river Doubs, then headed steeply up, opposite Maison-du-Bois, climbing by road and by paths through the woods, from 780m to 1,000m. After a steep climb, we sat having a well earned tea break. It was beautifully tranquil, a lovely moment of quiet with only birdsong punctuating the silence. After the descent to Les Alliés, we set off in the wrong direction, but quickly realised the error of our ways. Part of our problem was, that we were relying too heavily on following the red and white markers, without checking on the map. Hereabouts there were red and white markers everywhere, since there were several other paths, not just the G.R.5 that we were following. It was a long and beautiful descent to Pontarlier.

As we waited for the Youth Hostel to open its doors at 5.0pm, we were just brewing up, when into the car park swept a couple of large German BMW motorbikes. They halted side by side in unison, and the riders in full black leather gear stepped off them, again in unison, like some motorised ballet, flipped up the lids of their tail boxes and immediately opened up bottles of beer and started getting them down. Whilst I like my tea, the sight of the amber liquid disappearing down their throats, was almost more than I could bear. Once installed in a bedroom to ourselves, we became aware of the overloud strains of opera, which I presumed came from the radio of the Germans in the next room. Later when we came back to our room, the disembodied radio sounds were still continuing but now they were talking in French. I had to come face to face with my unreasonable racial prejudice, when I realised that the sounds actually came from our own radio, which I must have inadvertently switched on when unpacking, as there it was talking away to itself in my pack.

Day 10: Pontarlier
We woke to rain, and decided to stop over at Pontarlier and do the domestics, washing and shopping. At the hostel, there was no competition for the use of the tiny kitchen. We watched a bit of TV that evening, quite a novel experience. France was beating Tonga at rugby, rather predictably it seemed to me, though the enthusiastic French commentator made it sound like an epic victory. As I drifted off to sleep, I thought of my mother, whose 90th birthday had been celebrated that day at Oswestry, and hoped that it had gone off alright.

Day 11: Pontarlier - Lac Saint Point, Malbuisson
By 8.0am the sun was coming through, so we hoofed it down the road to La Cluse et Mijoux. Here we picked up the G.R.5 at the Fort de Joux, a castle perched high on rocks, at the junction of three valleys. Thereafter we had a steep ascent, through Le Crossart wood, to reach a lunchtime stop with excellent views over Lac de Saint Point. Then a superb walk in strong sun, through meadows above the lake, brought us to a campsite right by its side at Malbuisson. Cooking on the ground outside the tent is never an easy operation, but once we had eaten, we took the rest of our wine and glasses down to a seat at the edge of the lake. It was a perfect sunset, with fishermen on the lake, kids playing on pontoons in the water and the two of us gazing out over the idyllic scene. But the night was cold and dewy, which had us thankful for dawn and a cup of tea.

Day 12: Malbuisson — Mouthe
We went up and over the wooded top to Fouillon et Loutelet and walked along the valley using a disused railway track as far as Les Hopitaux Neufs. The *gîtes* along the G.R.5 at Le Grand and Le Petit Morond were closed, so we decided to go road-ways to Mouthe. We slogged down the highway in broiling sun, through Metabief, given over to 'le ski', with lots of new chalets and blocks of flats. The saving grace of this road-walking was that we were following the young and beautiful river Doubs, with its rolling open meadows and wooded tops above. At Gelim, where we joined a more major road, Betty and I raised our thumbs together, and instantly got a lift in an Alfa Romeo with a young ski champion, who set us down in Mouthe. Because

there was no affordable accommodation in the village, we trekked the three kilometres out to a campsite at the source of the river Doubs, and slept beside its rushing waters.

Day 13: Mouthe — Chapelle-des-Bois

The source is a mighty torrent, which issues from the limestone cliffs. Sometimes the course of such rivers has been traced many kilometres underground. This was a particularly magical spot, which we were glad not to have missed, because, having issued with such force from the rock, the river begins its above ground course by wandering lazily amongst a peat bog, before collecting itself for its journey through the lovely water meadows, which we had seen the previous day.

We climbed through woods to the new ski centre at Le Lernier, now off-season and empty of people. Our route took us through woods and meadows in the briefly warm sun, and then we were once again trekking up hill through the dank sunless woods of Bois Bannal. Here patches of snow lingered high up in the woods, and through and around these, grew masses of near-white and pale-purple crocuses. There is a very special quality to these mountain flowers which come up through the snow, as if out of dead ground. The potent combination of their fragile beauty and the power of nature makes them a wonderful surprise in a dark and gloomy place. Though fairly tough going, we kept up a good pace to reach the summit at 1200m. Thereafter it started to rain, and rained on and off as we descended to Chapelle-des-Bois, which we reached soon after 4.0pm. As this was a distance of 20 km. from Mouthe, done in seven hours, we felt that we were at last beginning to get into our stride.

Day 14: Chapelle-des-Bois — Le Bief de la Chaille

The formidable ridge of the Risoux escarpment, over which the path went, looked decidedly uninviting. The air was pregnant with rain and we thought better of submitting ourselves to an inevitable and prolonged soaking, so we went by road to Les Rousses and walked to the Youth Hostel, where we were the only customers. We heard barking from upstairs and eventually a rather touselled young man poked his head out of the upstairs window. Though clearly of a philosophical turn of mind, he lacked the essential bonhommie, or experience of pretending it, to make a good *guardien*. This was a 'green' establishment, recycling waste, making compost and generally encouraging care for the environment, at least in theory. It was plastered with posters about AIDS and, generally on this damp May evening, had a cheerlessness about it that was hard to shake off. We tried to imagine it in high summer with crowds of young holidaymakers there enjoying themselves, but the attempt failed. At least we were able to light a fire, but there was not enough wood to keep it in for long.

Day 15: Le Bief de la Chaille — Nyon
Rain once again! We watched orienteers out in the downpour with their maps, searching for their route, as large rivulets streamed down the window panes. Eventually we decided to ring for a taxi. Back in Les Rousses we found that there were no buses from there, but an hourly train service ran from La Cure to Nyon, across the border into Switzerland. So in spite of all our avoiding and delaying action, aimed at not walking in the rain, we found ourselves doing just that to reach La Cure. The journey down to Nyon on the shores of Lac Léman, should have given us spectacular views of the Alps, but all was obscured by low cloud and rain.

Ben & Betty's field kitchen

Useful information, addresses and bibliography

Tourist Office: 2bisRue Clémenceau, 90000 Belfort. Tel.03 84 55 90 90.

Youth Hostel 2, Rue Jouffroy, 25300 Pontarlier

Youth Hostel Le Bief de la Chaille, 39220 Les Rousses

Youth Hostel 6, Rue de Madrid, 90000 Belfort

Airport Basle\Mulhouse \Fribourg.

Train stations in Belfort and Nyon.

Autobus from Belfort to Fesches-le-Chatel.

The Jura — map locations: Belfort, Fesches-le-Châtel, Vandoncourt, R. Doubs, St Hippolyte, Fessevillers, FRANCE, La Cotote, Villers-le-Lac, Vieux Chateleu, Montbenoît, Pontartlier, Malbuisson, Mouthe, SWITZERLAND, Chapelle-des-Bois, Bief de la Chaille, LAC LEMAN, Nyon

Key to maps
— G.R. or Pilgrim Route
------ Our alternative
- - - Public transport
-·-·- National boundary

Footpaths of Europe, Walking the GR5: Vosges to Jura

Walking Europe from Top to Bottom. The Sierra Club Travel Guide to the GR5, by Margolis & Harmon

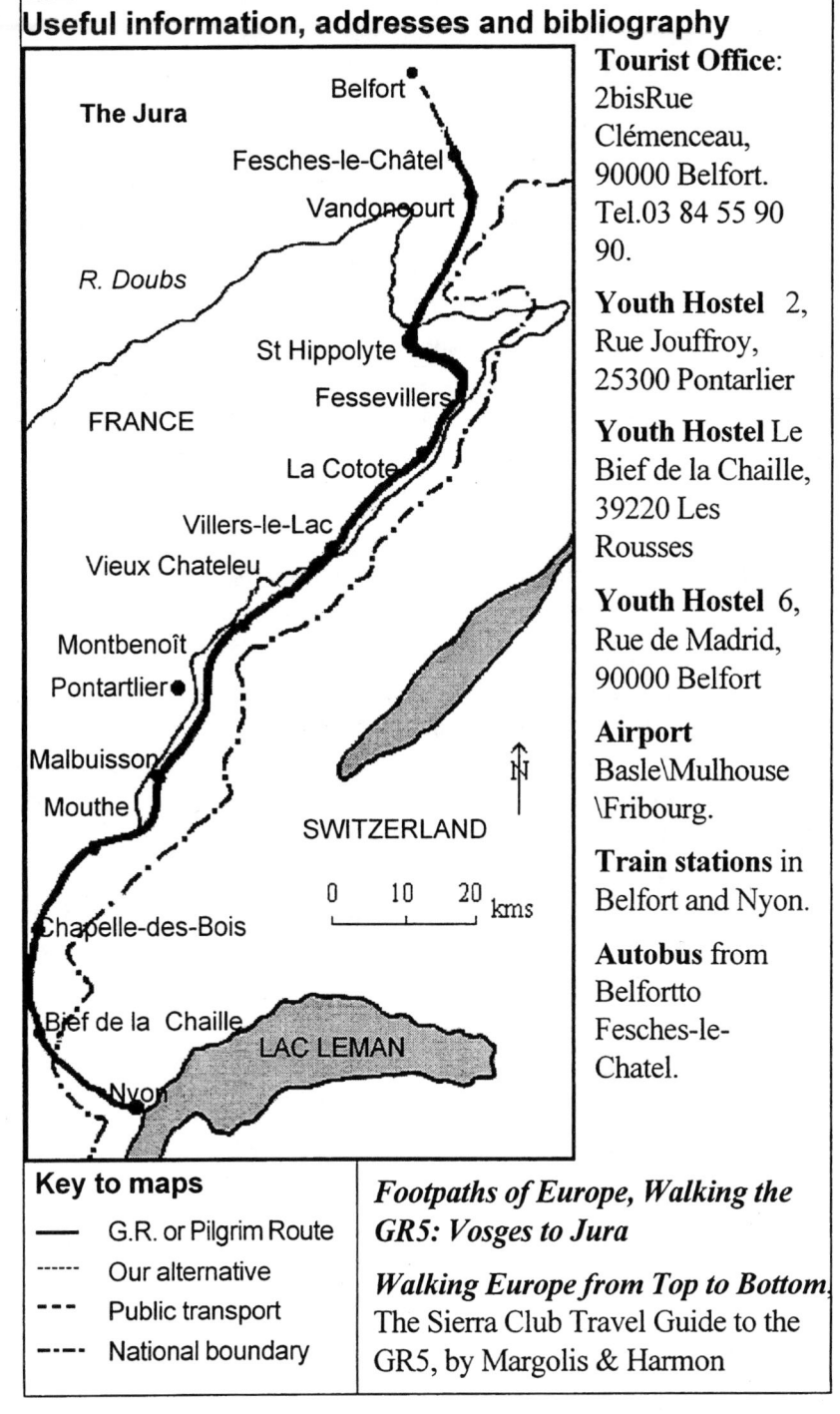

THE ALPS
~ VERTICAL LANDSCAPES AND SNOW BLOCKED PASSES

We neither got psyched up to, nor correspondingly let down by, the Alps. Robbed of views of them from the Jura and then from Lac Léman, we had not seen their snowy summits as we approached. For us the reality of the Alps was pass after pass still blocked, after unseasonably late falls of snow. So we had to go chasing our path southwards, from one mountain valley to another. This required large detours on foot, by train and bus, and by lifts when we could get them, to get round each mountain mass.

From Nyon we crossed by paddle steamer to Thonon-les-Bains, with the low cloud and drizzle persisting in obscuring all views of the Alps ahead. The crossing was enlivened by a party of elderly Swiss citizens on an outing, who were determined to have a good time. At Thonon we camped near the lake, beside a nature reserve around the outfall of the river Dranse, and one of the few places in Europe where beavers are still to be found. Drinking a bottle of local wine with our meal that evening, we noticed that it came from the nearby estate of the Duc de Savoie. Here, we were in Haute Savoie, now firmly part of eastern France. However in 1720 the Duc de Savoie became the King of Sardinia and as recently as the last century, Savoie was an independent kingdom, which included Sardinia and a large part of what is now northern Italy.

Our first day of walking up into the mountains was to a mere height of 1000m, but we went off with high hopes and a touch of trepidation, to start our assault on this fabled mountain range, in the knowledge of the many that had preceded us. We thought of Belloc crossing the Alps in a light suit and mac, taking no heed of the difficulties, with his mind set on his goal of the Eternal City of Rome. And then of John Hillaby pounding this way, in complete disbelief of Belloc's account of his crossing of the Alps. We thought also of the Ostrogoths, Huns, Romans and of Hannibal and his great crossing into Italy. In fact, though the Alps are a formidable range, throughout history, the makers and breakers of empires have continuously crossed back and forth through their passes. Our Sierra Club guide gave it a tremendous build-up, 'For the megawalker, the Great Crossing of the French Alps along G.R.5 is one of the supreme experiences of hiking anywhere on earth.'

As we climbed the final stretch up through wooded slopes from the valley of the river Dranse to reach our *gîte* at Les Clouz, we came upon a sight unique in all our thousands of kilometres of walking on G.R. footpaths. There was one of the *balisageurs*, the behind-the-scenes workers, with his pots of red and white paint, waymarking the footpath. Though seldom seen at their work, they are the unsung heroes of the footpath network. Without their efforts, even with the best maps in the world, you would be hard-pressed to find your way. This one was Jean Schmidt, who ran the *gîte*. He it was, who struck the first blow towards shattering our illusions of completing the whole of the G.R.5 footpath through the Alps, when he warned that unseasonally late falls of snow, had meant that many of the passes remained blocked, even though it was now June. A phone call on our behalf to the next *gîte* along the route confirmed that the pass at Le Dent d'Oche was impassable. That night the spectacular view ahead, miraculously cleared just before dark to show snowy summits to the east where our route should have taken us.

By morning, cloud had descended again with fine drizzle as forecast. So began the first of our long, depressing detours in search of the next point to the south, where we might pick up the path again. At Chamonix there is a Weather and Advice Centre for walkers and climbers, from which we got the news that all passes in that area over 2000m were likely still to be blocked. As our route included several passes over this height, we reluctantly decided we would have to make another detour to arrive at Modane, south of the Vanoise Massif. While at Chamonix, the clouds cleared briefly and gave us a glimpse of Mont Blanc, gleaming in the brilliant sunshine, recalling Rimbaud's 'lances of proud glaciers, white kings'. Some people staying at Chamonix told us that they had been there for two weeks and it was the first time they'd had a clear view of the peaks.

At Modane we were roughly 130 kilometres nearer to the Mediterranean and felt confident that we would be able to take up our path again. But when the official in charge of the camp site rang on our behalf to the refuge on Mt. Thabor at 2500m, the tale was once again of snow. 'But', he said with a malicious gleam in his eye, 'If you get up there before 10.0am, the snow will still be frozen hard enough to walk on' — knowing very well that this would mean leaving by 4.0am in the dark and walking a path where snow obscured the waymarks. Relenting a little, he told us that he had heard that Col Galibier beyond Valloire, was open. So ever hopeful, we set off to walk through the Forêt d'Orelle and on by Valmeinier, one of the closed up ski towns, to reach Valloire for an attempt to cross this col and rejoin the G.R.5 at Refuge Druyière.

The Alps

We were somewhat sickened to hear that it was indeed true that Col Galibier **had** been open. The snow ploughs had gone out especially to open it up for a cycle race the Sunday before but now, we were told by the uninterested girl in the Tourist Office, the road would have become totally blocked again. There was nothing for it but to admit defeat once again and get down to the valley to begin the tedious process of a series of trains and buses to get us to our next hope to the south at Montgenèvre. Here we stayed at the *gîte* of an English couple, John and Judy. John gave us the encouraging news that all high spots on the G.R.5 to the south should now be passable. He advised that we did the first leg past Briançon to Villard St. Pancrace the next day, so as to reduce the following day's stint over the Col des Ayes to Brunissard.

Table of Distances	
1. Montgenèvre - Villard de St. Pancrace	15.0km
2. Villard de St. Pancrace - Brunissard	22.0km
3. Brunissard - Château Queyras	8.0km
4. Château Queyras - Ceillac	21.0km
5. Ceillac - Guillestre (bus)	15.0km
6. Guillestre - Vars-les-Claux	16.5km
7. Vars-les-Claux - St. Paul-sur-Ubaye	16.0km
8. St. Paul-sur-Ubaye - Jausiers	22.0km
9. Jausiers - Bousieyas	34.0km
10. Bousieyas - St. Etienne-de-Tinée	22.0km
11. St. Etienne-de-Tinée	(rest day)
12. St.Etienne-de-Tinée - Roya	17.0km
13. Roya - Refuge des Longons	28.0km
14. Refuge des Longons - St. Sauveur-sur-Tinée	36.0km

Day 1: Montgenèvre — Villard St. Pancrace

For a change it was a beautiful sunny morning, and we picked up the *balisages* of the G.R.5, greeting them like long lost friends that we had almost given up hope of seeing again! It was a beautiful wooded walk down the valley towards Briançon, only marred by going wrong. We were striding out along a forest track, chatting away, when suddenly we were confronted by a young armed soldier barring our way. He explained that they were having target practice at Fort Dauphine. Having found the G.R.5 we had carelessly gone and lost it again, as we should have turned off to the right down into the valley. He politely sent us back to find it, and we eventually arrived at Briançon over the spectacular military bridge. The whole place was bristling with 18th and 19th century forts, protecting France's eastern frontier at this vulnerable point. Briançon, on a rocky outcrop at the meeting of five valleys, had for centuries been a frontier post guarding the Col de Montgenèvre, one of the oldest and most important passes into Italy. The previous night, John had told us that his friend, who kept the village bar at Montgenèvre, had a collection of pre-Roman and Roman coins from around the village. The local tradition was that **this** was the pass by which Hannibal crossed into Italy.

We had to wait until 6.0pm before setting off for Villard St. Pancrace because we wished to consult the mountain guides about the state of the path ahead. They told us the old familiar tale of snow, but while we were still in their office, in came two lads who had come over Col des Ayes that very day. Yes, there was plenty of snow, but it was not impassable. Our hearts rose. Armed with food and more fuel for the globetrotters we walked out the six kilometres to the *gîte*, cautiously optimistic after our hopes had been raised and dashed so many times.

Day 2: Villard St. Pancrace — Brunissard

At long last we crossed over our first alpine col. High up the valley there was a ramshackle collection of timber houses where we found some shelter for our picnic before pushing on up to Col des Ayes at 2477m, having started at 1242m. We had to struggle through snow across the path in two or three places on the way up but it was nothing too serious. It was exhilarating to be in the snow with brilliant sunshine and crisp clear air. For us this was an historic moment. Two young couples with husky dogs reached the col at the same time as we did. On the south side, the snow was rather more dicey since the path was, in parts, completely obliterated. Below the snow line, as we made the steep zigzag descent, our path was accompanied by masses of pasque flowers and yellow and dark blue pansies, which seemed to sprout out of the bare rock.

Pra Première could be seen far below us, a flat area of brilliant green grass with wooden barns in its centre, surrounded by mountains — a magical and unexpected spot after descending from a region of snow with barren rock and sparse vegetation. We found the *gîte* at Brunissard after several hours' descent through woods and had it completely to ourselves. Sitting out in the brilliant evening sun, we ate our supper. As soon as the sun disappeared behind the mountains at about 8.30pm the temperature dropped abruptly.

Day 3: Brunissard — Château Queyras

Going through meadows and woods to La Chalp, we were joined by a wire-haired dog who tagged along for several kilometres, as far as Lac de Rone, an idyllic lake amongst pine trees. We were beginning to wonder how we would get rid of him, when he spotted a party with their picnic spread out and abruptly abandoned us to investigate.

Château Queyras was an extremely impressive medieval fortification set on a rock at a junction of valleys. We found a camp site along the valley and cooked our supper, crouched in the lea of the shower block, keenly watched and nudged on the back of the neck by a husky dog, which belonged to the camp *guardienne*. A French couple told us that the next day's col, Col Fromage was quite clear of snow though they had heard that Col Girardin at 2700m, further south, was still impassable.

Col Fromage

Day 4: Château Queyras — Ceillac

It was a fine morning with heavy dew, and a long but beautiful walk took us up through woods interspersed with meadows. We emerged from the woods on to open grassland, nearing the head of the valley. From the grassy slopes we then climbed up to a rocky ridge, which we thought was Col Fromage from the deep sink holes in the tufa rock, like gruyère cheese. So we took triumphal photos of one another, thinking that we had reached another landmark along our itinerary. But a young Dutch couple who had just come from the true Col Fromage told us that it was another half hour or so onwards. To get out of the wind we picnicked in one of the sink holes and then walked on. The bright, crystalline, off-white tufa gave a lunar look to the landscape, especially where it had eroded into deep wide channels. Above the path to our left, rose two giant pinnacles of bare rock, Pointe de la Selles (2745m) and Pointe de Rasis (2844m). From them great spreads of scree, devoid of vegetation, stretched down to our path and below. We threaded our way across the scree and came suddenly to the wide grassy ridge of Col Fromage, itself at 2301m.

The difference between this col and Col des Ayes under 200m higher was marked. That extra height meant that the snow had remained, whereas at Col Fromage people were lying on the grass sunning themselves and admiring the view of snow capped peaks. We descended steeply towards Ceillac on a path zigzagging through the scree, retained with wooden boards and posts and planted to either side with larches, in order to try and arrest avalanches, which clearly are a serious problem thereabouts.

Ceillac at 1639m was a proper village with cow shit on the streets, from which huge, wooden, double doors opened on to multi-purpose barns. There were sheep in pens being injected. By contrast to the stone buildings of the village, the ski shanty town on its edges appeared jerry-built and boarded up. We shared our *dortoir* at the *gîte* with a young Parisian who had just arrived to walk the Tour de Queyras.

Day 5: Ceillac — Guillestre

At Ceillac we had the bad news confirmed that Col Girardin, which was on our next stint, was indeed still blocked by snow. This was a real blow because we had just enjoyed two superb days walking on the G.R.5 only to find that we had to make yet another detour. The 7.0am bus would take us down the steep valley to Guillestre. It was late arriving, there was only one other passenger beside ourselves and the driver was in a tearing hurry. He drove at breakneck speed through 15 kilometres of uninhabited wild gorges with pine forests to either side of the ravine, which at intervals had been eaten into by landslides. Betty was not at all happy with the driver's nonchalant way of taking one hand off the wheel to scratch his head, while negotiating the hairpin bends.

At the Youth Hostel, we parked our bags and, since nobody was around, we brewed up tea at a table in the shade, as by now the sun was very hot. Seeds from the poplars in the garden were blowing everywhere, and the sweet scent of the philadelphus in full bloom, wafted across to us. Without our packs we wandered down into the impressive valley of the river Guil and passed the fort of Mont Dauphin, constructed at this strategic point to protect the frontiers of France. The fort, standing on a natural promontory with sheer cliffs, at the junction of the rivers Guil and Durance, was built by Vauban. This 17th century engineer was given the task of protecting France's frontiers with massive brick-built forts. During our long walk, we came across his work several times at points of strategic importance. The rock of this promontory is a sort of conglomerate, in which giant rounded boulders are set in a core material, which produces a hard, but easily weathered formation. Fantastic pinnacles of weathered rock produced a dramatic landscape. The most imposing of these was named *La Main du Titan*, as it looked like a huge hand with stubby fingers and thumb, gesturing to the sky on top of a 100m column. By the river Guil, we watched a group of English skilfully manoeuvring their kayaks on the swift water. The lanes around Guillestre were filled with masses of sweet smelling honeysuckle and dog roses.

Day 6: Guillestre — Vars-les-Claux

From Guillestre, the nearest point to get back to the G.R.5 was at St. Paul sur Ubaye. After a steep climb up through woods, following the river Vars, we came to a stone mason's yard, where we asked if we could use their shady stone table and benches to eat. Roaming cockerels approached, seeming to expect some crumbs. In a delapidated corrugated iron shed, the workmen pushed huge granite blocks mounted on rails, towards the screaming vertical blades of a circular saw. We came across a spectacular variety of orange lilies as we crossed the bridge over the river. Then steeply up out of the beautiful wooded valley, we emerged into the hot sun and high meadows at Vars St. Marcellin, where we stopped briefly to drink the clear cool water issuing from the newly built village fountain. This was entirely constructed of wood and surrounded by tubs of brightly coloured flowers. Vars-les-Claux was another ski town, with virtually nothing open.

Day 7: Vars-les Claux — St. Paul-sur-Ubaye

We climbed to Col de Vars, the start of the Parc National de Mercantour, where there were rows of trinket shops around a large car park for tourists to admire the view. This was our reward for a long and demanding climb, as the panorama opened out expansively to the south. Moving on swiftly, we watched helicopters ferrying equipment to workers on the lines of pylons above us, as we descended on the road.

At St. Paul-sur-Ubaye, we shared the very pleasant accommodation there with a lone French walker, Hubert, who had followed the G.R.5 over from Ceillac via Col Girardin that day. It had been a nightmare he said, as he had gone up to his thighs in snow every two or three steps over the col. Our advice had been that it was still impassable, whereas Hubert had been told that it was alright. He said that he certainly wouldn't have tried it, had he know what it was going to be like. And what is more, he had met walkers who had turned back from the cols Mallemort and Vallonet, which lay on the next day's stint for us. We couldn't believe that having just re-found the red and white markers of the G.R.5, our plans had to change again. Whoever would have believed that snow would still be blocking passes this far south and well into June. Now we would have to walk down the valley to Jausiers, cross over the Col de Bonette to regain the G.R.5 at Bousieyas. This was a real low point in our journey. Not for the first time we wondered whether we should head south for the Mediterranean, giving up on the Alps altogether, but this we were reluctant to do.

Day 8: St. Paul-sur-Ubaye — Jausiers

At Jausiers, we stocked up before pressing on towards Col de Bonette. This would reduce the very long stint for the following day. We climbed on the road for an hour or so, and found a place to camp wild. Perhaps because the weather was hot and overcast, we were plagued by flies and mosquitoes. Even though it was a beautiful spot, the insect life made it impossible to appreciate it. Cooking outside the tent was an ordeal. Having got thoroughly bitten while we gobbled down our food, we did at least manage to keep the little devils out of our inner zipped compartment.

Day 9: Jausiers — Bousieyas

After the previous night's seemingly imminent storm, the weather was in fact sunny, so we packed up and were off by 7.30am. We speculated about where Hubert might be. Was he still at Jausiers or was he storming up the hill about to catch up with us at any time? On one of the many hairpin bends, we stopped for tea and were wished *bonjour* and *bon courage* by cyclists, straining hard on their pedals as they toiled up in low gear. These reciprocal good wishes continued as each one passed, giving us a fellow-feeling which spurred us on. One exclaimed, 'Are you going right up to the top with all that on your backs?' They were taking part in a three col event, tackling the Col de Bonette first. Though the walking was hard work, it was very rewarding, as we climbed up through successive plateaux of pastures. A highlight, which can only be appreciated fully by those who have camped rough the night before, was the luxury of an all-over wash in a beautiful stream in the hot sun. It was incredible that the water we were washing ourselves in, came from the melting of snows higher up the mountains, and yet it was pleasantly warm in the rushing stream.

Once again we saw crocuses poking through the snow, both white and purple, and the delicate, purple frilled-edged, flower that the French call *la petite soldanelle*. After passing the forts and barracks of successive frontier campaigns, we reached the col by 3.0pm. There was deep snow as we approached and snow ploughs had cleared the road itself, leaving a wall of snow about three metres high. We had convinced ourselves that we were ahead of Hubert, having seen no sign of him. It was really quite cold as we approached the pass, so we paused for tea in a sheltered spot before we started the long descent from this our highest altitude of 2800m. Though our highest, this col gave us no great feeling of elation as the previous two had, mainly because it was a road crossing and it was jammed with motor bikes and cars.

When we arrived at the *gîte*, who should be sitting there but Hubert, quietly triumphant. He had started at 6.0am from Jausiers, reached the col by 12.0 and had arrived down at Bousieyas by about 3.0pm - some walker. He was carrying about the same weight as us, though in fairness we might mention that he was at least 15 years younger! Hubert shared his bottle of wine with us that night. This had been our longest day so far at 34 kilometres.

Day 10: Bousieyas — St. Etienne-de-Tinée
We rejoined the G.R.5 and went up and over the Col de Colombière. The descent into St. Dalmas de Selvage was long and very steep. At times the path went across landslips in a hairy sort of way. We composed ourselves with cups of tea and lunch once had we reached some firm and level ground at the edge of the village. From there we decided to take the road the last few kilometres into St. Etienne. We arrived dishevelled and in a lather of sweat and bumped into the dapper Hubert, who had got himself installed in a hotel as he had arrived too early for the *gîte*. St. Etienne-de-Tinée was a real town, unspoilt by *le ski*, set at the junction of two steep wooded valleys.

Day 11: St. Etienne-de-Tinée
The Festival of Transhumance was taking place that day in St Etienne so we made it a rest day. It was an occasion when all the shepherds celebrated the moving of their flocks to their summer pastures. A wonderful experience and a chance to see many of the skills of this mountain region in action, smithing, shearing, leather-working, cheesemaking, breadmaking, roofing and hut building, and lots more. Shepherds had brought their long-suffering sheep, which were standing in pens, packed close together in the hot sun. At lunchtime the restaurants put on a special meal, and everywhere was packed with people sitting out at tables, under awnings which lined the streets. The crowds seemed to be made up mainly of local people from the surrounding towns and villages, dressed up in their Sunday best, together with the shepherds and their families. They far outnumbered us tourists.

There are, in these parts, an increasing number of wolves that have spread from the Italian mountains and this was a major talking point at the festival. Staff of the Parc de Mercantour were there with their displays. These were concerned with the protection of wolves and maintained that they were not as bad as their reputation suggested. On the other side, the hunting fraternity *(la chasse)* had displays showing the damage the wolves can do. These opposing views led to a public debate between the hunters and shepherds on one side and the conservationists on the other. At the *gîte*, opinion favoured the shepherds point of view in the debate about the wolves. It was felt that the shepherd's lot was hard enough without this added hazard.

Day 12: St Etienne-de-Tinée — **Roya**

There was a long, very steep, and for me, very arduous ascent through the woods. My middle back was aching, but as usual with steep climbs Betty was in her element, and went into overdrive. We paused for tea on the way up, and were passed on their way down, by a very fit looking French couple. I looked at them enviously, feeling ancient! At the top, when we stopped for a picnic, I thought I heard the sound of English voices below. It was a party of three men doing the G.R.5, a little each year. This year having just started at St. Etienne, they hoped to complete it.

After Auron, we climbed up to the Col du Blainon (2011m), through woods, criss-crossed by the cables of ski lifts. Our *balisage* had not been made clear at the bottom of this climb, and we felt that the footpath had lost out to the needs of the more flashy and up-market sport of skiing, with great swathes of the wood cleared for pistes. At the top we came out on open grassland and made the long descent through disused terraces, with barns, mostly ruinous, to stop part way down at Chapelle St. Sebastien. This chapel, long disused, set in amongst all these terraces, like them belonged to a vanished era of *la vie montaignarde*. The chapel was now given over to graffiti, mainly amorous but including a large and recent one saying, *mort aux chasseurs*, (death to hunters).

Roya is a small hamlet at the end of its valley, with high wooded cliffs all round. Other walkers had told us that the *guardienne* at Roya was an excellent cook. She lived up to her reputation. Her stewed rabbit and cannelloni was really delicious and it gave us a welcome break from cooking. We shared a table at dinner with two Parisians, Albert and a younger man called Dominic, who came each year to the Alps to have a walking holiday. Dominic was quite sociable and extolled the virtues of walking in France, where everywhere he went there was beautiful countryside and good food. By comparison, the older man, Albert, was altogether stiffer in his manner and less communicative. Betty noticed that he served himself first to everything that arrived on the table and remarked later that she felt sure that he was used to being waited on, hand and foot, by a devoted wife. Dominic, on the other hand, chatted up our hostess shamelessly and was fulsome in his praise of her cooking. You felt she was well used to both. Olivier, a young Frenchman, who we first met at the *gîte* at St. Etienne, was also at Roya but he was cooking for himself.

Day 13: Roya to Refuge des Longons
Our hostess needed to go into Nice early, which suited us well because we wanted to make an early start to a long day. So breakfast was at 5.30am. Albert and Dominic were off first and, at his request, we woke Olivier at 6.30am as we left. The first two were heading for Beuil, and the rest of us were bound for the Refuge des Longons. The bridge over the ravine at Roya had been swept away, so we had to negotiate the torrent, equipping ourselves with sticks to steady us as we crossed. On the far side there was an energetic scramble up a wet and muddy landslide. The first two hours up to a shepherd's hut, through woods and across another ravine were strenuous but magnificent. Albert and Dominic were setting off from the hut as we arrived. While we were sitting quietly drinking our tea, we had an excellent view of a group of marmots. These engaging little creatures, somewhat like oversized hamsters, have a habit of sitting up in a begging position to survey the scene. An area of cultivated ground close to the hut, provided them with a playground where they were sunning themselves on the rocks, fooling around and making their now familiar shrill calls. As we, in our turn, came to push on, Olivier arrived at the hut. We went on up, crossing snow twice as we went.

We were climbing steeply through a bolder-strewn landscape with little vegetation, when we came quite suddenly, to one of those vivid green, silent alpine meadows, with a stream flowing through it, and with nothing to disturb its peace except our passage. As we climbed on up from the meadow, the snow was difficult enough to negotiate in parts to show just how dangerous it could be. A couple of times I went in up to my knee, which was no great problem, but I thought back to Hubert negotiating Col Girardin on his own, and could easily see why he would not want to chance it a second time.

Olivier had overtaken us before we reached Col de Crousette at 2480m. It was a barren, rocky spot and he waited for us there to tell us that he was going to climb Mont Mounier to see if he could see the sea, which our guide said was sometimes possible. At our highest point there was a monument but we were too busy watching our tenuous foothold on the steep and treacherous scree slope, to worry who or what it was commemorating. Somehow in this landscape it was just bound to be a tragedy of some sort. For Betty, this near vertical landscape was bad news as it brought on her vertigo. For me, it had a grandeur that I would not have missed, but for both of us it was not a place to linger.

From there, suddenly the view ahead and down, opened up to reveal a vast, lifeless rocky plateau right out to the horizon. To our eyes it could not be called beautiful, but it will remain forever memorable. It was impressive in its extremity and its austerity and was a region to pass through as swiftly as possible. As the view of these barren wastes opened out, we could see our way ahead and far below, and on it a thin dark line. As we watched, this line moved slowly towards us and gradually we could see that it was made up of humans who in fact were moving very quickly. It turned out to be a caterpillar of 20 or so young soldiers, who had come up from Beuil on a route march to the top of Mont Mounier. There were cheerful greetings and exclamations of amazement that anyone would do this sort of thing voluntarily!

Within a moment they were gone, and after this brief and cheery exchange, the baleful and inhuman grip of the landscape lost its hold on us and we felt able to eat. We then continued our flight across the plateau, where a little vegetation here and there, was just beginning to establish a foothold. There was no place to shelter from the wind, until we eventually came down to Col des Moulines, to another world with grass and flowers. Far down below us on our right we could make out Albert and Dominic beetling down to Beuil.

Olivier came past us saying as he went, that there had been no view of the sea from the top, but he too had met the soldiers. We carried on through fairly level meadows until the village of Vignols where our route took a wide detour to the north, to follow the sides of a valley along which were many pinnacles in soft yellowy stone. We could see that Olivier had lost the waymarks and was heading down into Vignols, instead of keeping up on the flank of the valley. We tried shouting but he was out of earshot.

By this time we were very tired and still had another climb to get onto the plateau of Longons, at the far end of which was our night's lodging. The climb was again steeply up through shale on precipitous slopes and not surprisingly brought on again the feelings of vertigo. When we got up there it was another world as these upland meadows often are. A wide expanse of grass was revealed, on which were no animals and just one shepherd's hut. We trudged across this level but tussocky expanse for two or three kilometres to reach the refuge. As we approached it, there were a few cows and donkeys. It had been built on the site of *vacheries* (cow sheds), which had been destroyed by an avalanche in the 1950s. Eventually Olivier turned up, an hour or so after us. We had done 11 hours which was more than enough over this very testing terrain.

Day 14: Refuge des Longons — St. Sauveur-de-Tinée
When the refuge operated as the Vacherie de Roure, up to the 1950s, the cattle from the village of this name were fattened up on the wonderful grass of the plateau pastures during the summer. In this way the village got its cheese supply. These cheeses must have been hard won, since not only was there the threat of avalanches, but the journey up to the plateau from the valley was long and arduous whichever way they went.

This was certainly the most remote refuge that we came across. It was only occupied from May to September and supplies came in by helicopter. The *guardien* drove his cattle and donkeys along the road to get there, a journey of 30 or more kilometres. Before we left, the *guardien* and his wife told us that they had observed a couple of golden eagles nesting in the crags above. We set off to make our way down to Roure, where we hoped to buy food for lunch as the pantry was nearly bare — no bread, no cheese and only four teabags. Off the edge of the plateau we plunged even more steeply down than our ascent of the evening before. On through woods, we came to a spot where we could see, across the other side of a ravine, the path making its tenuous course through a precipitous bank of shale. Olivier was just negotiating this, and the sight brought Betty's vertigo to crisis point. There was no way that she could go on, so we turned back, and when she had recovered a bit we made our way back up to the plateau, sheltered in a little byre, since by now it was raining, and cooked up some packet soup. Restored by this and the sun's reappearance, we retraced our steps of the day before over the plateau and down the other side, back to Vignols. This was another ghost village with one or two of the old houses being done up. As we walked down the track from Vignols, Betty became more or less her old self again, pointing out flowers we hadn't seen before and puzzling over the vertigo.

She felt cross with herself and tried to explain to me what it was like. 'It doesn't help at all', she said, 'To know that the fear of heights is totally illogical and that there is no real danger; in fact it makes it worse. As I climb higher, which I really enjoy doing, some internal mental calculator makes me feel more and more insecure, and I start to anticipate vertical slopes and precipices round every turn. My legs begin to tingle with the fear of these long before they appear. The anticipation is usually far worse than the actual negotiation of tricky sections of the path. After yesterday's steep climb I lay awake dreading the descent to the valley and when we came to the point where we could see the tiny laden figure of Olivier, crossing that loose shale, which spilled down to the valley below as he walked, it was just more than I could bear, my legs turned to jelly. I didn't want to move either forward or back, and I only felt safe sitting and holding on'. Chatting away, we tramped on for ages before we came to Rubion, a village perched on the side of the mountain which we suddenly came upon through a rock tunnel.

We headed down towards St. Sauveur by road. It was a hard slog but a most amazing descent with soaring cliffs of different types of rocks all round, clothed in pines and larches almost to their summits. These cliffs were all at about 2000m and we descended to 450m at St. Sauveur. All told we must have done about 36 kilometres that day with very little food. Porridge for breakfast, soup for lunch and sustained at intervals with sweet coffee and dates. However we reached town in not too bad shape apart from being a little footsore.

We were able to buy some vegetables there and make a soup from some of the ingredients we had been missing, leeks, carrots, potatoes. The old ladies from the neighbouring houses sitting out on their walls chatting, observed our comings and goings from the *gîte*. Two Parisian girls arrived and left early the next morning heading for Beuil on the G.R.52. As for us, we had decided to bus the rest of the way to Nice, about 70 kilometres. Betty had an urgent need of some less vertical landscape and we were both ready for some really hot sun and sea.

Useful information, addresses and bibliography

Footpaths of Europe:Lake Geneva to Mont Blanc: GR5, GR5E, GR55

Footpaths of Europe:Modane to Larche: GR5, GR50, GR54, GR541

Footpaths of Europe:Walking the GR5: Larche to Nice

Walking Europe from Top to Bottom, The Sierra Club Travel Guide to the GR5 by Margolis & Harmon

The Path to Rome by Hilaire Belloc

Walking through Europe by John Hillaby: Paladin Books 1974

Maison de la Montaigne: Advice and Weather Centre, Chamonix. Tel. 64.50.53.03.40.

Le Cairn Pension, 05100 Montgenèvre, run by English couple, 12km from Briançon

Youth Hostels, Route de la Gare, 'La Rochette', 05600, Guillestre and Le Mas des Loups, 04850 Jausiers
Airports at Grenoble and Nice
Trains: Gares SNCF at Briançon, and Nice
Tourist Offices: Acropolis Esplanade Kennedy BP 4079 - 06302 Nice Cedex 04. Tel.04 93 92 82 82 and 1 Place du Temple, BP.49-05105 Briançon. Tel.04 92 21 08 50

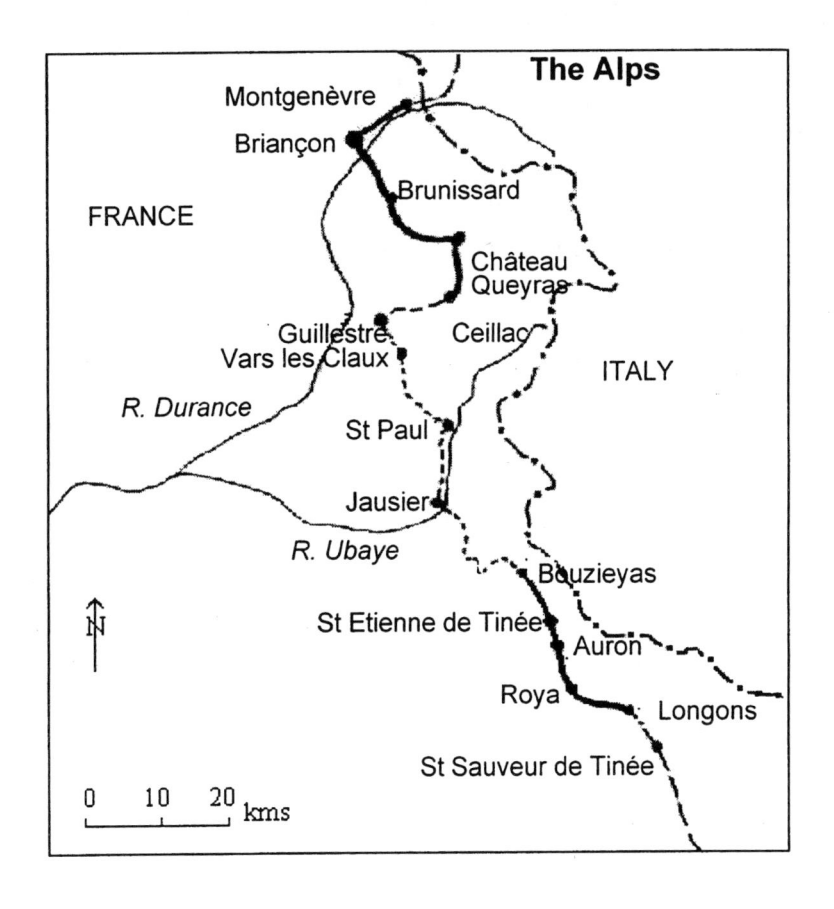

Key to maps - page 27

NICE AND THE PRE-ALPS:
SUDDENLY SUMMER

Much to our surprise, we really liked Nice. Yet our three day sojourn on the Mediterranean was enough for a rest and a change. In this section of our walk to La Palud we encountered, for the first time, the heat of summer and the beginning of the French holiday season. The Pre-Alps proved to be amongst the harshest and most hostile terrain of our whole walk, yet while amongst them, the mountain eyrie of Aiglun stands out as one of the most memorable places we stayed. Travelling west, the contrasting landscape of the Gorge de Verdon, with its water-worn rocks and boulders, was a vivid testimony to the power of wild nature.

It was a real treat to shop in Nice's old town market for our evening meal. We chose from a large variety of cooked dishes — there was a Sicilian aubergine and tomato dish which we particularly liked, mouth-watering olives with carrot and chilli and excellent wine from the barrel. The Youth Hostel had a pleasant garden on the hillside overlooking the city and the sea, where we ate the goodies.

An Irish family arrived — a mother with two bolshie kids and her blind sister in tow. They had just flown into Nice from Dublin and we chatted to them over supper, sharing a big bag of cherries. Though we got on famously, they left us in no doubt of the unpopularity of the English in Ireland. Sheila, of the Irish party was diabetic as well as blind. There were some moments of drama in the morning, as an ambulance and a paramedics car arrived with lights flashing and Sheila was whisked away to hospital. She had gone into a coma, but they had got to her in time, and by evening she was back at the Youth Hostel, chatting and eating her supper, as if nothing had happened.

Day 1: Nice — Aspremont
It had been a lovely break but our itchy feet were urging us onward. We spent the morning in the post office where we set up a temporary office to deal with our mail. We had a lovely lot of letters, and a

package with our topoguides and maps for the stretch across Provence to the Rhône.

Table of Distances

1. Nice - Aspremont	12.0km
2. Aspremont - St. Jeannet	14.0km
3. St. Jeannet - Grasse (part by bus)	34.5km
4. Grasse - Greolières	29.0km
5. Greolières - Aiglun	19.0km
6. Aiglun - St. Auban	24.0km
7. St. Auban - Castellane (by bus & lift)	22.0km
8. Castellane - Camping de Rougon	24.0km
9. Camping de Rougon - La Palud sur Verdon	12.0km

We picked up the start of the G.R.5 at Aire St. Michel and followed it along old cultivation terraces, between lovely, sweet-smelling golden broom. In typical Mediterranean fashion, nearly all species of vegetation now had prickles. So, scratched and blooded, we found our way down on to the road and pounded along it to Aspremont, a beautiful village set high in the hills. Aspremont's castle was a motte and bailey built in the 11th century, when it became the centre for large estates. Just before dark, we walked up to the castle mound and looked west over the soft, velvety outlines of hills, which disappeared as night fell.

Day 2: Aspremont — St. Jeannet

After so many weeks in the company of the elusive G.R.5, at Aspremont we turned our faces to the west to follow the G.R.51. Our route took us down a long descent into the valley of the river Var, via footpaths and minor roads. An occasional sighting of the bridge across the busy N202, down which we had travelled to Nice on the bus a few days before, provided us with an effective landmark. It was the only one for miles and took us across this highway and over the river Var, on our way towards Gattières. The day was hot and humid, so we stopped for a siesta in a leafy lane, after which we had a sweaty climb to Gattières and on up through cultivation terraces and little farmsteads set in amongst olives and vineyards.

Having reached the top of the ridge, we turned to look back, south-eastwards towards Nice, but because of the haze we could only see the near coastline of the Var estuary. St. Jeannet was a beautiful mountain village with streets far too narrow for the heavy traffic. Above the village towered the vertical rock-face of Baou de St. Jeannet.

Day 3: St. Jeannet — Grasse
The day started with shopping for ratatouille, which, together with boiled eggs made an excellent basis for our picnic lunch. Because we had no details about any sort of accommodation at Gourdon on the G.R.51, we took buses from St. Jeannet into Vence and on to Tourette, in order to reach Grasse by nightfall.

In a park where we ate lunch, we were accosted by a French professional 'gentleman of the road' called Chris (pronounced Chrees), who asked to borrow our knife. After a moment's hesitation, since it was a vital piece of our equipment, I handed it to him and he took it away to the other side of the street where his belongings were. My misgivings were misplaced since he promptly returned it to us. He had an ancient and dilapidated frame rucksack which was coming seriously apart, looking as if it had nothing very much in it. Chris had that deeply weathered look of those who spend their lives outdoors, and was quite smartly dressed with newish jacket and jeans with white trainers. An ex-miner from northern France, who had been made redundant when the mines closed down, he now travelled the length and breadth of France, quite often staying at monasteries, picking up casual work when he could get it. He had done fruit picking and had worked at Lourdes, pushing the chairs of the infirm on their way to take the waters. Once a year he returned to visit his two married daughters in northern France. Someone had given Chris his bus fare so he wisely waited for the bus to Grasse, whereas we set off jauntily walking down the road.

But fate overtook us in the shape of massed black storm clouds, which began to deposit their load upon us in enormous raindrops. We found inadequate shelter for a while under a tree, but as the rain came heavier accompanied by spectacular thunder and lightning, desperation made us remember a little shelter we had passed a couple of hundred metres back. In those few minutes, the road had been turned into a swiftly flowing river and we were soaked before we reached it. But at least once under its shelter we were able to brew up, and avoiding the leaking roof as far as we could, sit out the storm in relatively dry conditions. As we watched, the rain turned to hail with stones the size of marbles. After about an hour and a half, the rain let up enough for us to walk on with squelching boots, feeling pretty damp and chilled. We had just about got our circulation going again when we came to a place where we could catch the bus. It was the same impassive driver who earlier in the day had dropped us off in Tourette and he showed not a flicker of interest or recognition at our reappearance in this sodden and bedraggled state. We arrived at Grasse around 6.45pm and tumbled gratefully into the Hotel Oasis right by the bus station.

Grasse styles itself as the Perfume Capital of the World. Perhaps this is where all the lavender ended up from the fields we walked through later. The old quarter of the town had become a north African ghetto and we would have liked to try African food here, but the atmosphere was one of exclusion. This was one side of the town, the other side which it presented to the tourist was of a prosperous centre with public parks and gardens, large hotels and department stores selling the perfumes.

Day 4: Grasse — Greollières

From Grasse we left the G.R.51 and struck off north on the G.R.4. We climbed the road in hairpin bends to the point where the path should have been. After tracking backwards and forwards we eventually plunged into the scrub following a vestigial path with no markings, since our map showed us fairly precisely where the path should be. Our faith in the map was justified as a little further up the hill we found the waymarks. We had quite a fight getting through thickets of bramble and wild rose. Eventually we reached the Plan de la Malle, one of a series of bare limestone plateaux. This very inhospitable, rocky landscape with scrub pines, was covered with *proprieté privée* notices.

We continued to climb and skirted round an observatory, formed of a collection of semi-circular white domed buildings, in strange contrast to the bleak and wild landscape. From there, was a long and difficult descent on a loose rubbly path which brought us toCiprières, an attractive village where we had hoped to stay. The only accommodation was at the chateau which had been converted into a four star hotel. All around the narrow, pretty streets were artists with their paints and easels painting the attractive houses with their window boxes of red geraniums. Since there was no humble accommodation for the likes of us, we reluctantly trekked on, steeply down hill again, seeing Greollières, our night's lodging just as steeply uphill on the other side of the wooded valley. We arrived there totally exhausted after an endlessly zigzagging upward path, at the end of a 12 hour day. This was one of the occasions when we felt that the time of six and a quarter hours given in the topoguide, must have been achieved by fit, and unladen 20 year olds going at a run. They had got to be joking!

Day 5: Greollières — Aiglun
This was an unremittingly hard day, starting with a steep ascent without any cover from the hot sun, via innumerable zigzags. This brought us to a plateau of jumbled rock and pine scrub, through which we picked a seemingly aimless route, pursued and surrounded by a large retinue of flies. We stopped to have a picnic by an oratory, rather improbably dedicated to Our Lady of the Snows. In that fly-infested midday heat, snow seemed a far off but inviting prospect. Presumably she was there to invoke snow for the new ski resort just to the east at Greollières-les-Neiges. In fact in this savage landscape, where you felt it would be only too easy to get lost, it was for once a little reassuring to see the familiar, rather monstrous architecture of a ski resort.

We continued up a short steep stretch to a small idyllic plateau, with long lush grass, before plunging over the edge to start the steep downward path. This was a crippling descent, very hard on the knees, but at least we now had pleasant cover from the sun in the form of mature beech trees. The descent seemed not only steep but interminable, a lot of it on loose shaly ground, that threatened to floor you at every other step. About halfway down, the view opened up to reveal before us the terraces and ruinous buildings of the abandoned hamlet of Vegay. There was one large level meadow across which we could see a cherry tree laden with fruit and a rusty iron bedstead below it, the last evocative trace of the people who had lived here. I went across to pick cherries, but had hardly started when the bees and flies descended like avenging ghosts, and I gave up the attempt. The place had an atmosphere almost of being watched. It was very remote, about one and a half hours from the bottom of the valley and the many terraces, built with such labour, were now completely overgrown. As we learned later, it had been occupied from medieval until recent times, people having gradually left until the last inhabitant, perhaps the owner of the iron bedstead, had finally left the place empty of people about 30 years before.

We followed the old road which had been built to this hamlet, a mammoth labour of construction. A crossing of the Vegay stream gave us an idyllic tea stop with beautiful clear pools, a little waterfall and lovely cool water. We completed the descent, swallowed up in woods again and walked a little way along a blissfully level track by the Esternay river following its meanders. All too soon we had to leave this to climb steeply again to reach Aiglun with its Gîte Auberge. This we reached after a hard, but memorable, eight and a half hour day.

We shall not forget Aiglun, a tiny village clinging to the mountain side, with the almost vertical peak, Clue d'Aiglun above. There was little more there than a cluster of houses and the Gîte Auberge. One archway over the road with heavy double wooden gates was all that had been required in the way of fortification, as the sheer mountain side was so near vertical. The Auberge, the principal building of the village, was partly built over this archway. That night we had a wonderful meal there: pistou provençal, a delicious soup with beans, garlic, vegetables and herbs; roast lamb, new potatoes and salad. The place was packed and it was obvious that people had come from far and wide to sample its excellent food. The meal was accompanied appropriately by the music of the troubadours. After this wonderful dinner we wandered out and sat alongside the old folk, on the long benches by the narrow road through the village, marvelling at the view of the descent we had made out of the sky.

Day 6: Aiglun — St. Auban.

At breakfast the music was Frescobaldi's — the choice of the aubergist. He was pleased that it was appreciated. After the last two days of stiff walking, we decided to diverge from the G.R.4 path and take the road to St. Auban, some 24 km away. The first part of the road walking was spectacular. We descended to the bridge over the Esternay, high over the rushing torrent, which had smoothed the rocks in its passage down the narrow gorge. In the Auberge there had been pictures of the previous wooden bridge being manoeuvred into position. It was an unbelievably difficult spot to fix a bridge; but it was done. It was Aiglun's lifeline.

The road was only just wide enough for one car and several times we had to flatten ourselves against the rock face to let someone pass. We walked on until just before midday when the sun got too strong and we found shade in the square of the village at Le Mas which also had a welcome fountain. We watched the locals setting their tables outside for Sunday lunch as we ate our picnic on a stone bench in the cool.

We reckoned on arriving at St. Auban around 6.30pm. Just as we had set ourselves to this target, a van slowed and stopped in front of us. It was the lass from the Auberge at Aiglun offering us a lift. So we clambered in. I was in the back with the packs and her dog named

Gold, so named because he liked beer and particularly Fischer's Gold. I renamed him Monsieur Gold out of respect for his good taste. He was a splendid, large, Dr. Seuss-like dog, who, the previous night, had wandered amiably in and out of the Auberge. Our driver was most impressed with our plans and thought we ought to tell the journalists! She dropped us by a camp site at St. Auban.

Day 7: St. Auban — Castellane
As we had been told that there were no buses that day, we were very surprised to find one coming up behind us, and flagged it down. We declared our hand straight away and asked him how far 39ff would take us, as that was all we had left. Without saying he motioned us on. In fact he took us all the way to the main road, the N85, put us down there and wouldn't take any money. This was an auspicious start, but then our luck seemed to be running out as we stood trying to thumb a lift for two hours in the hot sun. We had more or less given up hope, when a young man in a sports car stopped, and took us right to Castellane. The piece of road we were travelling on, was, he reckoned, one of the worst in France for landslides. Our route brought us down out of the Pre-Alp mountains to the valley settlement of Castellane. We thanked him as he set us down in the square of this fairly touristy small town. His parting words were in praise of the water of the town's fountain. It was well known for being the best water for miles. We tried it out straight away and agreed.

The *gîte* was tucked away down a lane by the river. Though there was a large kitchen it was only for catering, so we set up our field kitchen and cooked under a large awning with tables and chairs in the garden. The menu was potatoes and french beans with fresh sardines. We were watched at intervals by the cheerful young *guardien*, who seemed intrigued by the way we cooked. Later we wandered into the square to hear a live band playing.

The river Verdon at that time of year was a wide shallow torrent, but its banks of huge boulders, piled high, showed how it must have swelled with the winter melt water. In the central square there were fiercely contested games of boule. It made a change to be tourists wandering around this little town with its shops and narrow streets.

There had once been a defensive wall, the surviving bits of which were built into later houses. Castellane was the first place where we encountered the excellent rosé fruitée, wine with a distinctive fresh and fruity flavour, which we were able to buy loose.

Day 8: Castellane — Camping de Rougon (Carajuan)

There was a steady climb by the hamlet of La Colle after which a Roman road took us all the way to Chasteuil, hugging the contours of the mountain side with steep or vertical drops from time to time on its outer side. This didn't excite Betty's vertigo because it was a good wide track. Just before we reached Chasteuil we exchanged greetings with a French couple. The man seemed to be making rather heavy weather of it and remarked to me; *C'est dur, unh?*, to which I obviously made the wrong reply; *Non, pas mal*, meaning to reassure him about the path ahead. Betty said she was sure he was a fellow vertigo sufferer, and he wanted me to put them off going further. Anyway they didn't go much further, since they were back in Chasteuil before we had finished our cup of coffee at the cafe, and he confirmed Betty's diagnosis by saying to a fellow Frenchman that he didn't like the steep sides to the pathway so they were going to try a different walk. Chasteuil had suffered the same desertion as many of the mountain villages, but here a group of craftsmen and women had repopulated the place. They were making pottery, doing leatherwork and woodwork and growing herbs for sale. Chasteuil was approachable by road and had set itself out to attract the tourists.

We climbed on up to the col which was a natural grassy amphitheatre with many old terraces around it. There were no animals and no people up there, yet it was a place with a presence, communicating that curious sense of being watched. From there we clambered down the mountain side to arrive at Rougon and were pleased because we thought we had arrived early at our camp site. But the locals assured us that there was no camp site there. We talked to two French couples who were also expecting to find a camp site, having bivouacked the night before in the Canyon de Verdon. We continued down to the main road, where we found a sign pointing us to the Camping de Rougon. So much for our early finish and the peace and quiet of mountain walking. It was five kilometres of road trudge past the unspeakable Point Sublime, a spectacular view point of the Gorge de Verdon, which was completely spoilt by a massive infestation of coaches and cars. The tedium of the road walk was relieved by a striking view of a snake. It was in a trap to take run-off water from the road and because it was deep we felt safe enough to watch it as it slid slowly out of sight. It was large, perhaps a metre or so in length, yellow with black markings.

Day 9: Camping de Rougon — La Palud-sur-Verdon

As we had decided to road walk to La Palud rather than take the G.R.4 through the Canyon de Verdon, which we knew to be very vertiginous, we set off by 5.45am to beat the sun and the cars. The same road that the previous night had been hideous with traffic, was absolutely quiet as we retraced our steps to Point Sublime. An occasional fisherman could be seen by the river far below. The water was vivid blue-green, and to either side of it the limestone cliffs were shrouded in mist, only their tops emerging into the sunlight. The whole effect was like a Japanese print. Point Sublime, a great expanse of bare rock, was at that time of the morning devoid of cars, apart from a little clutch of motor homes huddled together as if for protection.

We walked on at a good pace and arrived at La Palud at about 9.15am, having covered the 12 kilometres of our short day's stint to bring us to the Youth Hostel. We had phoned ahead to book in at the hostel for a couple of nights, since the next day was Bastille Day, France's national holiday. We were just in time to stow our packs before the Hostel closed until 5.0pm and were free to float round the countryside, taking in the incredible shapes of the mountains, with their successive ridges of limestone and little plateaux in between, rising up to the wall of the canyon itself. That evening we had an excellent *plat du jour* at a restaurant in the village: *Daube aux Cèpes,* a beef stew with fungi, accompanied by little squares of polenta, with bread, wine and coffee.

There were free drinks and music in the square to celebrate the eve of Bastille Day. An accordionist who started things off was alright, but the band that followed, ineptly named *Les Nuances* was dominated by an elderly, immaculately dressed medleyist on keyboard who implacably hammered out one old chestnut after another without pause, without a change of tempo, and without once turning to face his audience. We left at 10.00pm as a procession of torch-bearing cyclists rode down the twisting road of the mountain side into the village — a spectacular display.

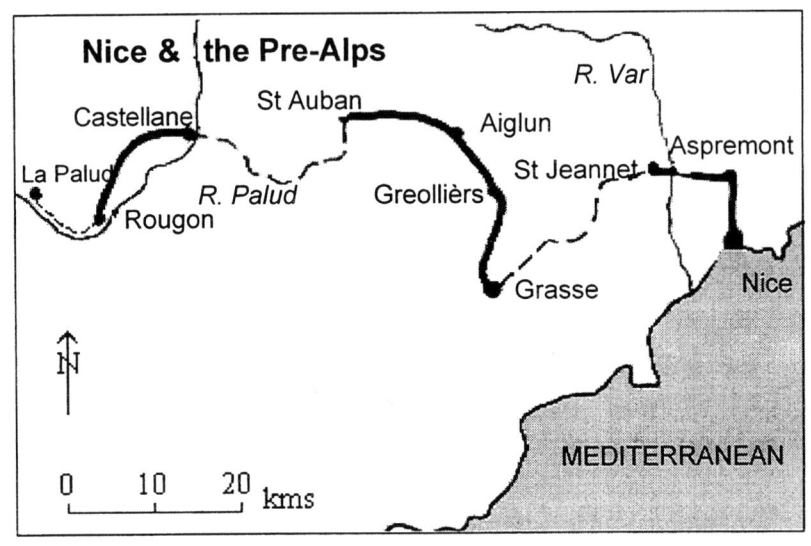

Key to maps - page 27

Useful information, addresses and bibliography

Topoguide 506: Balcons de la Méditerranée (GR51)

Topoguide 401: La Haute-Provence par Les Gorges du Verdon (GR4, GRP)

Fédération Française de la Randonnée Pédestre, 14 Rue Riquet, F-75109 Paris. (for topoguides and walking info.)

Youth Hostels, Route Forestière du Mont-Alban, 06300 Nice and Route de la Maline, 04120 La Palud sur Verdon

Airports at Nice and Marseilles

Train stations at Nice and Marseilles

Autobus between Marseilles and La Palud sur Verdon

Tourist Offices: Acropolis Esplanade Kennedy BP 4079 - 06302 Nice Cedex 04. Tel.04 93 92 82 82

and Rue National, BP.8-04120 Castellane. Tel.04 92 83 61 14.

Syndicat d'Initiative: Le Château, 04120 La Palud sur Verdon. Tel.04 92 77 32 02

PROVENCE IN THE HEAT OF JULY

This section of our walk revealed to us the dramatic contrasts of the Provençal scenery. On the high plateaux and broad plains, there were abundant crops, interspersed with the arid, almost soil-less, rocky mountains in between. When it was not hazy, the brilliance and luminosity of the light contributed a vibrant quality to the landscape.

During this period, we encountered the greatest heat. Water became of the utmost importance, as did the fountains in the villages. We appreciated the subtly different tastes of the water along the way, and particularly enjoyed that which came from natural springs, straight out of the rock. It was important to make an early start, so that from the cool of dawn we became gradually used to the increasing heat of the day. With the heat, the noise of the cicadas rose to a crescendo that was almost deafening, and at every step, small brown crickets or grasshoppers, jumped to reveal startlingly bright scarlet wings, which disappeared as they landed. Though we often found the intense heat taxing, paradoxically we both found that we enjoyed it enormously. It was, by turns, tiring and exhilarating.

Table of Distances

1. La Palud sur Verdon - Les Salles(20km by bus)	36.0km
2. Les Salles - St. Andreaux	20.0km
3. St. Andreaux - St. Croix	15.5km
4. St. Croix - Riez	18.0km
5. Riez - St. Martin des Brômes	16.0km
6. St. Martin des Brômes - Gréoux-les-Bains	8.0km
7. Gréoux-les-Bains - Manosque	14.0km
8. Manosque - Céreste	28.0km
9. Céreste - Oppedette	16.0km
10. Oppedette - Roustrel	17.0km
11. Roustrel - Rousillon	24.0km
12. Rousillon - Gordes	13.0km
13. Gordes - Fontaine-de-Vaucluse	23.0km
14. Fontaine-de-Vaucluse - Maubec	12.0km

15. Maubec - Mérindol	28.0km
16. Mérindol - Lamanon	29.0km
17. Lamanon - Eygalières	28.0km
18. Eygalières - St. Rémy de Provence	12.0km

Day 1: La Palud-sur-Verdon — Les Salles

The village was dominated by a square castle with round towers at each corner, partly ruinous, but in the process of being preserved. Conferences on pollution and the ecology of the region were held there, and the marshes were being turned into a nature reserve. As we walked in the afternoon, there was thunder and then rain. It had cleared by the evening and we sat, along with the elderly locals, watching the traffic squeeze its way through the narrow streets — motorhomes, caravans, cars, coaches and motorbikes. No wonder they needed conferences on pollution.

As the weather was very hot, we made up our minds to make a detour from the G.R.4, so as to spend a couple of days by Lac St. Croix, before picking it up again on the far side of the lake. From La Palud, we needed to go first of all to Moustière, a distance of 20 kilometres, most of it on a busy road along the vertiginous Gorge de Verdon. So as not to prolong the agony by walking, we took a bus. Moustière was a centre for the production of faience pottery, a beautiful village high up on the mountain side, so beautiful that it was seething with tourists. The elegant, fine porcelain was on display everywhere, with its delicately fluted edges and handles, decorated with genteel scenes from a bygone era.

We swam in Lac St. Croix, and the water was superbly fresh and an unbelievably bright blue-green colour. Then, on the way down the east shore of the lake, we crossed the spectacular dam over the river Verdon, looking down on tiny kayaks far below on the water. It was getting dark as we approached Les Salles, which advertised itself as the youngest village in France, a novel description after the usual claims of villages and towns to a long history. It had been established on the shores of this artificial lake, created by Electricité de France (EDF) for electricity generation.

Day 2: Les Salles — St. Andreaux

The mobile-homes were still sleeping peacefully as we left the camp site at 6.30am, and made our way to the *boulangerie*, for what had become our favourite breakfast; *brioche aux raisins* with orange juice and coffee. These *brioches* were buns of coiled, freshly baked dough, sweet with raisins and confectioner's custard, and glazed on top.

We spotted a footpath marked as the G.R.99, which looked as if it would give us a short cut back to the G.R.4, keeping us close to the edge of the lake. We found the red and white markers, running along a good track which, on this Bank Holiday weekend, was full of parked cars of family groups, enjoying the lakeside for a day out. Suddenly the track round the lake, which had seemed so promising, came to an abrupt end. We could see that the red and white markers continued, but they took a narrow path up the rocks and we only hesitated for a few seconds before following them. After all the red and white markers indicated an official footpath. But little by little it turned into a series of rock chimneys, ever more difficult to negotiate and clinging to the edge of the sheer cliff face of the lake. It would have been a difficult path at any time, but laden with full packs it was impossible. The problem was that the prospect of returning over what we had done already, was just as daunting as going on. However, when the path showed no signs of becoming any easier, we settled in desperation for the only other option; to clamber up to the plateau above us and see what that had to offer. The answer was not much, but at least it was not life-threatening. The terrain was rock-strewn, with pine trees and prickly scrub and no visible track.

We took a compass bearing on the direction we wanted to go from the map, and set off to trudge cross-country. Our main concern was to avoid returning to the precipitous edge of the lake. Having achieved Betty's childhood ambition to get completely lost, the whole idea suddenly seemed to have lost its charm. We followed one track after another, until we found one which continued for kilometre after kilometre, up hill and down dale but we had no idea where we were. At last, to our enormous relief, we saw a group of buildings, cars and people, who were amazed to see these two exhausted figures staggering out of nowhere. We asked if they could show us on our map where we were but we had walked right off the bottom of our Michelin map. Our 'short cut' had, in fact, taken us miles too far to the south.

We set off in the direction they indicated and managed to get a lift part of the way in an already crowded jeep. When we were dropped off, it was getting dark and it was obvious that we couldn't reach Boduen that night, so we pitched camp in the first flat, grassy field we came to. We would solve the rest of our problems the next day.

Day 3: St. Andreaux — St. Croix

Nothing beats a cool, quiet, early start to the day and we were off by 5.45am, completely refreshed after the previous day's fiasco. We headed down to Boduen on the lakeside, the place that had eluded us so completely the day before. There we got breakfast and shopping, before heading off around the lake to the mighty barrage and hydro-electric station; an edifice of massed concrete constructed by EDF.

We hoofed it down to St. Croix with a following of enthusiastic flies. On an old terrace in the municipal camp site they were still taking an intense interest in our activities. On the next plot to us was group of young cyclists. Judging by their youthful exuberance and the number of empty bottles around, we thought we were in for a sleepless night. By 8.0pm there was virtually no one down by the lake and everything was closing up, in spite of this being, perhaps the most popular French holiday week. We polished off our wine by the lakeside and were quite ready for bed ourselves. Our neighbours were, after all, surprisingly quiet, or we had drunk so much wine that we didn't hear them!

Day 4: St. Croix — Riez

Having re-victualled, we climbed from the lake and the village up to the level top of a plateau. By minor roads and tracks, we made our way to Roumoules to rejoin the G.R.4., walking through fields of barley, maize and lavender to the market town of Riez, set in its lush river valley. We stayed at Hôtel des Alpes, an old, rambling place, no longer smart; the wooden panelling faded and worn with age and the broad, bare floorboards worn smooth by the passage of many feet. There were long corridors that sloped at alarming angles and from our window we looked out on the luxuriant growth of peach and plum trees along the river.

Day 5: Riez — St. Martin-des-Brômes

The stalls and awnings were being set up for the weekly outdoor market, under the trees in the main square. This was our first experience of a Provençal market, with all its wonderful variety of colourful fruit and vegetables. Local farm cheeses were on sale, including many varieties of goats' cheese. There were butchers, with rabbits and poultry hanging from the awnings of their stalls, and fishmongers, displaying all the Mediterranean variety of fish, large pink lobsters and tiny translucent shrimps, mounds of inky coloured mussels, milky-white squid, as well as all the glittering array of whole, silvery fishes of all shapes and sizes, constantly sluiced with water to keep them looking fresh. Tables were devoted entirely to honeys, including the local lavender honey. Local pottery, pots and pans and the brightly coloured traditional frilly skirts, in all shapes and sizes, were also on sale. It was a scene, bustling with life and energy. Stall-holders shouted their wares and called loud greetings to one another. Crowds of housewives were concentrating on testing the fruit and vegetables and tasting little proffered slivers of cheese and sausage, before making their purchases.

Our route took us, first by road and then by track, along the verdant valley of the Colestre, with water meadows and abundant willows and poplars. We passed a castle, converted into a hotel and then turned abruptly at right-angles to scramble steeply up a rocky path onto the plateau again. Once up there, flies in droves pursued us over the open tops, amongst barley fields and lavender, and then into woods of scrub oak with no view out. The heat was fiercely concentrated in this narrow, cleared band between the trees.

St. Martin was dominated by a formidable Templars' tower, the first of many such remnants of this medieval order of military Christians, which we were to encounter in these parts. The tower stood on a hill above the familiar maze of narrow, cool streets of the village.

Day 6: St. Martin des Brômes — Gréoux-les-Bains

The same geology prevailed - beds of five metres or so of pebbles and cobbles, loosely concreted, sometimes in clay, sometimes in a harder matrix, alternating with bands of reddy-brown soil of about the same thickness. This looked like a most unpromising material for cultivation, but, as we had seen, it did in fact grow luxuriant crops. After a magnificent walk over a wide plateau, the path then led us down to the river and along its broad, stone-filled bed with a shallow, harmless spread of water, so unlike the mighty torrent of the Verdon, seen in the gorge.

Gréoux-les-Bains was filled with French holiday makers, the heat was intense, 36 degrees centigrade, and the newspapers were talking about a heatwave. We stayed the night at the municipal camp site, where the clientele were mostly *curistes*, here to take some form of water therapy. A large party of French campers were sitting in the dusk, taking it in turns to sing or recite.

Day 7: Gréoux-les-Bains — Manosque
The way out of Gréoux repeated the, now familiar, pattern of the climb up to the plateau top, then down into the wide valley of the Durance river, last seen at Guillestre, where it was a swift torrent. Now the river course had become a broad strand of boulders and gravel, with tangles of uprooted trees from the spring melts, and a swift deep channel of blue-green water, snaking its way across an expansive fertile plain, planted with vast apple orchards and barley. It was so hot that when we reached the town, we had to find shade and water urgently and make a brew-up to recover a bit. Then we drank another litre and a half of water, this time chilled Evian water, as we made our way through the old town to the Youth Hostel. We were getting to be connoisseurs of good water, and this rated high. Two months before when we had passed by Evian, close to Thonon-les-Bains, nothing could have been further from our minds than drinking chilled water.

This was the home town of the much-loved writer, Jean Giono, who died about 1970. His books were, above all, a celebration of Provence, and such was his fame that he had a main street and some local wines named after him. We had seen a mime of his story, *The Man who Planted Trees,* some ten years earlier — a poetic story delivering a strong green message.

One small kitchen served for everyone at the hostel, so we decided to have a *paella* which we could cook in just one pan. Betty observed with some amusement that one rash young woman, who wanted to impress her friends, decided to cook pancakes with a variety of different fillings. She can't have been used to cooking at Youth Hostels. Monopolising the kitchen which others were waiting to use, she roped in the rest of her party to do different tasks to assist her, with all utensils being commandeered. We retired before they actually got any food.

Day 8: Manosque — Céreste
As we arrived in Pierrevert, the great wine growing village of this area, around 7.0am, they were setting up the stalls for a Sunday bygones and bric-a-brac fair but we went straight on to Montfuron after a long pull uphill. From there it was an easy ridge walk to Montjustin, a yuppyfied village, whose castle was being restored with European funds. Nearing Céreste, we had views of the formidable looking ridge of the Lubéron ahead, which we knew we would have to cross in a few days' time.

The *gîte* in Céreste was delightfully well equipped. Not only were there the usual facilities, but a bottle of wine and cooked food in the fridge too. Since there was no one in the *gîte*, no luggage and no sleeping bags, we assumed that this had been left behind by people who had departed — an especially welcome find, as it was Sunday and all the shops were closed. So eventually we tucked into some excellent couscous and chicken left in a dish, congratulating ourselves on our timely good luck. But as we were stuffing our faces, we heard someone bound up the stairs. It only took his momentary look of shocked surprise, for us to realise that this was the maker of the couscous. As we found out, he was the young temporary pool attendant, living, for the summer, in the separate upstairs flat. Never has anyone so graciously accepted the unwelcome sight of someone uninvited, eating his food. Brushing aside our clumsy attempts to apologise, he smiled, sat down and ate with us, further entering into the spirit, by helping us drink the wine left behind by a party of Strasbourg walkers.

Day 9: Céreste — Oppedette

A small country road led us to a shady lunchtime stop at the priory of Carluc. A French couple, seeing us looking hot and sweaty, came over to us and asked if we had found *la source*, which they said, had beautiful water. We found the spring — a deep pool of lovely, cool, clear water to drink, and sit beside for our picnic. Carluc had been a sacred site from prehistoric times onward. In the fifth and sixth centuries AD, there was a cemetery of rock-cut tombs attached to the church, which itself had been established, and then neglected, several times, over the many centuries of its occupation. The presence of a spring of really cold clear water in these dry limestone hills, would be enough to account for the sanctity of the site.

Having refreshed ourselves, a long hot ascent on a mixture of roads and stony tracks brought us to Oppedette, where the *gîte d'étape* was the tiniest we encountered. It had four bunks, showers, loos and cooking facilities in one cool, cellar-like room.

Day 10: Oppedette — Roustrel

As we left the village, mist was swirling up from the valley to this tiny settlement, with the promise of another hot day. There, we left the G.R.4., which heads north at that point, to continue on the G.R.6 in a more westerly direction. We followed the road down to cross the Gorge d'Oppedette, a mini version of some of those which we had seen, but very wild and completely without water. After the gorge, there was a long steep climb to Viens, typical of the *villages perchées*, with its hilltop position clinging to the edge of a precipice, its castle, its church and its narrow streets.

The area known as mini-Colorado is an amazing landscape of sandstone cliffs and pinnacles of all colours, from white to deep glowing red, with greens, browns and yellows as well, all in amongst pines and box shrubs. Where the terrain allowed, there were cultivated fields, mostly cherries and vines, with occasional rows of almond and walnut trees. As we approached Roustrel, we came across a couple who were gathering different coloured sands into containers, to make pigments for painting.

The *gîte* was in a restored 17th century castle, which also housed the Mairie and an exhibition hall. The electricity went off as Betty was cooking, and she had to finish off on our globetrotter stove outside, to get enough light to see what she was doing. Judging by the candles in the kitchen, this was not the first time that the cooking had been interrupted in this way. We ate outside on a semi-circular tier of seats, in the company of a motley assortment of dogs and cats, who obviously used this as a regular meeting place. We then retired to our double bed in the base of one of the four corner towers of the castle. It sounds very romantic, but in fact it was absolutely stifling, as there was no way of opening the window. Apart from us, there were only one or two other people who inhabited rooms in this huge building. During the night, after one or other of us had flushed the loo, there was a prolonged and thunderous clanking of pumps, which were drawing water from a deep well below the castle to fill header tanks in the roof.

Day 11: Roustrel — Rousillon
The baker opened at 7.0am and we were there to get freshly made chocolate croissants. The bread was still being baked and you could see the flames from the wood fuel in the background. Our path took us above another château on the side of the Plateau de Vaucluse, which we then came down to cross, amidst vineyards and fruit trees, mainly cherries, but also almonds and apricots. In fields too small for machinery, lavender was being cut by hand. We bought a melon for lunch, from a farm by the roadside where they were growing, and found a shady spot in Gargas. After we had eaten, we spread our sleeping mats on the metal benches and dozed, gazing up at the multiple leafy umbrellas of the plane trees above. A group of locals, men and women, brought their chairs to sit in the shade beside the road above us.

The afternoon's stint through pinewoods provided some shade, and when we came to the ochre quarries just east of Rousillon, a great hole opened up before us and what looked like toy machines were working far down in the bottom of this crater. Just in time we found a sign telling us that our route was diverted.

Rousillon was a very picturesque place, too picturesque for its own good, since there were far too many of us tourists about. The story goes, that a troubadour came to the castle of the count of Rousillon who was obsessed by hunting. While the count was away, the troubadour made courtly advances to his wife. When the count found out about this, he butchered the troubadour and served him to his wife. She then died of a broken heart, and from that time on, the rocks around Rousillon were stained blood-red.

Day 12: Rousillon — Gordes
It was a splendid walk down from Rousillon through woods and eventually on to the plain, to make our way between fields of sweet-smelling melons, being harvested a few feet from our noses. A steep climb then brought us to another *village perchée* at Gordes, with its castle and church dominating the hilltop. In deep shade below the castle in the main square, we ate, watching a party of young children having baguettes doled out to them and eating these with great concentration, sitting on the steps of the church. The square was full of restaurants and cafés, with brightly coloured sunshades. At the neighbouring café, there was an exceedingly dissolute-looking waiter, who had the affectation of turning away from his customers, as if hurrying off to get their order, then pausing and shouting it back to them over his shoulder to confirm. Each time he appeared he seemed to be leaning further back, as if just about to fall over backwards. However he kept going, and was still there continuing his performance in the evening.

We walked the two kilometres out from the village to find Camping des Sources and set up next to a young English couple who had walked down through France in about eight weeks. It was rare to meet up with fellow long distance walkers. In Gordes that evening we ate at the Bistro des Artistes where jazz was advertised. Two girl violinists came, did some spirited excerpts from the classics and went round with the hat. Maybe jazz came later, but we had to climb the hill to sleep, because we had an early start in mind for the next day.

Day 13: Gordes — Fontaine-de-Vaucluse
The walk along the valley side to the Abbaye de Sénanque made use of the old cobbled track to this 12th century Cistercian house, which is

still in use as a monastery. Its setting at the head of a valley, with its gardens and lavender fields, was most impressive. On the way up through box and pine woods, we stopped to watch a black snake ahead, disappearing unhurriedly into the bushes. Once we had gained the ridge, it was level walking round the top of a valley by a lone deserted farm, Basse Pouraque, set amongst small pastures. We pressed on through sparse scrub until we started to descend a bank of scree. Our path took us through a wild and desolate canyon, where all the trees had died. The heat was fierce and it was intensified within the walls of the canyon. Once again, as with other remote spots, we had the feeling of being watched. We could easily imagine this setting being used for a spaghetti western with the baddies lying in wait above.

We were in segregated dormitories at the Youth Hostel that night. I awoke to look out on a velvet sky full of stars, with bats swooping silently back and forth.

Day 14: Fontaine-de-Vaucluse — Maubec

This Youth Hostel was unusual in being run on rather old-fashioned lines. They still retained the way of allocating tasks to be done before hostellers left in the morning. At breakfast we talked to a pleasant German family who had broken their journey at Vaucluse and would arrive in about six hours at their holiday destination in the Pyrenees. For us, walking this distance would take about three months! The quality of the journey **had** to be more important to us than the arriving.

After the hot dry countryside, the broad deep-green expanse of the river Sorgue at Fontaine, with its water wheels, made a totally unexpected contrast. The river Sorgue was famous in antiquity because no one knew its true source. The start of the river appears to be a still, rock pool of vivid blue-green water, below vertical limestone cliffs about 200m high, but the true source of the river lay hidden far within the mountain. Strabo, the Greek geographer, mentions it as one of the wonders of the world. Even today with modern diving equipment, Cousteau and others have only penetrated the rock caverns behind the pool to a distance of some 250m. But in fact the river drains a vast area of the Plateau de Vaucluse. It was early used to power paper mills, which pounded wood to pulp, and the surviving mills are open to the public as a tourist attraction. Roman remains at Fontaine, in the shape of fluted Corinthian columns, incorporated into the Carolingian church, suggest that there might have been a temple there, close to the source of the river. In the middle ages, Petrarch lived at Fontaine and wrote about it in *Traité de la Solitude* and about his famous love affair with Laura in *Canzione*.

After lunch we set off on a supposedly short stint to Maubec but managed to make it rather longer by losing our way across the heathland east of Lagnes. We walked some distance beside the Mur de la Peste, a dry stone wall with occasional deliberate breaks, as access points, with little guard chambers beside them. It was built to try and check the spread of the plague, but it was not clear at what period. Notices told us that this wild country was where the Maquis le Chat resistance group, was formed and operated in 1943. We managed to make our way with the aid of map and compass, to pick up our route again further on, and continued by vineyards and apple and cherry orchards, across the plain of the river Coulon, to Robion.

At first we thought we had the *gîte* at Maubec to ourselves, but when we opened the fridge there were several sealed packages inside, which, after our experience at Céreste we left strictly alone. Their owner turned out to be a fanatical fisherman overnighting there before a competition on the following day. He opened up the plastic boxes that we had seen in the fridge and insisted on showing us their contents of writhing maggots, large red ones and small green ones. But we were so hungry that this unappetising sight hardly put us off a splendid meal of *gnocchi* and *ratatouille*, followed by *crème fraîche* and apricots with Côte du Lubéron rosé, absolutely **the** local wine. We were able to show our fellow guest how to operate the water heater for the showers, and discovered that he had been coming there for eight years without ever figuring out how it worked. By this time we had become quite expert in overcoming the idiosyncrasies of different heating and cooking appliances, which we encountered along the way.

Day 15: Maubec — Mérindol

Our main objective was to get up and over the Montaigne de Lubéron, the massive ridge of limestone, which we had seen from afar to the east and had skirted to the north. We started with a cool, pleasant woodland path at the foot of the mountain. This developed into an up-and-down scramble over ridges on the mountain side, before we emerged at Oppéde-le-Vieux, a semi-ruinous medieval settlement built on crags. Some of the fine old houses had been restored to make attractive dwellings. It had clearly been an importance place in medieval times, since some of the abandoned houses had finely moulded door and window surrounds. We walked down the worn rock surface of the extremely narrow main street, with the shells of these stone houses to either side, and out through the town gate. Then we began our ascent proper, and though it was still early in the day, we agreed that neither of us had ever sweated so much. When we got to the top, I could literally wring my shirt out.

Our topoguide referred to *a-pic dangereux* (dangerous cliffs) in the next stretch, so we decided to take the road and forest tracks, which gave us a less steep but much longer route to descend the other side of the mountain. But with vertigo and heavy packs we preferred this cautious option. We rejoined the G.R.6, then turned southward, to follow the bottom of a gorge with narrow sides which, with no view out, seemed to go on for ever. At last we came out into a wide valley with grassland and vineyards, so different and civilised-looking, after the harsh and bare landscape we had travelled through for the previous six or seven hours. At Mérindol, the village *fête* was on, and we managed an early round of the stalls, before crashing out, after a day of around 28 kilometres.

In the 16th century, there were still heretics in these parts, called Les Vaudois, following the 12th century teachings of Pierre Valdo of Lyon, which called for a return to the simple way of life. The established church put an end to what they saw as unacceptable beliefs, by issuing the Arrête de Mérindol in 1540, which ordained that this town and others in the area such as Oppéde-le-Vieux, which followed this heresy, should be razed to the ground. As we had seen earlier that day, Oppéde had never recovered.

Day 16: Mérindol — Nostradamus Campsite, Lamanon
We wended our way across the plain of the river Durance, by fields of

espalier pears, apples and vineyards, interspersed with vegetables, all with an elaborate system of leats for watering. Even the clover fields were being watered. We crossed the bridge over the Durance river bed, very wide there, with baulks of gravel and sand, through which a narrow snaking stream of water wove its course. Uprooted trees, left high and dry, showed what the river could do when in full spate.

In Mallemort we took a bus to Lamanon and walked the 5 km. to Camping Nostradamus, a haven, miles from anywhere, set in a wide valley with intensively cultivated fruit, irrigated by swiftly flowing channels. There were trees laden with peaches and nectarines, which all looked luscious. On the camp site, the jollity was, for once, provided by a happy van load of English, who arrived, set up their tents and started kicking a ball around. It was a hot night and we drifted off to sleep to the sound of bongo drums.

Day 17: Lamanon — Eygalières
A road walk of one hour brought us to Eygières (not to be confused with Eygalières). We were there by 8.0am in time to pick up cheese and fruit from the market and carry on along a track to Aureille. This was good walking; the track ran along a rise of ground, which continued upwards to form the shadeless Alpilles on our right, and on our left sloped gently down to the great verdant plain of the Bouches du Rhône, which was spread out before us. We pressed on towards Eygalières, past the Mas de la Vallongue, with its long straight valley, lined by mountains on either side. The vineyards stretched in regular rows to its far end, where the estate house could be seen. As we approached Eygalières, we passed between the dramatic fin-like peaks of the Alpilles, having seen them for the past few days getting nearer and nearer. They formed a series of narrow, bare, rocky tops in a row and looked very much like insubstantial stage props in the intense light and heat of that afternoon. In the past, the troubadours 'borrowed' (as our topoguide untranslatably said) the Col de Vallongue, and met at the Château de Romanin, a castle set in this mass of barren rocky outcrops. Perhaps they 'borrowed' some wine from the Vallongue Estates too, to get them in good voice.

On the camp site that night there was no shade for our tent at the Camping à la Ferme, but there was a roofed area attached to the house providing shade, with tables, chairs and a fridge. The Provençal couple who ran the place, were proud that their language is now taught in schools. There are cultural and linguistic connections with the Catalans and the flags have the same red and yellow stripes. As we were preparing our food, in the shade of the lean-to, the *guardien* gathered there with his wife and cronies at the aperitif hour, to demolish a bottle of Pastis. It was drunk in tall, straight glasses with water and lots of ice. One of the company, a short, ginger-haired and freckled fisherman from Toulon, was keen to hear where we had walked in the Jura, an area he knew and liked.

Day 18: Eygalières — St. Rémy de Provence

Instead of following the G.R.6 we opted to try and find our way to St. Rémy along the Canal des Alpilles, which ran close to the camp site. The canal was for irrigation and had leats going off to the fields to either side. Most of the way to St. Rémy, perhaps about 10 kilometres, there was intensive cultivation of tomatoes, aubergines in polytunnels, melons and fruit trees. Quite a lot of the fields had shelter belts of evergreens and tall bamboo hedges about four metres high, in between the rows of polytunnels. It was a great pleasure to have some easy walking on grassy paths on the level, where we could walk side by side and chat, in contrast to the many kilometres of difficult rocky paths, where all the concentration goes into making sure of the next foothold. Along this stretch by the canal we noticed thistles with bright yellow flowers and scabious with glowing deep red ones. I never before realised how elegant and sweetly scented the white flowers of 'old man's beard' are. Our path followed the canal all the way to St. Rémy.

Useful information, addresses and bibliography

Fédération Française de la Randonnée Pédestre, 14 Rue Riquet, F-75019 Paris (for topoguides and info on walking) *Topoguide 401*: La Haute-Provence par Les Gorges du Verdon (GR4, GRP) and *Topoguide 601*: De La Montagne de Lure aux Alpilles (GR6)

Youth Hostels, Route de la Maline, 04120 La Palud sur Verdon and Parc de la Rochette, 04100 Manosque and Chemin de la Vignasse, 84800 Fontaine-de-Vaucluse.

Airports at Avignon and Marseilles.

Train: Avignon nearest SNCF station to St. Rémy de Provence.

Autobus: Marseilles to La Palud sur Verdon. and Avignon\St Rémy, Gare Routière d'Avignon, 5 Ave. Monclar, Avignon. Tel.04 90 82 07 35.

Tourist Office: Place Jean Jaure, 13210 St. Rémy de Provence. Tel.04 90 92 05 22.

Syndicat d'Initiative: Le Château, 04120 La Palud sur Verdon. Tel. 04 92 77 32 02.

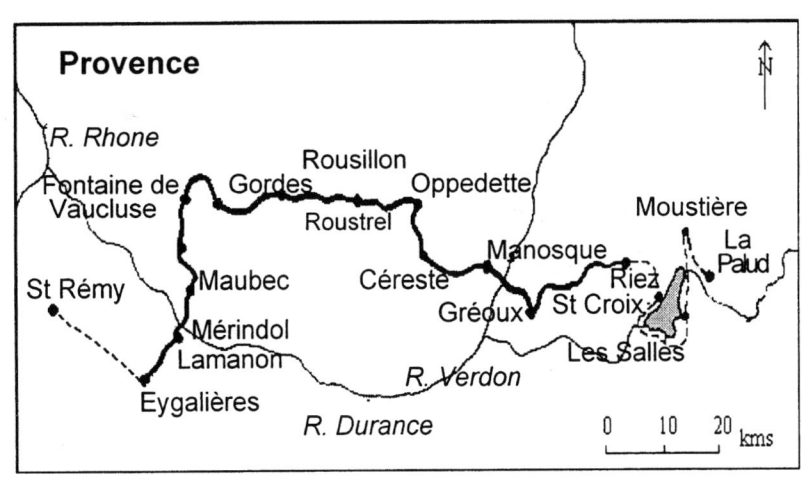

Key to maps - page 27

Provence

The Rhône and the Cevennes

This section of our journey took us from the orchards and vineyards of the Rhône, along the gorges, heaths and river banks of the Gardon, up and over the wooded Cevennes. The Gardon was a revelation. We hadn't experienced rivers that behaved as strangely; that, during the summer are intermittent streams running over one stretch of the river bed, and totally dry at another; and that are roaring torrents in the autumn or spring. The mountains of the Cevennes were just as beautiful as everyone had said they would be. The whole area was a holiday centre for walkers and bikers particularly. The old hard way of life had largely disappeared. Sweet chestnuts are still grown in large quantities there. Though we walked along the old drove ways we saw no sign of sheep, and forestry was the major activity.

Table of Distances

1. St. Rémy de Provence - St. Etienne de Grès	16.0km
2. St. Etienne de Grès - Tarascon	12.0km
3. Tarascon - Remoulins	24.0km
4. Remoulins - Collias	13.0km
5. Collias - Pont St. Nicholas	15.0km
6. Pont St. Nicholas - Moussac	22.0km
7. Moussac - Vézénobres	13.0km
8. Vézénobres - Anduze	19.0km
9. Anduze - Colognac	20.0km
10. Colognac - Les Plantiers	19.0km
11. Les Plantiers - Mont Aigoual	23.0km
12. Mont Aigoual - L'Esperou	10.0km
13. L'Esperou - Le Vigan	21.0km

Day 1: St. Rémy-de-Provence — St. Etienne-de-Grès

Everywhere in St. Rémy there were beautiful reproductions of Van Gogh's paintings and a centre in the town was dedicated to his work. Over several years he spent time at a monastery close by. Walking in the intense light and heat of Provence made us appreciate all the more, the vivid way Van Gogh conveys the qualities of light and sun, which are so special to this landscape.

We picked up the G.R.6 again on the outskirts of St. Rémy and walked the long straight drag, up to the remains of the Roman town of Glanum, some three kilometres from the present town, tucked just underneath the summits of the Alpilles. There was a triumphal arch and monument, with the usual sculptures of victorious Roman soldiers killing unfortunate natives. Continuing on along the G.R.6, we climbed high above the Roman remains, through woods and box scrub, amongst the fantastic rock fins of the Alpilles. Our path brought us to a near vertical rock chimney, worn smooth and slippery with the passage of many people, down which a series of iron rungs led to a natural hole in the rock to continue down to a small artificial lake. I descended part of this in full pack, then took it off to return for Betty's. Our topoguide made no mention of this little excitement which was clearly meant for younger *sportifs* than us, presumably without backpacks too. We wondered how many more of these tricks the path ahead had up its sleeve. Having decided not to find out, we beat a retreat back down to St. Rémy. We had already realised that it would be possible to continue along the path beside the Canal des Alpilles and by this time we were quite happy to take up this duller but safer option. In fact, the walk along the canal was pleasant and shady and the wildflowers were abundant with particularly striking yellow and pink balsams and yellow flag irises.

Day 2: St. Etienne-de-Grès — Tarascon

We hit the road just after 7.0am for the last leg of our journey to the Rhône, starting with fairly busy roads made all the more trying by very heavy, hot and overcast weather. Once we had regained the banks of the Canal des Alpilles, we had a pleasant enough walk right into

Tarascon, where we arrived just in time to stow our packs in the Youth Hostel, before it closed for the day.

We made our way across the Rhône to our *poste restante* rendezvous of Beaucaire on the other side of the river. It was great to hear from so many of the family and from Thea, our Dutch walking companion, who had made it to Nice, using her indomitable cheek to hitch a number of lifts in between stints of walking and stretches by bus and train.

After eating at the hostel that evening, we wandered out and around the old town, which is virtually a north African ghetto of narrow streets with shuttered windows, as we had previously found in Grasse. We came across an open air showing of a film in one of the squares, which was apparently laid on free. We sat down amongst the locals and got hooked, then were horrified to find when it finished that the time had slipped by unnoticed and we found ourselves locked out of the hostel which closed up at 11.30pm. This wouldn't have been so bad if the film had been worth it but it was a load of rubbish about a diver who wanted to become a dolphin. After losing our way in the maze of unlit streets in the old town, we eventually found a hotel by the station, where we were lucky to get room for the night, as they were just closing up.

Day 3: Tarascon — Remoulins

We slipped back into the hostel for breakfast and nobody had missed us. A couple of Dutch lads, doing a course on land and water management in Holland, were currently working on a nearby farm, irrigating the fruit and maize crops with water from the Canal des Alpilles. From them we learnt that the canal had been constructed specifically for irrigation in the 18th century, and runs from the river Durance to the Rhône. It is closed off for two weeks in the winter for cleaning.

As we said farewells, the *guardien* congratulated us on being such good hostellers, little knowing of our truancy. The air was clear after rain and we crossed the bridge over the Rhône to start our next major leg of the journey, north-westwards along the G.R.6. While we were sitting by the roadside having our picnic lunch, a car passed slowly by. The driver appeared to be very interested in us, since he was craning his neck out of the car window. Like the re-run of a silent film, the car reappeared again coming slowly backwards, then stopped beside us. The driver asked all sorts of questions, and once he had heard our story, declared that we were mad and abruptly drove off. We thought that was the end of the matter, but within a few minutes he was back with a passenger. *This is Benoît, my son-in-law*, he declared; *He has brought a bottle of wine for you from his vineyard.* Benoît handed us the bottle and shook our hands. His father-in-law, Claude, who was visiting from northern France, asked if we would like to see the *caves* where the wine was made and, when we said yes, bundled us into the car.

In a few minutes we had arrived at the Domaine de Parc Saint Charles where Benoît introduced us to his family and then showed us round the whole works. He had a beautiful stone house, and all the wine-making went on in the stone barns of the estate, arranged round a large courtyard. There were 24 stainless steel vats, each containing 15,000 litres of wine, and his vineyards surrounded the house which was set on a little hill. He grew nothing else but vines apart from a few olives, just to make oil for the family. Benoît showed us the presses which were used to make the white and rosé wines. The red was made by simply allowing the grapes to ferment out in the vats, and the grape residue was then shovelled out and recycled for a second wine making. We clambered up and down the gantries to explore the whole process, which included the bottling and labelling, which was all done on the premises. We were given a sample of each of the wines to taste, and very good they were too. In the old days he explained, the harvest was gathered by 50 or so people, who had to be fed and put up at the house. Now, two men and a machine, of which Benoît was very proud, did all the work in a shorter time, and, he said, made a better job of it. The visit ended with a reluctant daughter being dragooned into playing her accordion for us. Photos were taken and Claude returned us to our route. We continued on our way only slightly the worse for wear, and eventually reached Remoulins after crossing over the river Gardon. We had Benoît's wine with our supper and it was really excellent, fruity, full of flavour and we could tell this was far superior to the wine we usually drank. A further measure of its quality was that Betty found herself sleeping with her feet on the bedhead!

Day 4: Remoulins — Collias

We started off along the road to the Roman aqueduct, Pont du Gard, and joined the hundreds of other sightseers, to gaze in admiration at the massive arched structure, which we crossed in following the G.R.6. This impressive example of Roman engineering, which still survives intact, was built by Agrippa in AD 19. Its purpose was to span the river Gardon, north to south, carrying the water supply for Nîmes, from its collecting point further north-west at Uzes. You only have to look at the way in which the rocks in the river bed are worn smooth to understand the tremendous power of the autumnal surge of water. No wonder this aqueduct was built so massive. At that time, in August, we were seeing it at its lowest, when parts of the river course were completely dry.

After putting up the tent in the camp site at Collias, we went off to get supplies, and to have a look at the river Gardon. There, it had plenty of fresh blue-green water, in marked contrast to the sluggish flow at Pont du Gard. There was a wide pebbly shore from which people were swimming and while I joined them for a dip, Betty watched the kids scrambling up the rocks on the far bank and diving into the deep water.

Day 5: Collias — Pont St. Nicholas

Walking over the tops above the Gorge de Gardon, through dense scrub oak and ilex, with a myriad of paths crossing it, miles from anywhere, we came across a concrete table about four metres long, with a drawing of a boar inscribed into the surface at the centre of it. The word *'assassins'* was scrawled across it. There were chairs stashed in the undergrowth, and two stools conveniently placed by the table, which served us nicely for a tea break. The table was set at the edge of a little clearing, where the *chasseurs* would come to lay out their kill, and gloat over it before roasting it over a fire. No wonder the *sangliers* keep themselves out of the way. We heard noises on this trek through the scrub which we thought might have been made by the *sangliers*, but we never saw any sign of them. We compared notes later and both of us independently had thought that we heard little pig-like squeaks and grunts and rustlings in the scrub. But of course they are normally nocturnal and very wary of humans, so it may have been the power of suggestion.

We journeyed silently on until we started the descent on the north side of this wilderness of scrub, when suddenly we had views out to the Cevennes in the distance. As we came down into the valley, the contrast between the highly cultivated vineyards there and the wasteland above was extreme. The danger of sudden rises of water in times of flood was indicated by vertical measures at the roadside, as a warning for motorists, showing how devastating the river could be when in full spate. At the bridge itself there was a boarded up church and a group of buildings with overgrown walled gardens. According to our map, this was the site of a former convent. It was amazing that there the Gardon was a completely dry river bed, but with a vigorous vegetation growing along its course. A particularly striking plant grew to about two metres high, with large white trumpet flowers and a fine border of poplars and willows lined the banks. We stayed at the Chaumerie, probably once the farm belonging to the convent by the bridge, now a shady auberge set amongst trees a little distance from the main road to Nîmes.

Day 6: Pont St. Nicholas — Moussac

Unlike yesterday, we had views out over the dry river bed with occasional small pools, but otherwise a wide rocky channel. As we walked, we could hear the distant sound of artillery from the south where the army have a large area for military exercises. After Russan, where we stopped for provisions, the valley of the Gardon opened out. Our path took us first through cultivated fields, then through old gravel quarries and finally through a wooded area of considerable size with shacks dotted around in it. We came to one spot on the river where the water was caught in a succession of pools with lots of fish in them. There was a man fishing for carp, who emphasised that it was purely for sport not for eating.

As we approached the camp site at Moussac, we met Wolfgang and Margaret, who were delighted to meet fellow walkers, their first since starting the G.R.6 at Tarascon. This was the friendliest little camp site that we came across. There were just two caravans and two tents under the trees by the river. Showers and loos were those of the village football team. There was an elderly Nîmois couple with a caravan, who told us how to put our tent up to get the best advantage of the breeze. Another caravan was owned by an Indian from Beaucaire, who played a nice line in South American music, which, apart from his own country's, he liked the best. We all talked together and the elderly couple were invited to eat with the Indian and family. That night was the start of the village *fête* but the star singer and his orchestra, looked, from the posters, as if they would be pretty dire, so we went to the local bar, had a coffee, listened to the 'Gypsy Kings' on the juke box and watched the folk assembling. The young were gathering at a temporary bar set up outside. Pastis seemed to be the drink. Inside the café, a troop of dogs, of all shapes and sizes, kept us all amused with their comings and goings. We retired across the Gardon by the footbridge to the camp site before the *fête* had really got under way. During the night we could hear the ploppings of fish and bird calls from our tent. The Gardon was a proper river again here.

Day 7: Moussac — Vézénobres

Our path took us into Cruviers-Lascours, where there was a huge and ugly distillery. Lascours itself was decidedly up-market, a rather twee village of stone houses, done up for holiday homes. Sitting on a bench there, brewing up a cup of tea, we felt we were lowering the tone, when the 'lady of the manor' appeared, showing some potential customers around. We reached Ners through vineyards with much of our path making use of tracks created by the workers in the fields. From here we detoured from the G.R.6 to reach the *gîte* at Vézénobres which was up a steep climb into the medieval village, and housed in a beautiful old terraced cottage. The German walkers were already installed and had gone off in search of a bank. After we had eaten, we climbed up to the top of the town, where we had a magnificent view in all directions, just as the sun was setting. From the orientation table located there, we could identify our next major objective, the Cevennes mountains, which were again clearly visible to the north-west.

The *guardien* came to collect our dues when he returned from work and stopped for a chat. He said that he did the *balisage* for this sector of the G.R.6. He and his fellow walkers were having trouble with the markings being erased by hunters. They wanted the country to themselves so as to avoid the risk of shooting people rather than wild boar, he explained. He had walked by himself along the Canal du Midi for a week, carrying all his supplies, so as to be independent of civilisation and in order to 'empty his mind'. Though he got 'blisters the size of egg yolks' in the process, he told us that he put 'mind over matter' and didn't allow them to put him off. This didn't sound at all like our kind of walking but we let him know how much we appreciated the work on the *balisage*.

Day 8: Vézénobres - Anduze
Our stint took us through lots of fields of fruit, including kiwi fruit and white peaches. Being another hot day, a lunch time swim in the Gardon was very refreshing. We watched a couple of kingfishers flashing to and fro just above the water, on the far side of the river, displaying their distinctive iridescent blue plumage.

The *gîte* at Anduze was conveniently placed in the centre of town. We were met at the door by a man with long grey hair and a small black dog, who installed us in a bedroom on the top floor. However we were soon ousted from there when the *guardienne* arrived and explained that it was booked. So we had to bring our packs down to the dormitory on the ground floor. The man with the dog, it turned out, was a long-term resident who got ticked off for trying to be over-helpful. We cooked up and ate in a little courtyard, where the 'elderly Chrees', as we christened him, sat working on drawings, listening to the radio with his little black dog at his side. Every so often he would go out, sporting a briefcase with the dog trotting beside him. We found some *harissa* in one of the shops in Anduze, which inspired me to make a hot, spicy vegetable dish based on ratté potatoes, aubergines and peppers. *Harissa* is a brown fiery paste of North African origin, made from chillies and flavoured with spices — excellent in small doses.

Anduze is styled, 'Gateway to the Cevennes', and was full of touristy shops and choked with traffic but we could get our supplies in the relatively quiet, narrow streets of the old town. The Templars were in evidence again. There was an Auberge des Templiers in the town. They were great landowners thereabouts as well as in Provence. Anduze was also notable for being a centre for non-conformism, as was the whole of the Cevennes. Stevenson, writing in the 19th century about these parts in *Travels with a Donkey*, tells of the *camisards*, non-conformists who held out against Catholic persecution, rebelled, slaughtered their repressors and were quelled with savagery.

Day 9: Anduze — Colognac
We plunged into the wooded hills of the Cevennes, taking 20 kilometres to climb steadily from 130m at Anduze to 570m at Colognac. We were walking mainly through sweet chestnuts, which made a pleasant change. The *gîte* was one side of the bar and the *épicerie/ boulangerie* was on the other, very handy, and all run by the same people. This was just about all there was in this sleepy little village. The supplies at the shop were very restricted; no fruit, not many vegetables, no wine and no Export 33 beer either! Betty, with her flair for improvisation, managed to make a country omelette, which incorporated a tin of flageolet beans, and produced a chocolate mousse from what was in stock. There were enough beans left over to mix with dressing for the next day's picnic.

Day 10: Colognac - Les Plantiers
The fact that, early the next morning, bread was being baked on the premises next door in such a tiny village, says something about the importance that the French attach to their daily fresh bread and croissants.

The route from Colognac was up through shady lanes with stone walls on either side and sweet chestnuts all around. The rock was a sort of crumbly, gritstone or granite, with lots of quartz. These leafy lanes, characteristic of the Cevennes, were the old sheep tracks (*drailles*) along which the flocks would once have been taken to their summer pastures on the mountain tops. High up above the tree line, views out to the north were misty but splendid, with layer upon layer of mountains visible up to Lozère. We made for the Col Max Nègre, then descended by track and road to the Col de l' Asclié, which was an access point for cars. A *source* was marked at this spot, and we had hoped to get some cool spring water, but it turned out to be a miserable little trickle coming out so low to the ground that the guy before me in the queue, had to bend his plastic bottle in order to get water into it. There were others waiting, including an extremely thirsty looking dog, so I left them to it. We had after all enough water to make a cup of tea. From there we made a detour of about eight kilometres by a quiet wooded road to reach the *gîte* at Les Plantiers, which for these parts, was a metropolis, with a bar, a hotel and a restaurant.

Day 11: Les Plantiers — Mont Aigoual
Having lost most of the height we had gained the day before, by going down to Les Plantiers for a night's lodging, we climbed steeply up straight away from the valley, past the church of St. Marcel de Font Fouillouse to emerge above the tree line on to a splendid ridge. We were heading for Aire de Côte to pick up the G.R.6 again. It was a beautiful walk amongst the heather, with views out to the north over several wooded ridges, on to the bare higher slopes of Lozère.

At Aire de Côte we picnicked at the tables of the *gîte* and watched groups of walkers setting off and returning. This was a popular spot and was the crossing point of several G.R. paths. For some time I had been carrying two, one and a half litre, plastic bottles of water each day in my nosebag. Where there had been a fridge the night before, I had frozen these and they would remain semi-frozen until lunch time. By packing the wine, salad and fruit between these frozen bottles, I was able to deliver chilled rosé and water and keep the other foodstuffs cool in the heat of the day. Not a bad service for out in the wilds!

The climb up to the summit of Mont Aigoual at 1580m, was a good even gradient, sometimes in replanted pine, sometimes beech. There were lots of family groups on this route, ascending and descending. At the top were many more people, since it could be reached by car, but though they were swarming on the tower of the observatory and all over the mountain's broad top, there was room for everybody and still the landscape reigned supreme. It was a huge and expansive top with breathtaking views to all compass points. The *gîte* was right on top, next to the cafe and the observatory. We shared a dormitory with another couple and a young French mum with two kids, who had walked up from L'Esperou, our next day's destination. In the dusk we sauntered out to see the last of the sunset. It was a very special place. A great end to a good day's stint.

Day 12: Mont Aigoual — L'Esperou

I was up soon after 5.0am and became aware in the half-light of movement outside, so went to look. It was the dawn patrol, a collection of 15 to 20 people, all very quiet. Some had tripods and cameras, some were standing and others were sitting in their cars waiting, while more people walked up the slopes to join the gathering. I waited with them as the first light along the horizon spread and coloured, brilliant fiery red, then broadened out to give light to the deep, deep blue cloud-mass around it. It seemed to take forever for the top edge of the sun to burst through. Meanwhile we could see the Mediterranean, as a pale line of light to the south, and the dark furry outlines of the plateaux to the north. Then layer upon layer of dark blue velvety outlines of mountains were silhouetted briefly as the sun rose. I strolled around this great top, savouring the moment, listening to the bells of the cows grazing on the broad grassy slopes.

At this point we left the G.R.6 and turned off to the south-west on the G.R.7 for L'Esperou before descending to Le Vigan.

Day 13: L'Esperou — Le Vigan

A descent of 1000m took us down to the valley of the Arre and the first town since Anduze a week before. It was a great descent, steep and wooded for the most part. At one point we heard some curious squeaks high up above us which continued to get louder and closer, but it wasn't until about 15 minutes later that we saw two mountain bikers slowly negotiating downward on the rocky path behind us. We greeted one another as they passed us. It was obviously father and son, with the son deftly controlling his bike over the difficult surface, making it stop and move on as he required obviously in total command of his machine. The father, by comparison, was finding it heavy going and it was his bike that was producing the squeaks that had preceded them. We heard the squeaks continue on down the mountain side gradually getting fainter. Then once again the total quiet of the woods surrounded us. We stopped at Prat Coustal, which was a ruinous mountain village in the process of being made habitable again by a lot of young workers, who were lunching outside at tables set in the shade. Calls of *bon appetit* and *bonne route* were exchanged.

At the *gîte* at Le Vigan we found that we were sharing with a woman who had come for the national Aikido (non-violent form of self-defence similar to Judo) seminar, which had been held there annually for several years.

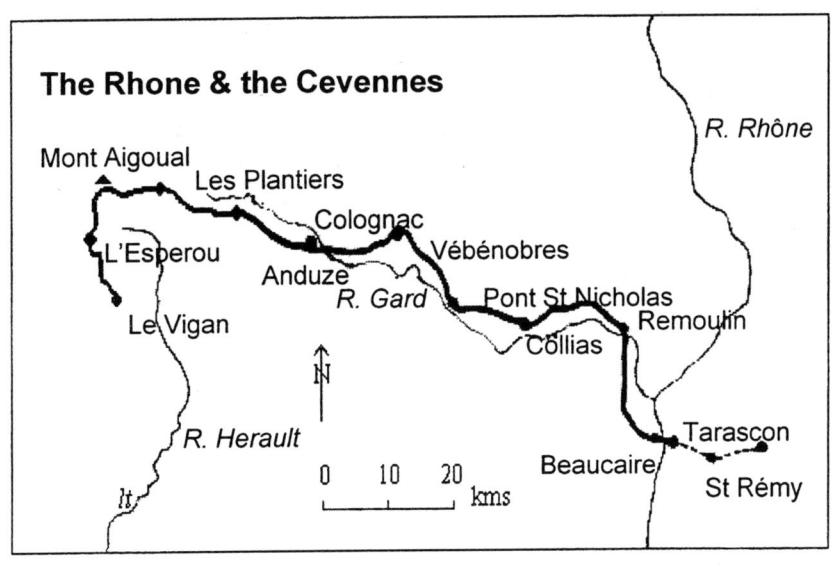

The Rhone & the Cevennes

Mont Aigoual
Les Plantiers
Colognac
L'Esperou
Vébénobres
Anduze
R. Gard
Pont St Nicholas
Le Vigan
Collias
Remoulin
R. Rhône
R. Herault
0 10 20 kms
Beaucaire
Tarascon
St Rémy

Key to maps - page 27

Useful information, addresses and bibliography

Topoguide 601: De La Montagne de Lure aux Alpilles (GR6)
Topoguide 603: Du Rhône aux Cevennes (GR6, GR42, GR60, GR61, GR62 & GR63) and *Topoguide 716: Traversée du Haut-Languedoc* (GR7, GR71 & GR74)

Youth Hostel, 31 Boulevard Gambetta, 13150 Tarascon.

Gîte d'Etape Municipal, 1 Rue de la Carrierrasse, 30120 Le Vigan. Tel.04 67 81 01 71.

Airports: Avignon, Nîmes\Arles|Camargue,Montpellier.

Train stations: at Avignon, Montpellier, Nîmes.

Autobus: Avignon to St. Rémy de Provence, Montpellier to Le Vigan, Nîmes to Le Vigan.

Tourist Offices: Place Jean Jaure, 13210 St. Rémy de Provence. Tel.04 90 92 05 22 and Maison de Pays, 30120 Le Vigan. Tel.04 67 81 01 72.

CROSS COUNTRY TO CARCASSONNE

In this stretch our path took us across a variety of countryside, sampling different terrains, but not exploring them in depth as we had with the Cevennes. The most distinctive landscapes were the high wild plateaux of the *causses* and the enormous gorge of the river Vis. Thereafter we crossed a number of ranges of hills *en route* for Lamalou-les-Bains. Pic de Nore gave us an unforgettable panorama south to the plain around Carcassonne and to the Pyrenees beyond.

There was an excellent market at Le Vigan where we found really good Cantal cheese and some superb Sicilian olives, flavoured with garlic and basil. We also found one of the best breads we have yet had on our travels — a wholemeal loaf with walnuts. To cap it all we found good loose red wine. During the day the *gîte* filled up with people arriving for the Aikido seminar. Among the 200 attending was a teacher from Washington DC who came every year. In the evening, we checked out our onward route for the next day and when we returned to the *gîte*, we found that everyone was out. So we retired to bed in the empty dormitory and were only just aware of the return of all the Aikido students, who slipped into the building quietly and almost noiselessly got themselves into bed. All praise to the discipline of Aikido!

Table of Distances

1. Le Vigan - Navacelles	24.0km
2. Navacelles - La Vacquerie	20.0km
3. La Vacquerie - Lodève	22.0km
4. Lodève - Dio	17.0km
5. Dio - Lamalou-les-Bains	15.0km
6. Lamalou-les-Bains - Olargues	15.0km
7. Olargues - St. Pons de Thomières	12.0km

8. St. Pons de Thomières - Labastide Rouairoux	12.0km
9. Labastide Rouairoux - Refuge de Nore	28.0km
10. Refuge de Nore - Villeneuve Minervois	22.5km
11. Villeneuve Minervois - Carcassonne	21.0km

Day 1: Le Vigan — Navacelles
Starting off south along the river Arre, we had a very pleasant walk to Arèze, followed by a stiff climb through chestnut woods to the plateau of the *causses*, an arid landscape of dried out grass with sparse scrub oak and box. Out in the middle of the huge high plain, there appeared dramatically before us an almost complete circle of stones, standing between one and two metres high, around a larger stone at its centre. Circles like this may have been prehistoric religious sites, but no one really knows what rituals were enacted. Thankfully they remain unexplained, an enigma to fire the imagination. As we paused to wander round this circle, we were conscious of its powerful presence.

From Blandas, we were quickly at the edge of the plateau, peering down into the depths of the Gorge de Navacelles. The G.R. path looked too precipitous, so we took the road around, and down a tortuous way, to reach Navacelles in the bottom. As we walked, the dramatic scenery was lit up from time to time by lightning and thunder reverberating around the sides of the gorge. Though we were walking through steady rain, we were not at the centre of the storm.

Day 2: Navacelles — La Vacquerie et St. Martin de Castries
In the Gorge de Navacelles, the river Vis forms a number of oxbows as it winds its way between high limestone cliffs. Around the village, one of these oxbows had silted up, giving rise to an accumulation of cultivable land whose crops fed Navacelles. As we had walked down, we had seen many uncultivated terraces, which in the past had been carefully built up with stone walls and little buildings. By this time it had become a half-abandoned settlement, the only one for miles at the bottom of the gorge, now sustained mainly by tourism. We set off walking up through some of the abandoned terraces to follow the

G.R.7 south along the gorge, climbing higher and higher up the cliff side, towards St. Maurice Navacelles. It was a wild and lonesome scene, with the path accompanied only by scrub and shale, running halfway up the side of the gorge. From it we could look down on a luxuriant growth of mature trees of all sorts, which lined the sinuous course of the river in the bottom. Once up on top, there was a reserve devoted to the reintroduction of vultures. Several of these birds of doom perched on a frame looking huge even from a distance.

On a circular stone seat, surrounding an ancient oak by the castle at St. Maurice, we picnicked, before crossing over the Causse du Larzac to La Vacquerie, a village of many horses for hire for *'promenade au cheval'*. We were admitted to the *gîte* of the Club Alpine by a friendly and helpful lady and had the place to ourselves.

Day 3: La Vacquerie — Lodève
Over night there had been thunder, lightning and it had rained cats and dogs, and it was still raining a little when we took the key back to the friendly *guardienne* of the *gîte*. As we set off we noticed that several doors were decorated, in the local custom, with wide-spread pale gold Carline thistles. The walking was fairly tedious, by forest paths. Rain came on more heavily and we stopped for shelter and a cup of tea, brewed up in the cab of an enormous tractor, standing by an area of cleared woodland. Sheltering later in a large stone-built *bergerie*, now partly ruinous, which had been used for trysting, we noticed one graffito which particularly appealed, *Yolande, mon âme pour la vie. Robert 1961*. One of the beams had a date of 1667 on it, and all around the interior was a continuous bench seat. This was one of a series of large *bergeries*, presumably used for shearing and branding the sheep in the old days. We pressed on into Lodève, by a steep, wooded descent, and just got registered in at the Hotel Croix Blanche before the heavens opened again.

Day 4: Lodève — Dio
We set off up the road to a radio transmitter upon the open hill top. There were superb views down to Lodève and the previous day's walk down through wooded slopes and to the plateaux of the *causses* behind them. It rained on and off after that and we had nearly got to

the Chapel de St. Amant, out in the wilds, when it started to pour down, so we sheltered in its porch.

From there on the terrain changed as we started to descend. We began to get real soil instead of rock, sometimes a deep reddy-brown with lumps of iron ore in it. When we reached Dio about 6.30pm, there was no restaurant/bar as our topoguide indicated. It was a really tiny place dominated by a huge ruined castle. The *gîte* had a welcoming bottle of red wine, though otherwise it left a lot to be desired. It was an old converted school that had a Dickensian air about it, rickety iron bedsteads, broken windows and toilet, and a dark and dingy air. But it soon took on a more cheerful aspect when we got some food and wine inside us. When we went to pay our dues, Mme. Cadeaux asked us where our donkeys were. When we said we were our own donkeys, she laughed and explained that they had quite a few English visitors arriving with donkeys. Locally advertised donkey treks were obviously popular.

Day 5: Dio — Lamalou-les-Bains

We followed the donkey turds down off the mountain and felt a sympathy for them as we negotiated the narrow, bolder-strewn path. At least we were doing it voluntarily! Once down in the valley, we were mainly back among vineyards. There we met a man collecting snails from the edge of a field of lucerne. He told us that he kept them for three weeks in his cellar. At the end of that time he sprinkled them with *gros sel* and washed them in several rinses of water, then boiled them. After that he took them out of their shells and mixed them with garlic, butter and parsley. Wishing him *bon appetit*, we continued on to La Tour sur Orb. From this river valley, we climbed up to the fortified village of Boussagues, into an extremely fertile area, with gardens bursting with produce, fields of fruit and vineyards. We collected some delicious wild figs, to have with our picnic in a disused builders yard, incongruously placed amongst all the orchards.

Descending into another river valley, we crossed over the medieval Pont du Diable, a really enormous structure, very solidly built and making a high arch above the river. Then we were up and over the next mountain side to La Sequestrière and down through woods to Lamalou, where lo and behold, the municipal camp site was directly in front of us, without any need to search for it.

Enquiries at the Tourist Office confirmed that the next few stints of the G.R.7 were without any possibility of getting provisions along the way. Also, the first place to stay would come after a very short stint followed by an extremely long one. The girl we spoke to suggested the alternative of using the railway line instead. This carried a little tourist train that only ran twice a day between Bedarieux and Mons, and she gave us the times. Beyond Mons you could walk the disused line as far as St. Pons de Thomières, she had done it herself. This was very useful advice, which we decided to follow. It would give us places to stay, shops for supplies, and we could pick up the G.R.7 later.

Lamalou was a real health cure centre, based on the healing properties of the water of the rivers Usclade and Vernière. It makes wide ranging claims for the treatment of conditions affecting the central and peripheral nervous systems, rheumatic and arthritic conditions and for the treatment of impotence. Certainly there were a lot of people whizzing around in electric buggies, and manoeuvring themselves on crutches. Unlike Grèoux, this was not an up-market spa and the sight of so many people with health problems prompted sympathy and a certain morbid curiosity. We were thankful for our continuing good health. However, the local youth were shooting-up in the Japanese gardens as we returned to the camp site. Right alongside all this expensive health care, the young were busy with their own solutions to other problems.

Day 6: Lamalou-les-Bains — Olargues
This was a day of level walking for a change, along the railway line. We timed our tea stop so that we were off the line when the morning train to Mons passed. You could hear it coming up the valley for quite a distance, repeatedly sounding its whistle, which echoed from side to side of the wooded slopes. At Colombier-sur-Orb station, we picnicked on the overgrown platform and were there when the train returned. We waved and the driver stopped to ask if we wanted to get on, but he was going the wrong way for us. After Mons station we

were on the disused section of the line. As we approached Olargues, we saw a disused railway bridge spanning the gorge. Betty could tell from behind that I was distinctly unhappy about the drop, because of the way I placed my feet on the rails. I could see all the trees in the gorge below, moving in the wind, and it seemed as if the viaduct was moving too. It gave me a taste of what Betty's vertigo must be like, though unaccountably crossing this bridge was no problem for her.

Having got directions, we walked down into the valley bottom to find the camp site. The *guardien* advised how to pitch our tent to cope best with the Mistral, which was blowing hard. We had to hang on to everything as we erected the tent, and the showers were most uninviting with blasts of coolish wind coursing through the building. We went back into Olargues to find something to eat but met a distinctly chilly reception at the Hotel Larzac, which had been recommended by the camp site. There was just one elderly customer troughing away in one of those stifling panelled dining rooms, which you meet in fusty old-fashioned hotels. The proprietress clearly didn't want to serve us, so we departed and eventually settled for a snack meal at a centre promoting regional products. In general we got a decidedly unfriendly feeling about Olargues, the way people were in the bar, and the stony looks of the old men sitting on the pavement, who looked, not so much at you, as through you. We went to bed with the wind still howling round our tent.

Day 7: Olargues — St. Pons de Thomières
We walked up into Olargues from the camp site to get breakfast and provisions. There was a market stall selling real wholemeal loaves — quite a rarity. Since bread loomed so large in our diet it was great to have a change from the inevitable French baguette. I asked someone where there was a water source, and was directed to a metal stand pipe with a press button, which wouldn't produce any water. Typical of Olargues, I thought bitterly, but I was over-hasty. I asked a mournful looking man sitting on the wall, where I could get water, and his whole face immediately changed. He smiled and said yes, there were two sources, one further down the village and the other which I had just tried. I told him I had tried it without success, and his smile

broadened. *Il faut bien pousser*, and then in English *You must poosh 'ard*, he replied, with gestures to match. So I filled up the water bottles and we left Olargues on this pleasanter note.

This was our second day of walking along the railway and we wended our way on an overgrown track. We were just remarking that it couldn't often be walked, as we had not seen a soul in over 20 kilometres along it, when a figure appeared ahead. It was a witch-like figure in long dark flowing garments, a pair of worn slippers and carrying a sickle. Her grey-hair was drawn tightly back into a bun. As she drew closer her face broke into a smile and she told us she was out looking for *cèpes*, and was disappointed to have found only one. The best place to look was in the chestnut woods, but it needed more rain.

The tunnels were quite exciting, once or twice plunging us briefly into total darkness before we could make out the light ahead, and channelling strong cool winds down them. Intermittently it was a real struggle to fight our way through the jungle which had grown up along the line. The most effective team were the robinias and the brambles. They worked together so that while you were fighting off the sharp thorns of the robinia up top, the brambles were wrapping themselves lovingly round your lower legs. Just when we thought we had mastered all this, we would find that we were being tripped up by a loop of bramble close to the ground that had escaped our notice. Progress slowed to two kilometres per hour or under. Eventually, nearing Riols we decided that the road, even with all its traffic was a better bet.

St. Pons was a long, straggling settlement along the N112, which goes through to Béziers. We decided on a cheap hotel and opted for eating in, as the menu was quite cheap and it included *coq au vin* and wine. But the food was awful. The first course included tinned mackerel, all too frequently an ingredient of our picnics. The *coq au vin* must have been prepared in a proprietary 'cook-in' sauce, it was so dreadful. But all was not lost as the red wine was really beautiful, mellow and full-bodied, and half a litre was included in the price. So we had a second *pichet* which made us feel a bit happier. Our only companions in the dining room were an elderly couple that we thought might have been long term residents, from the way they were addressed by the waitress. The man had had his lower right arm amputated, and had an intriguing knack of distributing salt on to his food by pouring it on to his stump, and shaking it with a flourish from there on to his plate.

Day 8: St. Pons de Thomières — Labastide Rouairoux

It was spitting with rain as we had our brioche and orange juice on a damp seat outside the cathedral. This enormous edifice was fortified, with two towers. At its west end there were Romanesque relief sculptures, very like those at Lincoln, with a scene of the Last Supper and the Crucifixion. During the religious wars of the 16th century, it had been partly burnt down.

We gritted our teeth for road walking down the N112, but in fact, it was very rewarding. The country opened out from the wooded hills we'd had the last two days, to a broader landscape of rolling hills, with cereal fields going high up, and plantations of different conifers. The *gîte* at Labastide was on the camp site and the *guardien* was very proud that it had been built by the local Syndicat d'Initiative. Though new, it wouldn't score very high on our '*gîte* accreditation scheme'. There were two blocks at the top of the camp site, one for the bunks and one for the kitchen. The bunks were of canvas attached to a metal framework, without any mattresses. Its saving grace was that it had a good big table and benches and a wonderful view.

We spread out our maps on the big table in the kitchen to check our route ahead. There were three days to go to Carcassonne. The first night would be after a climb up to the unguarded refuge at Col del Tap, then we would leave the G.R.7 by Pic de Nore and join the G.R.36 descending to the south. There would be nowhere to buy more provisions after Labastide until we reached Pradelles Cabardes at three hours walking down from Pic de Nore, where our friendly camp staff told us that there was a shop. The gusty wind that we had been experiencing this last three or four days is called locally '*le vent d'autan*', the fool's wind. Since La Vacquerie the weather pattern had been changing. Apart from the wind there had been quite a bit of rain, but on the plus side there had been a wonderful blue clarity to the air, that was particularly noticeable looking round at the hills from the camp site at Labastide. It provided a perfect spot for taking all this in and we had our best display of stars yet, as well as perfect dawns and sunsets.

Labastide Rouairoux used to be an important wool manufacturing centre. All that was left were factories producing glittery and gaudy specialist yarns for creative work, such as embroideries and tapestries. There were quite a few north Africans around who perhaps worked in the factories which we saw spreading up the valley to the south.

Day 9: Labastide Rouairoux — Refuge de Nore, Col del Tap

To make sure that we got to the unguarded refuge in good time, we were up before first light. We picked up the *balisage* of the G.R.7 on the south side of the town. It was beautiful walking up through beech woods on old paths, and we emerged from the woods just before Sales. We pressed on up to the ridge of Montaigne Noire at 1000m, which we followed for several kilometres. Fontaine des Trois Évêque was where three departments meet, Tarn, Hérault and Aude. The fountain named after the bishops of these three departments was dry and the bishops therefore deserved to be defrocked, as this is the only water source for miles around. It was too cool to linger there and we passed on to a bunch of weathered rocks on the ridge, which, a little oddly was picked out as a 'view point'. It was **all** good viewing, but it had to be taken in on the hoof as it was too windy to stop. After the ridge, there was a haul up through woods on forestry tracks, where we were given a cheery greeting by a forestry worker, stacking lengths of tree trunks into piles.

The refuge appeared suddenly in the beech woods in front of us. It was quite a shock to see that a battered wooden shack was to be our night's lodging. There was a large fireplace, benches, table and a bunk bed. It was a good morale booster to get the fire going, since this was going to serve for both cooking and lighting. We set about collecting wood, and seven loads lasted us for the evening and early the next morning. As we were gathering wood and feeding the fire, we had a visit from a man from Mazamet, a neighbouring town, with his two young cousins from Toulouse. He had obviously come to check up what was happening, seeing the smoke from the chimney. He said that he had himself stayed at the refuge in the past. He often came up to see the fantastic views from the Pic de Nore. Occasionally you could see from end to end of the Pyrenees, the Mediterranean to the south and the Auvergne to the north. In 1936, when the Spanish civil war was on, he said that you could see cannon fire in the Pyrenees from there.

Day 10: Refuge de Nore, Col del Tap — Villeneuve Minervois
We walked the short distance from the refuge to the junction with the G.R.36, and followed it up to Pic de Nore, with its red and white television transmitter looking like a rocket about to lift off. The light was good that day, though not perfect. We saw the Mediterranean as a line of bright light and the Pyrenees were like fairy tale mountains with fantastic snowy peaks visible above the cloud line. Carcassonne lay before us in the broad valley like a fabled city of towers and walls, some 40-50 kilometres away.

There was no shop at Pradelles Cabardes after all, which was quite a blow because our supplies were almost used up, but we got a coffee and brioche at a cafe there. The proprietor told us that the only place with a shop before Carcassonne, which was anywhere near the route of the footpath, was at Villeneuve Minervois. This was vital information, on the strength of which, we replanned our route to make a detour off the G.R.36 to reach there that night.

The descent was beautiful with open views to the Pyrenees all the way. Fortunately we always carried emergency supplies and so we had tinned mackerel, two-day old bread, and sweet coffee for energy, which all tasted good because it was eaten in such a marvellous spot. In retrospect this counts as one of our most memorable stretches of walking. We descended by a series of ridges with craggy outcrops of sandstone, a little reminiscent of Dartmoor but on a much vaster scale. Sweet smelling broom and gorse were all along our path, which swept us first up and over then down again, giving us panoramic views all the time to either side. The last few kilometres were a complete contrast, with their cultivated lowland slopes and vineyards. In fact

Villeneuve Minervois (familiar to us from wine bought in England) was completely surrounded by vineyards. This was an attractive small town by a river, with a shady main street and a choice of two or three hotels. It seemed geared towards wine tourists with its large *cave* on the outskirts.

Day 11: Villeneuve Minervois — Carcassonne

We set off west on a minor road through vineyards, to pick up the G.R.7 again. To our north were open vistas of the mountains from which we had descended the day before. Before Conques-sur-Orbiel we found our G.R. path again. Reaching higher ground we could see Carcassonne ahead of us and couldn't believe that it was still three hours away. This was an amazing view of the city, which looked from there, just like it must have looked in medieval times, with its wall and towers intact and rising out of the plain. Reaching the Canal du Midi, we followed its towpath for a few kilometres before striking off to cross over the river Aude by the Pont Vieux. We climbed the hill to enter the walled city, packed with tourists and trinket shops and found the Youth Hostel, right in the middle of it — a haven of peace and quiet.

Carcassonne was one of our *poste restante* addresses and we stayed four days (the longest time we had stayed in one place since leaving England). Pauline had come up trumps with a tape recorder, so that I could begin brushing up on my Spanish. We were also pleased to hear from Andrew and Paula who were continuing to enjoy life in our house in Barrow. It had been so hot in England that my brother had been umpiring cricket matches in nothing but his swimming trunks under his umpire's white coat.

As usual we met an interesting bunch of people at the Youth Hostel. There was a redoubtable, single Belgian lady, from near Vielsalm, which we knew from walking the G.R.5. She was on her way to meet up with her poorly sister at Lourdes. She spoke very distinct French, excellent to follow. All her sentences started or ended with; *Oui monsieur,* or *Bien sur madame*, as she talked volubly to one or other of the company. She enthused about everything and loved England. She had been to Hull and Ramsgate, and when she got back from this trip, she was off to Italy with an organised party. Betty started to speak French to a girl in the kitchen and discovered that she was a long-term American traveller, Shirl by name. She had started off with her boyfriend but she had sent him home because he was missing mummy! She thought that we were lucky that we both enjoyed the travelling life so much and because of our advanced age, felt compelled to take our pulses. She seemed reassured by her findings.

The defences of this hilltop town are complete, given judicious restoration, with inner and outer circuits. The church of St. Nazaire had splendid Norman arches and wonderful gargoyles and corbel heads, covered with human and animal subjects. The interior had been left plain, austere stone, such a pleasant sight after so many mawkishly done-up interiors, with their 18th and 19th century paintings. As we walked down into the modern town we came across a great frieze, recently painted, depicting episodes of the history of Carcassonne, in a similar style to the Bayeux Tapestry. It started with the Saracens and went on with the Cathars and the Counts of Trancavel to the twelfth century when it became a royal city. But in fact the history of this hilltop settlement started with Iron Age and Roman occupation. Beside the main gate to the medieval city were a collection of jugglers, musicians, living statues and beggars with their motley collection of dogs, all vying for hand-outs, just as it might have been in medieval times.

Useful information, addresses and bibliography

Topoguide 716: Traversée du Haut-Languedoc (GR7, GR71, & GR74)

Youth Hostel, Rue du Vicomte Trencavel, Cite Medievale, 11000 Carcassonne.

Gîte d'Étape Municipal, 1 Rue de la Carrierrasse, 30120 Le Vigan. Tel.04 67 81 01 71.

Airports: Nîmes\Arles\Camargue; Montpellier; Carcassonne.

Train stations: Montpellier, Nîmes and Carcassonne.

Autobus: Montpellier to Le Vigan; Nîmes to Le Vigan.

Tourist Offices: Maison de Pays, 30120 Le Vigan. Tel.04 67 81 01 72 and 15 Bd. Camille Pelletan, BP 842 - 11012 Carcassonne. Tel.04 68 10 24 30.

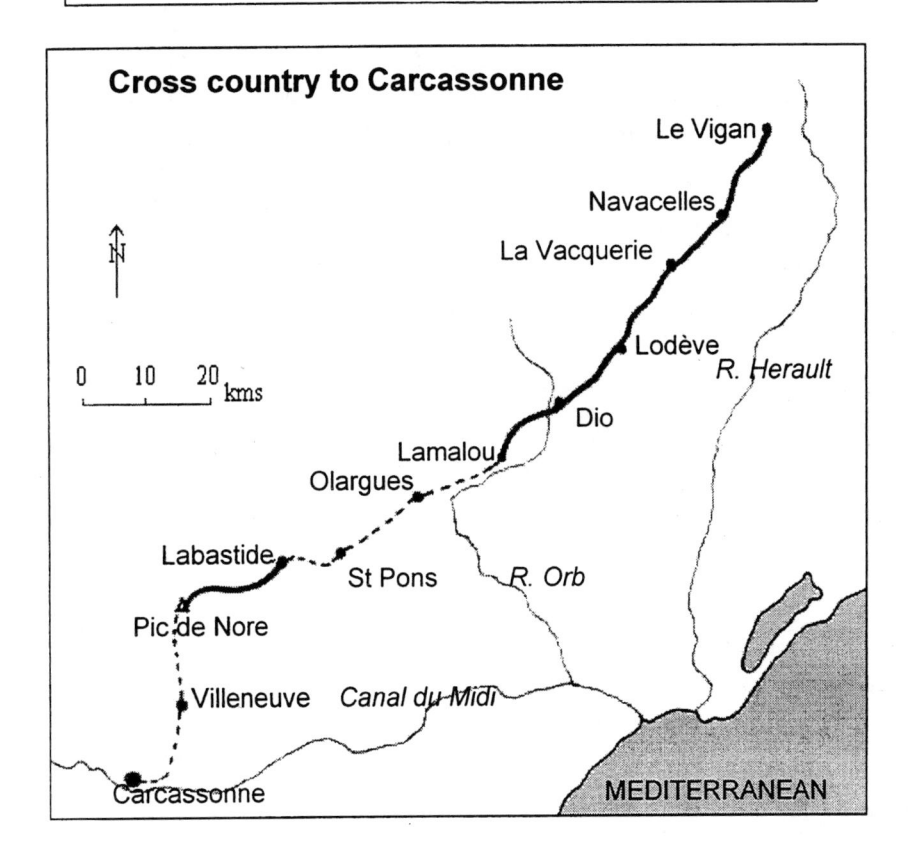

Cross country to Carcassonne

To Carcassone

LES CORBIÈRES AND LES FENOUILLÈDE

~ THROUGH THE VINEYARDS

Far from being just a gentle stroll through vineyards, we found ourselves having to do several stiff ascents to cross the high, barren tops, in between the productive valleys. For once we were definitely in the right place at the right time, to experience the start of the grape harvest and to sample some of the best wine that we encountered in France.

Table of Distances	
1. Carcassonne - La Fraissinède, Montlaur	25.0km
2. La Fraissinède, Montlaur - Lagrasse	14.0km
3. Lagrasse - Château Durfort	18.0km
4. Château Durfort - La Carcassé	19.0km
5. La Carcassé - Duilhac	10.5km
6. Duilhac - St. Paul de Fenouillet	10.0km
7. St. Paul de Fenouillet - Caramany	13.5km
8. Caramany - Perpignan (22km by bus)	37.0km

Day 1: Carcassonne — La Fraissinède, Montlaur

It was good to be back on the trail as we walked straight out of the Narbonne gate of the medieval city into the countryside. We crossed the motorway to a lake under local authority control. It was controlled to death, with notices, litter bins and footpaths everywhere. We got held up in Monze as the *balisages* weren't very clear, and petered out at either side of the village, leaving us to find our way by trial and error. Our route was up the western slope of the Montaigne d'Alaric. The path deteriorated into great lumps of loose stone and, after a level platform it plunged steeply down to the north, where we had to negotiate a three metre cliff of bare rock. From there on we were amongst scrub and dense tree cover, with only occasional views out to the Pic de Nore. At the Priory St. Jean we found a huge concrete table and bench which had been constructed amongst the ruins of the building, possibly used as a hunting lodge.

From there we diverged from the G.R.36, which followed the mountains, to take the quickest route to Montlaur and the *gîte*. We walked first through grassy meadows, no doubt formerly used by the priory, then into the wide open valley, with its vineyards ringed by mountains. The grapes looked almost ready but we were told they would need another two weeks. La Fraissinède was an isolated auberge, about three kilometres east of Montlaur and close to the slope of Mont d'Alaric. One of the farm buildings had been converted to make a very pleasant *gîte* which we had to ourselves, but there were no facilities for cooking. The auberge provided meals. Outside the *gîte* was an attractive garden, with tables and chairs and lots of flowers. Pots full of herbs were arranged around the large yard and were obviously used in the cooking. These made Betty feel quite nostalgic. It was a really great place to stay, where we were given a good dinner of *porc sauté*, accompanied by lovely red Corbière wine. We had started off at 8.0am and finished at 6.0pm. After four days of rest, this stint of 25 kilometres took its toll.

Day 2: La Fraissinède, Montlaur — Lagrasse
A little track from behind the auberge led us up on to the ridge where we rejoined the G.R.36. The path was accompanied by masses of a pale yellow umbelliferous plant which we had not met before. There was also a spiky shrub with yellow flowers whose scent was like that of mignonette, though the growth itself was entirely different. Other flowers too seemed to be specific to these mountains. The highest, easternmost point, Roc de l'Aigle, had expansive views north to the Black Mountains, east to the sea somewhere close to Narbonne, and south to the Pyrenees with all the hills and mountains of the Corbières in between. We were inspected from the air by an eagle, which must have decided we were a bit too heavy too haul off for carrion. From this high point there was a magnificent walk down the southern rocky spine, with near views over the vineyards all around the villages in

the valley. The story goes, that Montaigne d'Alaric may have been named after one of Charlemagne's companions, since he and his army were all around this area.

The route to Ribauté was through vineyards with advertisements for *dégustation* at various chateaux along the way. The chateaux there are more like our manor houses than the traditional English picture of a castle. The way over to Lagrasse was on tracks high above the road, where we found fig trees and almond trees by the wayside. We ate one each of the absolutely ripe, blue-black figs and gathered almonds from below the trees.

Lagrasse is in the heart of Corbières country, hence there were several *caves* in the village, each selling wine from their own particular estate. We got a litre and a half of red, *vin ordinaire* 1993, from the *cave* of M.and Mme. Cabanol, a small family concern. It was beautiful, mellow and fruity. We were in a wine lover's paradise. The village had many small squares and a tight-knit series of narrow streets going down to the river, in one of which we found our *gîte*, above Les Trois Graces Restaurant. We wandered down to the river and performed a Stone Age ritual, selecting suitable stones to crack open the almonds we had gathered. We chopped these almonds up and mixed them with sugar to sprinkle over our figs and *crème fraîche*. The taste was unforgettable, with a zest and bitterness almost over the top.

Day 3: Lagrasse — Château Durfort

This day was intended to be a shortish one, as our hostess at La Fraissinède had told us that there was a *gîte communal* at Maironnais. We tried ringing the Mairie there several times without success, but it was on the G.R.36 so we would find out details when we got there. Before leaving Lagrasse, I had a look at the abbey, which was founded by Charlemagne in the eighth century. Though there was little left of the original, this abbey had been important in his time, as one of the major religious houses on the fluctuating border between France and Spain. Hence its role was as much political as religious.

We went up over uncultivated tops of scrub and pine, remarking the extreme contrast between this wild scenery and the highly cultivated valley floors. Our route across the tops went by a well, complete with wooden capping, and containing lovely clear unlittered water. As luck would have it a mobile shop had just pulled up in Caunette-en-Val, so we were able to get some green beans for our evening meal. Maironnais was a tiny village and we puzzled a local by asking confidently for the *gîte*. He took us along to the Mairie, open by this time, to speak to a very helpful woman there. She said no, there was no *gîte*, but if we were desperate we could sleep in the church. Otherwise if we were prepared to walk on another seven or eight kilometres, we would find a *gîte* at Château Durfort and she would phone ahead if we wanted. Since it was only about 4.0pm, we took her up on her offer and when she had checked that we could stay there, we set off.

It was easy, if rather boring walking, on forest tracks, which hugged the contours round the meandering folds of the mountain side, to reach Château Durfort. There was the ruined chateau perched on a pinnacle and three other houses. The *gîte* was all locked up, so we tried the house opposite. The old man there, M. Orajous, said that we could stay there but we had to wait until his son came home from work to let us in. In the meantime we sat in the last of the sunshine on the patio preparing our french beans. His son arrived just as it was getting dark to let us in. He was very pleasant and affable and when I asked whether I could buy a bottle of wine, he said; *Oui, bien sûr, blanc ou rouge.* So we had a bottle of the lovely red wine from their own vineyards and this made the cassoulet and beans into a special meal. We slept soundly in this quiet and remote spot.

Day 4: Château Durfort — La Carcassé

Looking round at all the wild boar heads in the study, when we went to pay our dues, I remarked that we hadn't once seen one in our travels. So we were taken to see Mimi, their captive *sanglier*, who had been injured when young. She was now kept in a pen as a pet and came when called and ate the bread thrown to her. M. Orajous said that she would only come out for him, as otherwise she would smell us and be too nervous. Betty said, *Never mind her smelling us, we can certainly smell her!* She had a good but powerful pig smell and was a splendid animal with a long tapering snout, oval rib cage, longish legs and the beginnings of a thick grey-black winter coat. She had her back to the corner of the pen and M. Orajous said that this was to defend herself in case of danger, showing that she had not really become domesticated. Since harvest time was close, the vineyards hereabouts were protected with electric fences as the wild boar are especially partial to ripe grapes. We saw some domestic pigs later in the day and saw how much the proportions of the feral creature have been altered — shorter snouts, rounder bodies, shorter legs, less hair.

We followed the road round and picked up the *balisage* for Termes, another château, further on. We found that a considerable amount of path clearance and marking had been recently completed on this stretch. The footpath was up and down wooded ridges with some fairly abrupt climbs but also some splendid old tracks, completely enclosed in woods of box and oak. After an energetic morning, we climbed out of the woods on to the bare grassy top of Peyre Fouillère at 688m, where the wind was so strong we had difficulty staying on course. At Mouthoumet we phoned ahead to La Carcassé, a *gîte* which M. Orajous had told us about. Situated in a remote spot, high up in these wooded hills with their folded, secret valleys, La Carcassé was a muddle of half-finished buildings. A fire chief and his wife, who were doing the place up, were away for the evening and a friendly woman with lots of kids was standing in.

Day 5: La Carcassé — Duilhac

The fire chief was very much in evidence at breakfast. La Carcassé had been the home of this small, lively man in his 50s, since 1984. If they were snowed in during the winter and he was urgently needed, the fire service would send a helicopter to fetch him. He told us the folk tale of the origin of the name of Carcassonne. The city, occupied by Dame Carcas, a foreign princess, was besieged, so the story goes, for several years by Charlemagne. When they had only one pig and a sack of wheat left, she hit on the idea of sending out the pig, fed on the grain, to the besiegers. She then rang the bells of the town to suggest peace to Charlemagne. He agreed, as he thought they must still have plenty of food. La Carcassé itself had been a hamlet of perhaps 200 people once and had belonged to the Templars. It had been abandoned for 70 years when the fire chief and his wife had taken it over.

After walking for two to three hours in wooded terrain, we emerged into the open valley of Rouffiac des Corbières, surrounded by vineyards and gardens. Our lunchtime stop was memorable for a wonderful dip in the river Verdouble. After this we began the incredibly steep ascent to the Château de Peyrepertuse, which we had seen from the river, perched on the top of impossibly steep crags. The path climbed directly up from Rouffiac, and we looked back down on to the wonderful glowing orange tiles of its roofs. With her sixth sense, Betty had already realised that this climb might not be for her, so after scrambling quite a way up, she descended and went round by the road. I kept going in dense box undergrowth on this slithery, one in two path, wondering why I hadn't joined her. I came to some large boulders, between which the path squeezed and thought I could hear distant voices above. A little later, when I could eventually look out from the boxwood, I found that I was right underneath the crags on which the castle stood. The entry to it was by worn rock steps which went under the overhanging cliffs and up a narrow rock-cut path. I could see Betty far below, beetling along the road as I slowly rounded the crags to enter the castle.

Peyrepertuse was perched on a narrow fin of rock and, as I struggled up into the keep, I joined all the tourists milling around. They had come up by car on the other side. The view was stunning — you could see sunlight on the sea to the east and Château Queribus across the valley to the south, sticking up like a finger on another impossible crag. I spent some time wandering around in a bit of a daze, recovering from the climb and marvelling at this impregnable castle of the Cathars, which was, not surprisingly, never taken. I must have seemed a strange sight as I ambled about, drenched in sweat, with my backpack, amongst the motor tourists. Several people had video cameras and seemed more interested in videoing each other than the castle. One, an Englishman, appeared to be muttering to himself, as he pointed his camera, but in fact it was a running commentary. Overheard samples included; . . . *and now we can see some steps leading up to a curious little tower. . .*, The 'curious little tower' was a sentry post on the curtain wall, with a superb view out to the south through the arrow-slit. The beauty of the view would not have been appreciated by the wretched guard, especially with a strong southerly wind blowing through. Worse still was the gaping hole below his feet, down a vertical rock face. This hole was provided for the sentry to relieve himself, without leaving his post. I wondered if he had ever had the satisfaction of crapping on an approaching enemy.

The road walk down to Duilhac took longer than expected and Betty had already booked in at the *gîte*. It was a surprise to find it was nearly full, after staying in so many empty ones. But it was a Saturday night, and we met up there with the Sentier Cathar, a popular circuit of the Cathar castles. We met a monosyllabic, lone English walker of the Sentier Cathar, who was painfully shy. During the night I was trying to make sense of the Cathar heresy from the bits of information that I had gleaned, and decided to try to break the ice with this lone Englishman, if the opportunity presented itself, since somehow I felt sure that he would know all about it.

Day 6: Duilhac — St. Paul de Fenouillet
This proved to be a good hunch and when he came into the kitchen early, I asked him and he was away. Catharism, he explained, was a blend of Christianity and Buddhism, and had arrived from eastern Europe, where, in Bulgaria, the Bogomils (Friends of God) held similar ideas. Basically, the world and its creatures including humans, were the work of the devil. God's world and that of the spirit, was something separate, to be attained by leading a celibate and otherwise abstinent life. In part it was a revolt from the laxness of the established church, but it was also seen in northern France, as belonging to a separatist movement of a wealthy area, which didn't then belong to France. It gave the excuse to the established church and the state to work together, to annex what was to become southern France, on the pretext that Catharism was a heresy. Though Peyrepertuse was never taken, at Montsegur, another Cathar castle, which held out, an amnesty was arranged but not kept. The Cathars there were all burnt at the stake. At Béziers, the entire population of the city (several

thousand) was slaughtered — ostensibly all done in the name of religion.

The shortish stint for that day took us part way up to the castle again, and then over an unnamed col towards the Gorges de Galamus. Everyone had said that we must see this, but we had seen one too many gorges already, and preferred to make our way directly down to St. Paul de Fenouillet. By that time we had passed out of Les Corbières and into Les Fenouillèdes, defined by the bare rocky ranges north and south of St. Paul, and including the important vineyards in the valley of the river L'Agly. Muscat, a speciality of the vineyards around the town is a sweet desert wine, with a very pleasant aromatic flavour. We had enjoyed sampling the Muscat grapes, identifiable by their golden colour, so it was nice to try the wine.

Day 7: St. Paul de Fenouillet — Caramany

We had parted company with the G.R.36 the day before, in order to ensure that we had somewhere to stay between St. Paul and our projected next stop at Ille sur Têt. So, after St. Paul we joined the Tour de Fenouillèdes, a local walking circuit with yellow and red markers, instead the red and white which we'd been used to. This path set off up a gentle slope to Col de Lesquerde, giving us splendid views over the vineyards and the barren rocky spine to the north. Beyond this to the north-west, we could see the sinister black shape of Bugarach, projecting high above the surrounding tops. It looked as evil as the name suggested. The woman at the Mairie had booked us into a *gîte* at Caramany, where we were to meet the key-holder at 6.30pm. As it was only late morning, and we appeared to have only ten kilometres or so to walk, this seemed like a doddle.

But all was not as straightforward as it seemed on the map. After we left Lesquerde there was a tortuous route through vineyards, with a fairly innocent couple of downs and ups. But then we came to an up, which just kept on going, getting ever steeper and shalier. Neither of us were at all happy with this in full packs, and it got Betty's vertigo going. But we had no choice but to continue, as returning would be worse. Fortunately when it was done, the descent on the other side was less steep. We missed our route somehow, taking a wrong turning, south-west nearly to Ansignan, instead of heading south-east to Caramany. Finally we got down to the road in the valley bottom, and had to set our minds to about nine kilometres of road walking in just under two hours, to make Caramany by the appointed time.

We were much heartened, as we pounded along the road, to be overtaken by all manner of vehicles, carrying large containers of grapes toward Caramany. This was the first day of the *vendange* (grape harvest), and there we were right in amongst it. As we approached Caramany, we could see that all these assorted vehicles were heading for the *cave* at the bottom of the hill. We were able to buy some beautiful, mellow deep red wine that enlivened our humble supper no end. The shop had stayed open late, especially for the grape harvest and when we went in, the shopkeeper thought we had come for the grape picking.

Day 8: Caramany — Perpignan
Returning for more excellent wine, we got talking to the man who was weighing the vehicles, as they arrived with their grapes. He told us that machines were not used there to harvest the grapes, because the vines were grown too close together and the terrain was not suitable. The weekly schedule of grape varieties to be accepted on each day and at what percentage alcohol, was posted outside. Grape types included Syrah, Morvedre and Maccabeo.

We decided to take the quickest route over the mountains down to the main road at Ille-sur-Têt. The road climbed through vineyard after vineyard. It was cloudy, windy and threatening rain and by the time we reached Bélesta, it was raining seriously enough to make us take shelter in an old wash house with stone troughs. After Bélesta the countryside changed completely. All sign of modern cultivation ceased and we were walking through wild rocky valleys and craggy tops, with rounded granite profiles. Even here there were traces of an enormous number of old cultivation terraces, which had gone back to nature. The rain lent a romantic grandeur to the scene, especially when the sacred mountain of Canigou, one of the peaks of the

Pyrenees which we had been seeing on and off for days, appeared in the distance, lurking behind black thunder clouds.

As we started to descend, very gradually into the broad valley of the river Têt, we both noticed a decided softening in the air and a sweet smell. The climate, I guess was changing as we came out of the mountains into the ample and productive river valley. On the way down we passed through an area called Les Orgues (The Organs), so-called because the pinnacles of crumbly sandstone, glowing red, reminded someone of organ pipes. They were indeed a fantastic sight. When the Pyrenees were formed, in the Tertiary Era, the Têt valley received successive strata deriving from the creation of the mountain range. These formed an enormous plateau of fine sediments of granite dust and other larger debris. Thereafter storms, water channels and wind eroded these deposits, to form this weird landscape, which we saw with the dramatic backdrop of Canigou, as we came down into the valley. From Ille-sur-Têt the bus took us to Perpignan in half an hour and we settled for Hotel de la Poste et Le Perdrix, an old fashioned establishment with a splendid view out on the Narbonne Gate.

Once established in our hotel, we started our search for the *pied à terre* we had promised ourselves. We found a small student flatlet, available until the start of the University term, with a small kitchenette, bathroom and bed-sitting room and a shared courtyard at the back. To our great joy, Perpignan had a daily market, which revealed itself slowly, since its real live centre was not the covered part of it, with its ordered rows of permanent stalls, but a warren of minor streets around the covered market, where there were small shops and outside stalls. As far as we were concerned, the nerve centre was a narrow thoroughfare, where each lunchtime a large paella pan was heated with calor gas and a different dish was prepared from scratch with mouth watering aromas permeating the neighbourhood. One day a variety of seafood, mussels, cockles, baby crabs were being stirred with the aroma of wine and garlic in evidence; another day it was lamb's kidneys that were being cooked. The stalls around had all the ingredients available, lots of olives, spices and herbs, fruit, vegetables and fungi, and above all, the fish stalls, with live crabs trying to climb out of their container and live eels squirming in a tub.

One day a week there was an organic market with lovely breads. The guy who produced it, said you could read his bread like books. He decorated the tops with the ingredients that were also included, thus olive, hazel and walnut loaves could be identified. I was in my element as I discovered one *cave* after another offering loose local wines and we managed to sample most of them. After extensive tests we decided that our favourite was a red, Espina de l'Agly. One of the many *caves* was kept by a woman with a broad, ruddy, peasant face, who told me *Je vous fais goûter ce vin rouge*, which I chose to translate as *I am going to make you taste this red wine*. I like to hear talk like that. It was she who introduced us to the said, Espina de l'Agly, so full and fruity.

Without realising it, we had landed ourselves bang in the capital of Roussillon wines. It was quite an education for us, to learn how highly controlled and structured wine production was in this area, and no doubt throughout France. Crops could not be irrigated and the amount of grapes allowed to be produced on each hectare was strictly laid down. Particularly with the *apellation controllée*, as at Caramany, the grape types that could be used to produce a particular wine were specified. The precise growing area, and in which named communes, was laid down for the *apellation d'origine controllée*. All the detailed rules and regulations, governing wine production, are understandable in such a long-established industry. In classical times, Pliny the Elder praised the wines from this area, and there is now some evidence for wine production in prehistoric times.

While we had been travelling, we had registered that the *boulangeries* always had a wonderful display of fresh cream *gateaux* on a Sunday, when they would open just in the morning. It was a French tradition to buy these luscious, but fragile cakes for Sunday lunch. So many times we'd had to gaze longingly at them, and pass them by, since we couldn't hope to carry them with us. Our local shop had plenty to choose from, and we bought a fantastic concoction, of puff pastry base, with choux balls round the edge, filled with vanilla custard, coated with caramel and the whole thing decorated with *crème Chantilly*. Absolutely no concessions to being healthy, but what a wonderful way to go!

The town of Perpignan was dominated by a low hill, which was surrounded by the inevitable brick fortifications of Vauban, whose frontier works we were now familiar with. Vauban's 17th century work at Perpignan was the end of a succession of defensive works, which had started with the palace of the kings of Majorca in the 13th century. This was a short-lived kingdom, independent of the warring countries of Aragon, Catalonia and France. For a brief period in the late 13th and early 14th centuries, it controlled Mediterranean trade and held the rich wine and fruit growing area of the Perpignan valley. To modern day ears, it sounds like a tin-pot kingdom, named after an island now noted for cheap package holidays. But for a few decades, it held the balance of power, between powerful neighbours. One bizarre touch, was that the Princes of Aragon bred lions in the castle ditches, because, as kings of the animals they were symbols of the supreme power of the Princes. These lions were fed on goats which were raised in the castle meadows by nobles. From the massive defences of Vauban, still preserved as a tourist attraction, there were extensive views of the Pyrenees, the plain of the river Têt to the west and north and the Mediterranean to the east. A busker was playing his guitar and singing flamenco, under the austere brick vaults of the passageway leading up to the citadel. The acoustics were fantastic. The sound of this beautiful, sad and haunting music, with his harsh broken voice, seemed to be the music of the endlessly oppressed, making their lament at the castle wall of their oppressors.

There was an underlying feeling of tension, unrest and violence about the city. Perhaps it is there in all cities and we picked it up from having been so long in country places. There were burnt-out cars, police visible frequently, and soldiers with guns guarding the station. Apparently the latter was because of a recent terrorist bombing in Paris, by ETA, the Basque separatist movement. A prominent graffito on a wall in the town, added to these feelings — *Let us hang the last cop (flic) with the guts of the last priest (curé)*.

Our last day in Perpignan was one of considerable frustration. We started off by **not** catching the bus to Mont Louis, as we had planned. Having found the temporarily re-sited bus station, way out of town, we apparently got there in plenty of time, but no bus came. Then having walked all the way back into Perpignan to the train station, we excelled ourselves by managing **not** to catch the train either. Salvador Dali, for some unknown reason, thought that Perpignan railway station was the centre of the universe. In truth, it was a fairly depressing place, as stations go, the more especially with soldiers standing outside it. As we stood waiting in a freezing wind, Betty quietly said, *I wonder if they could have changed the clocks?* How right she was! We should have put our clocks back and were an hour ahead of local time.

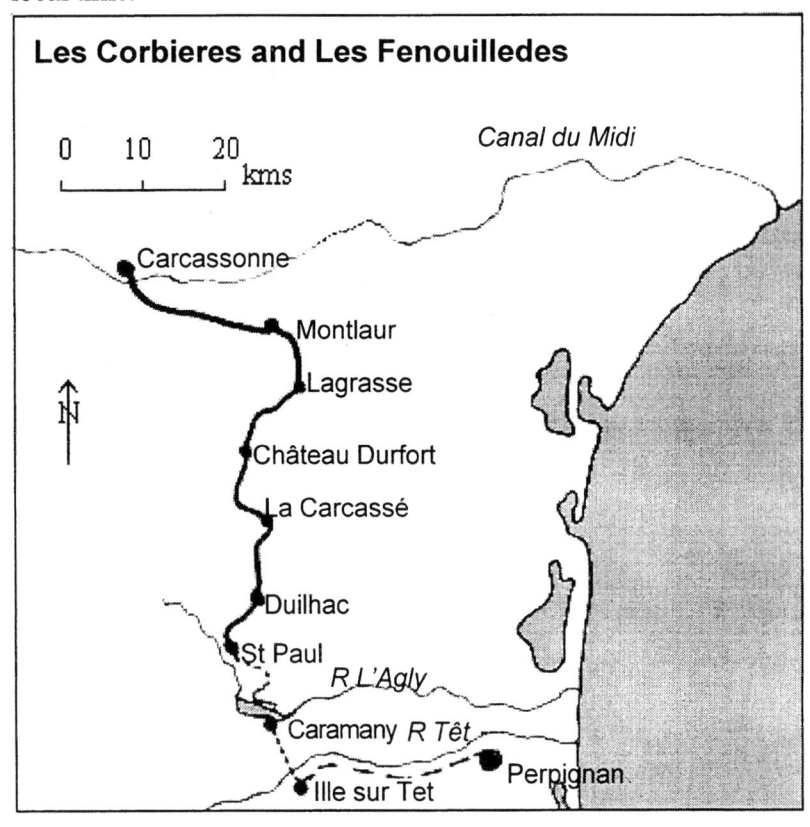

Les Corbieres and Les Fenouilledes

0 10 20 kms

Canal du Midi

Carcassonne
Montlaur
Lagrasse
Château Durfort
La Carcassé
Duilhac
St Paul
R L'Agly
Caramany *R Têt*
Ille sur Tet
Perpignan

Key to maps - page 27

Europe at walking pace

Useful information, addresses and bibliography

Maps IGN Series Verte 1:100,000 No. 72

Youth Hostels, Rue de Vicomte Trencavel, Cité Médiéval, 11000 Carcassonne. Tel.04 68 25 23 16

and Parc de la Pépinière, Ave de Grande Bretagne, 66000 Perpignan. Tel.04 68 34 63 32

Airports: Carcassonne and Perpignan

Train stations: Carcassonne and Perpignan

Tourist Offices: 15 Bd. Camille Pelletan, BP 842 - 11012 Carcassonne. Tel.04 68 10 24 30 and Palais des Congress, Place Armand Lanoux, BP 2155 - 66002 Perpignan. Tel.04 68 66 30 30

THE PYRENEES AND INTO SPAIN

There could not have been a grander approach to Spain, than walking down the long, broad valley from Mont Louis to Puigcerdà at its southernmost end. Before us all the time were the peaks of the Spanish Pyrenees, and when we reached them, it was a magic time to be in the mountains. Not only were the woods and forests changing colour, but it was also the season when nature yields up its wonderful annual crop of fungi.

Table of Distances	
1. Perpignan - Mont Louis (train)	72.0km
2. Mont Louis - Err	15.0km
3. Err - Puigcerdà	8.5km
4. Puigcerdà - La Molina	14.5km
5. La Molina - La Pobla de Lillet	16.0km
6. La Pobla de Lillet - Guardiola	15.0km
7. Guardiola - Santuari de Falgars	11.0km
8. Santuari de Falgars - Vilada	16.0km
9. Vilada - Berga	12.0km
10. Berga - La Quar	17.5km
11. La Quar - Sagas	14.0km
12. Sagas - Puig-Reig	15.0km
13. Puig-reig - Manresa (bus)	28.0km
14. Manresa - Sant Vicenç	12.5km
15. Sant Vicenç - Monistrol	14.0km

Day 1: Perpignan — Mont Louis
At the *boulangerie* where I got bread for our journey, the tubby young baker was conversing with two smartly dressed, elderly gentlemen customers, while his assistant, an old man, thin as a rail and wearing a

flat cap, went to and fro bringing out the loaves from the ovens in the back. As his customers turned to leave with their purchases, the young baker said to them, as if to children, with mock gravity and a wagging finger; *Soyez sage et portez-vous bien* (Be good and behave yourselves).

It was a brilliantly sunny morning, but windy still, as we headed up the Têt valley to change at Villefranche to the famous *Train Jaune*. This was a real frontier post set in a narrow cleft and dominated by a fort on the crags above. From there we really got into the mountains and the journey was spectacular by any standards. The train was absolutely full of school kids on an outing, who took little, or no notice of the scenery, so busy were they thumping and clouting one another. The single line rail track spanned incredible gorges and the children, briefly suspending warfare, took to screaming each time we crossed one, for the excitement of hearing their voices echoing back from the mountain side. During this journey we climbed from more or less sea-level, to 1400m at Mont Louis. The tops of the mountains were dusted in snow and dazzling in the late September sunshine. At La Cabanasse we happily left the school party to complete their journey by coach and plodded up into Mont Louis.

The *gîte* at La Cassagne was in an old farmhouse on the edge of a near vertical slope, with its farmyard enclosed by two enormous wooden doors. Our room had a little balcony with a sheer drop over the steep valley side and a panoramic view of the mountains. Betty cooked a splendid supper of stuffed aubergines and scalloped potatoes. While we ate, we talked to Henri, who was travelling with a pony and trap all round France. He was a loquacious soul, and good company but we could hear Yuki, his mournful spaniel, shifting and scratching her fleas all night long, on the bare boards of the room above us.

Day 2: Mont Louis — Err

Dawn over the mountains was mind-blowing. We had a cup of tea and kept looking out at this breath-taking sight as the mountains lit up with sunlight across the valley. It was going to be a lovely day. We saw Henri and Yuki off in the pony and trap, hotly pursued by the large, soft St. Bernard dog, which belonged to the *gîte*. It came back well pleased with itself and leant heavily against me when I stroked it, practically pushing me over. We set off from the *gîte* down the impossibly steep descent to get us across the valley to Planès, where we rejoined the G.R.36.

A long, steep climb through woods, brought us round the flanks of the mountain, L'Homme Mort. Betty spotted a *boletus* and then we found more that we bagged. A French couple were able to confirm what they were, and that they were good to eat, especially in an omelette. Betty was happy to try them once we had got a second opinion. She is always a bit suspicious of my identifications.

The views opened up, so that we could see the whole, broad plateau ringed with mountains. We could look back and see Mont Louis with a clearer understanding of the strategic importance of the fort. Vauban's work was brilliantly placed to control this long, wide and fertile plateau, where Spain starts. We could look down from the valley side on the little airfield at Saillagouse, from which light planes and helicopters operated at frequent intervals. What with the little train, and airfield and the national road, this valley was now only one hour, or less, from Perpignan. When Vauban was defending France's frontiers in the 17th century, it must have been a pretty remote area. We looked forward and south and could see the jagged summits of the Spanish Pyrenees at the southern limit of these high flatlands.

At the *gîte* in Err, there was a pleasant upstairs kitchen with long tables and a large fireplace. But the whole place was in shade and so, at this altitude, very cold. Barbara, the *guardienne*, said that she had quite a few Basques and Spanish coming to stay, but she didn't have people passing through, like us, walking into Spain. She encouraged us to light a fire to warm the room. The *boletus* took quite some preparation. They definitely needed their rather slimy skins taking off but the resulting omelette was delicious.

Day 3: Err — Puigcerdà

It was a short day's stint to get us over the border into Spain, but it was a great walk too, along the slope of the mountains overlooking a productive valley with a number of villages, each with their area of farmland with cattle, sheep and some arable fields. We could see Puigcerdà sitting up on its own hilltop on the other side of the valley.

We journeyed on to Bourg Madame, a rather dilapidated settlement on the French side of the border, and walked through the customs post into Spain, without anyone knowing or caring!

After struggling up the hill into Puigcerdà, we passed the school, where they were just returning for the afternoon. One of the kids shouted, *Do you spick ingleesh?* To which I replied in unctuous British tones, *Yes, I do actually*, provoking a gale of giggles. Betty spotted the G.R.4 topoguide, complete with map, in a bookshop. It was in Catalan, but the essential information was there in table and map form. This would at least get us four or five days towards Barcelona. That night we joined the throngs strolling around the streets, our first introduction to the Spanish custom of the *paseo*. The tapas bars were filled with tasty looking dishes of sea food and fungi. From the hilltop site of the town, we looked out at sunset on to a wild, ragged sky, with a livid fiery sun disappearing over the mountains. It didn't look like a good omen for the next day's walking.

Day 4: Puigcerdà — La Molina
The Sunday market at Puigcerdà was full of good things, stalls of cheese, olives, different salt fishes and a variety of fungi. We bought some quite delicate little golden fungi to try, called *trumpetetas*, some good, heavy wholemeal bread and not least to mention, some loose wine to slake the thirst *en route*. We quickly learnt that the Spanish word for *cave* is *bodega*. The particular one where we got our wine was a real temple to Bacchus. There were rows of huge barrels, a suitably dedicated barman, a counter and stools, and a couple of tables and chairs for those who were stopping, not just sampling. We settled for a red from the Tarragona area. Well stocked up, we descended the steep flights of stairs on the south side of Puigcerdà, taking in the terrific view of the Spanish Pyrenees ahead. All was clear and brilliant in the sun, such a change from the dramatic, stormy sunset of the previous night.

It was a relief to find that the waymarking for the Gran Recorrido, G.R.4, was absolutely clear and, as in France, marked with stripes of red and white paint. We decided to vary the G.R.4 route, by aiming for La Molina Youth Hostel, after Alp. This would give us two more even days, to arrive at La Pobla de Lillet. The walk to Alp was mainly on a minor road in farmland, where tractors and ploughs were out in the fields. We crossed paths with a group of Spanish walkers, old and young, and exchanged greetings of *hola* and *buenos días*. At Alp we cooked up the *trumpetetas*, which were good but not as tasty as the *boletus*. We walked beside the Riera de Alp, and eventually joined the road to La Molina. By the roadside in enormous letters was this graffito: SI UNA LEY ES INJUSTA NUESTRO DEBER ES DESOBEDECER LA — INSUMISION (If any law is unjust, our duty is to disobey it — no surrender). Who decides when a law is unjust and needs to be disobeyed? Such anarchic slogans need to be set in their context. The Catalans are proud of their culture and their language and have a strong wish for independence.

La Molina was a draughty ski town, with practically everything closed up, except a cafe and a grocer. The Youth Hostel was a pleasant new building with spacious sitting areas and paintings and posters on the walls, flowers growing and music playing. The warden was friendly and explained how we could rejoin the G.R.4 the next day going by way of another ski town, Super Molina. The hostel, which held 150 people, had been virtually full the weekend before, with people searching for fungi in the mountains. But on that evening there was only a handful of us.

Day 5: La Molina — La Pobla de Lillet

The warden drew us a diagram of our route and armed with that, we set off steeply up from the hostel into the forest. We were obviously following a path of the mushroom pickers, since there were discarded, upturned fungi, of several sorts on the mossy forest floor. But there were plenty more still growing up through the moss and to a mushroom freak like me, this was an extraordinary sight. Putting our packs down, we hunted happily for a while. Eventually we came to the ski piste above Super Molina, which our warden had told us to climb to meet up with the G.R.4. It consisted of a very steep, grass and rock slope, cleared between two bands of pine woods. It looked pretty formidable, even for us who by this time had got used to stiff climbs. It took all of fifty minutes to get to the top. The main problem was stopping ourselves from falling over backwards down the hill when we straightened up or missed our footing. This was a real danger given the weight of the packs on our backs.

Once at the top of the piste, the bare mountain tops were before us. At Collado del Pal at 2100m, our next landmark, there were great views to the south, as fold upon fold, peak upon peak, made a new panorama before us. Perhaps because of the splendour of the view, we went the wrong way at the col, not paying close enough attention to the red and white waymarks. Retracing our steps, we were thankful that it was a mere half hour detour. We plunged down the steep descent, thankfully very well marked, because for the first part, there was no path at all. We went down and down, over open grassland, and through thickets of box. Then through lovely beech woods, we continued steeply down to arrive at a disused cement works, one of the few landmarks given on the map, in this incredibly sparsely populated region. From there we followed a disused railway line the last two to three kilometres into La Pobla de Lillet. It was already getting dark as we entered the town, soon after 6.0pm, so we fell into the first *hostal* we found, where we had a small and basic room with an en suite bath, into which we blissfully sank.

Day 6: La Pobla de Lillet — Guardiola
It was a big mistake not to make sure that we found the red and white markers of our path as we left the town. Instead, we followed a road along the river and then a turning signed to the Sanctuary of Falgars which we knew to be on our route. It wasn't until we were nearing the top of our climb that we found waymarks. Though they were going up a forest track to the west and we couldn't square that with what the map showed, we felt sure it must be our route. The forest track led us up to a col in about half an hour and waymarked us to follow the track down the other side. It was a beautiful spot with little terraced grass fields sloping down into a wider valley with fields stretching beyond. The mountains with their forests encircled the valley. We were surprised not to be able to see the buildings marked at the site of the Sanctuary of Falgars, particularly as we had been passed on the way up by a coach load of tourists, presumably on their way to visit it. After the stiff climb up, we were, perhaps, too eager to be going down

hill again to check carefully. We had our picnic in one of the meadows, and then proceeded to follow the clear waymarking on a good descending track while we chatted.

After about an hour and a half we began to realise that there was a fair sized village ahead that we could not find on our map. Gradually the realisation came to us that we were no longer on our G.R.4 route but on a similarly waymarked alternative. This was the G.R.4.2, going west towards the valley of the Llobregat, instead of southward through the mountains as we wanted. The village was San Julia de Cerdenya. On making enquiries there we found that there was just one place to stay, and it was only open at weekends. Rain was now descending steadily and our nearest place for accommodation was four kilometres steeply down into the river valley at Guardiola. Looking down on the river Llobregat as we walked, we could see stands of tall yellow flowering daisies in the rocky river bed and its margins. Their bright yellow flowers made a great contrast to the prevailing rain and gloom.

Day 7: Guardiola — Santuari de Falgars

We set off up the valley feeling confident in our route. Looking back down at San Julia we saw the river valley beyond, and beyond that again the mountain we named 'twin peaks', actually Pedraforca — two evil looking prongs of rock, sticking up into the sky like a rude gesture. We went up past Clot de la Fou, a wonderful arc of descending terraced fields, with a little circular stone hut at the top. Then we started to go more steeply up into the woods and encountered the parked cars and vans of mushrooms hunters. From one of them I learnt that *tufones* were truffles. We had seen several signs *(recollido de tufones reservada)* forbidding the collection of these. By now we had lost our earlier confidence in our route, as there were several tracks we could have taken up through the woods. We asked someone the way to Collado San Miguel on the G.R.4 but they didn't know. There now seemed no way that this could be our path. We decided the only thing to do was to retrace our steps to the spot where we had picnicked the day before, and follow the markers back to the road, and on up it, to find the Santuari de Falgars, where we should have been at lunchtime the previous day! We found our G.R.4 path heading to the south from there but opted to stay at the Santuari over night as it was already 4.30pm.

This was a great big rambling stone building, set on the top of the hill next to the church, a most impressive sight. After we got ourselves installed in our room, very simply decorated, as befits a monk's cell, we began to hear the rumble of thunder. This made us very glad that we had been able to stay there as the heavens opened and rain bucketed down accompanied by dramatic lightning and thunder. On one especially loud crack of thunder, our lights went out, but fortunately not for long. Finding our way down to the dining room in the dark, could have been quite a problem along the winding corridors and several flights of stairs that we had climbed. The room we ate in was an enormous refectory, and one end of it was used by the family. There was a stove there beside which the children were playing, while grandmother and grandfather watched television. We were the only guests and ate close to the stove to keep warm on this rather chilly evening.

Day 8: Santuari de Falgars — Vilada

In the church, which was a place of pilgrimage, there were lots of candles burning and a panel with miniature plastic representations of different parts of the body: legs, arms, kidneys. These were offerings that pilgrims had made for the return of good health.

We climbed directly on the G.R.4, through beech woods quite gently, and then more steeply on cleared ground, up to Collado San Miguel at 1700m. This was where we were aiming for the day before. After that we were back into the woods for a fairly arduous rock-climbing ascent at the top of which there were fantastic views to the south, which were obscured with intermittent cloud and rain. We stopped for a drink on these heights at the concrete bases of a gun emplacement, where there was one small cross of pebbles and some withered flowers. Was this still a memorial to someone who died in the Civil War? When we got down to Castel d'Areny, at about 2.30pm, we made some instant soup in the drizzle and had the last of our bread and cheese with some sweet coffee, then pressed on down the road heading for Vilada, the nearest place to get lodgings. We stayed at Cas Xocolater (House of the Chocolatier in Catalan). Our host was a large and genial man, who spoke French fluently. He had several flats in the house, and for the following weekend he would be full with people coming out to collect mushrooms in the mountains.

Day 9: Vilada — Berga

It was a wild and beautiful dawn after the rain, over peaks of bare rock which looked like huge jagged teeth projecting from their flesh of woodland below. We needed information about the footpath further south, so headed for Berga, 12 kilometres to the south-west by the artificial lake, Embalse de la Baells, created by damming the course of the Llobregat. That evening wild mushrooms, *rovellones*, were being prepared at the restaurant, so we got a chance to try them.

When we phoned home, Betty pronounced the name of this town as 'burger'. Our precise, language-teaching daughter replied; ***That doesn't sound very Spanish!***. She was quite right, as we later found out it should be pronounced, something like 'Bairrrga'. Berga was a pleasant, untouristy place, on the side of the mountain and spread across a couple of ravines. Though it had not much pretension to beauty, it was the capital of the Berguedà and strongly Catalan. On a publicity map of the area, we found a route, of unspecified nature, marked from Berga, running eastwards through Pedret and La Portilla to La Quar, where we would pick up the G.R.4 again. Though we could find out little about this route, we decided to give it a go.

At the laundrette we met Danny, the Danish son-in-law of the manageress. He had met his Catalan wife whilst they were studying and had then settled in Catalonia. Through his mother-in-law he had got a job, though he said that normally the only way to get work was by knowing who to pay. The local expression was 'to be plugged in'. He spoke English well and apparently Swedish and German fluently, as well as Catalan. He was after a job with an expanding Spanish firm marketing potato crisps, where his languages would be called for. His mother-in-law was from Andalucia originally, but had been moved to Berga under Franco's regime. This was part of his policy of transplanting whole communities, in order to break up local patriotism.

Danny said that it didn't seem to have worked in her case because she was now a strong supporter of the separatist movement in Catalonia.

Day 10: Berga — La Quar

On this sunny Sunday morning, few shops were open, no *bodega*, no market, only the bread shops. We did eventually find a small kiosk with a variety of cold cooked dishes for sale and opted for a portion of meat with *rovellones*. When we asked the girl what kind of meat it was, she proudly produced her English to tell us that it was 'cow'. She had been across to London for a wedding in June, and had liked England very much. We travelled on, happy that we now had something for lunch. As things turned out it was lucky that our picnic was fairly substantial.

Our road out of town gradually disintegrated into a track, which led to a medieval stone bridge crossing a little river burbling over a rocky bed, where we paused to watch the flittering of a large group of day-flying bats. This was a wonderful sight, since in England you only see their nocturnal cousins, indistinctly in the gathering dusk. We pressed on up to the tenth century church of Pedret where some Spanish sightseers put us on the right path for La Portilla, walking with us as far as a rocky ravine. There they pointed the way across and drew us a little diagram in the mud. When we had got some way further on and had climbed up above the dense woods, they said we would be able to see La Portilla ahead. So we gingerly negotiated the ravine with its bare rocky sides and they waited until we had got up the other side to see that we were on course. We then waved goodbye and were on our own. After some while, we heard a car door and voices ahead, in the stillness of the woods. A rather suspicious old man and a young lad appeared. As chance would have it, we were at one of the few named places on our map, Cal de Santa Eugenia. The old man told us to follow the painted yellow circles which marked the path to La Portilla.

From the ruined hilltop farmhouse of Can Mascaró we could see a succession of similar ruins on hilltops down this broad and heavily wooded valley. Their terraces and meadows were once more being swallowed by vegetation and going back to the forest. Our path meandered amongst the dense undergrowth along the side of the river valley. Parts of it were absolutely idyllic with beautiful clear streams, around which lush and diverse plant life grew, but for the rest it was a struggle with brambles and undergrowth. Eventually and to our great relief, we arrived at an occupied house called Can Dou. The man of the house gave us directions for La Quar. We could see La Portilla clearly before us, a ruined church and buildings rising above the woods on a hill to the other side of the stream. After that he carefully explained to us, we would pass, one, two, three tops, until we came to La Quar, the fourth.

We arrived there as dusk was gathering, weary but expectant. With nothing to guide us, we took the track to the north, since our map showed a group of buildings some way along it. After a while we saw lights below us to our right and joyfully thought that this must be our *hostal*. As we reached the group of buildings, I asked a man outside if this was Hostal La Quar and he said; *No, this is not a hostal, we are having a family gathering*, and he knew nothing about any *hostal*. We realised that the *hostal* we were looking for must be at San Maurici, marked on our map about four kilometres to the south along the G.R.4. It was practically dark, so there was no way we could get to the hostal that night. On the first piece of level ground we came to, we pitched the tent by the light of the moon, which was full, very bright and white in a clear sky. Moon and stars are never so bright as when seen from high up in the mountains.

Day 11: La Quar — Sagas

It was a beautiful dawn with silhouettes of mountains to the east. We rejoined the red and white markers of the G.R.4 which we had left at Castel de l'Areny. Our route climbed on a forestry track and when we got to the top of the ridge, the path had been obliterated by the construction of pylon bases. The workmen saw that we were in difficulties and came to show us where our path went. There were calls of *buen viaje* as we found it and disappeared down into the next valley. It was a beautiful gradual walk down through fields and woodland to the *hostal* at San Maurici. We were all the time on the lookout for water, to fill our bottles and have a wash and eventually found a small spring coming out of the mountain side.

From there, on a pleasant track down through rounded natural sandstone terraces, we started to notice that most of the pine trees were burnt. Our next resting place was supposed to be at Sagas where we had booked a room at Hostal San Christoforou. But when we got to Sagas, there was nothing but a church and a large pig farm. We eventually found someone to ask. Although it sounded quite close by, it was in fact about seven kilometres. On arriving at the *hostal*, we got a cheery welcome from Maria, and were amply fed in a dining room with boar heads mounted on the wall. As Maria explained, they were not popular with the farmers, because they do a lot of damage to the crops. There was one particular trophy which was, as she said; "One womans and two bebays", with the added rather gruesome detail that their little trotters were also mounted below, upside down as coat-hooks. We went for a stroll, after eating, beside the Riera de Merlés, which was dammed just above the bridge, but below it, was a chaotic tumble of huge boulders. We slept with the sound of the river, a soothing continuum all night.

Day 12: Sagas — Puig-reig
Though it was a very mild morning, the fire in the bar was lit. The reason soon became clear, as workmen began to arrive for breakfast. Maria handed each a huge slice of bread, cut from large round loaves, and they toasted their bread at the fire with long toasting forks. Then they took a shiny oil can from the mantelpiece, drizzled olive oil over the toast and seasoned it well. At this point an older woman appeared from the back, with a plate of thinly cut ham to accompany the toast. To go with this, on the table, was placed a bottle of red wine and a soda siphon with glasses. These were obviously men who had already put in a few hours work. For us there were large slices of bread and marmalade and good coffee, and bought eggs and bread to take on.

As we left, Maria gave us a cheery wave. We went to deposit our rubbish in a skip at the back of the *hostal* and saw the skins of two or three boars in a wheelbarrow, ready for disposal. Wild pig would be on the menu that night at the *hostal*. We retraced our steps to pick up the G.R.4, which was re-routed. It was sad to see the landscape, for nearly 20km, so diminished by fire. All the pine trees in this area, down to the road to Puig-reig were destroyed. They were standing as black skeletons in a landscape of rounded, natural sandstone terraces, with cultivated fields in between. There were large areas of bare rock, where the soil had been flushed off by rain. The devastated landscape had already started to rejuvenate around the charred trunks. We followed a track, newly built since the fire.

We walked into the town down the valley of the Llobregat and found a cheap place to stay. The landlord's mother told us that we could eat there later, when her son returned. About 9.30pm he arrived and calmly set to and prepared food for us, and two others as well as his mother and himself. It was he who told us about the burning. No one knew why, but since the reports suggested that it started at about the same time in several different places, it seemed as if it must have been arson. The fires all started at 8.0am on 7th July 1994. Seven or eight fires had been lit. Lots of cattle were killed, and he gestured the horns with forefingers out sideways from the temples, and made mooing noises to get the point home — also pigs, done with oink-oink noises. Then he said four people had also died. It was a mystery whether this was politically motivated or not. Our landlord was a good person to learn from because he wanted you to understand and spoke clearly and not too fast. With his short grey hair, glasses and moustache, and neat dapper clothes, he seemed an unlikely person to be running a cheap lodging house. But he was calm and courteous, and he obviously took a pride in his establishment.

Day 13: Puig-reig — Manresa

Our map and guide cover had run out at Sagas, so with nothing available at Puig-reig, we bussed into Manresa, our first city of any size for a while. The trip took about an hour, along the valley of the Llobregat. The towns were not pretty, but there was quite a lot of industry visible. In a bookshop we discovered the excellent Catalonian 1:50,000 maps to guide us to Montserrat.

The Youth Hostel at Manresa was on the highest hill of the town and was an entirely new building, finished five years before. It was a beautifully designed building on one side of the former cloisters of a medieval convent. From it there was a stunning view of the extraordinary jagged pinacles of Montserrat, 'the mountain of the saw'. This was our next major objective, some 25 kilometres to the south.

The pinacles of Montserrat

Manresa was an interesting city with a turbulent history, situated at the junction of two rivers, the Cardoner and the Llobregat and became an important centre because of its position between the Pyrenees and the Montserrat mountains. Ravaged by the Muslims in 889, it was subsequently awarded the status of city by Otto I, king of the Franks, developing early as a centre of manufacture and trade. St. Ignatius of Loyola, founder of the Jesuits, lived in the city for about a year, before setting off for Palestine in 1523. Though his stay was brief, he made a great impression on the spiritual life. In the 17th and 18th centuries a group of religious buildings, La Cova, were consecrated to his memory. The city had more than its fair share of sackings. In the 18th century, the Spanish king Philip V, burnt the city because it sided with the Hapsburgs, as did Catalonia as a whole. Shortly after this, the French army of Napoleon ravaged the city. In the Spanish Civil War of 1936-9, it also suffered as so many places did. This constant succession of sackings is found in the history of many Spanish cities.

Day 14: Manresa — Sant Vicenç de Castellet
At El Pont de Vilomara, we rejoined the G.R.4. From there it was a good walk along the valley of the Riera de San la Creu. To either side of this tortuous river course, there were endless ruined terraces. The path crossed the dry river bed twice and at the second of these crossings another walker appeared out of nowhere behind us. He was Catalan, and from Terrasso, near Barcelona. It was nice to meet a fellow walker, rather rare so far in Spain. As he sped on ahead gesturing upwards, he uttered words that we guessed was the Spanish pronunciation for San Jaume, the name we could see on our map for the next landmark. We climbed steeply to this group of ruined buildings, a hermitage perched on the col between two valleys, with its church and living quarters. From there we descended by the lone church of Sant Pere de Valhonesta, in amongst a valley of cultivated terraces, then up and over the motorway to enter Sant Vicenç at dusk.

Day 15: Sant Vicenç de Castellet — Monistrol de Monserrat
Sant Vicenç looked hardly less dismal in daylight than it had by night, when the narrow streets had been dimly lit and uninviting. Our route took us twisting about on its tortuous approach to the Montserrat mountains. We climbed steeply, close under their jagged teeth, with cloud alternately obscuring and revealing the rocky pinnacles. These curious mountains must rank as one of the most memorable sights of our travels, and it was not surprising to learn that they are considered the spiritual home of Catalonia, inspiring generations of poets and writers.

Just as it came on to rain, we reached the monastery of Sant Cecilia and were glad to be able to shelter in the nearby Refugi Bartomeu Puiggros. From there on it was road walking and the volume of traffic put us off the idea of staying at Montserrat itself. Instead we took the long winding descent to Monistrol with every few minutes a coach passing us on the way down. We were down to Monistrol by dusk and the centre of this place gave just as gloomy an impression as Sant Vicenç, with its mean narrow cobbled streets and shortage of street lights. We decided to head for Barcelona, not on foot but by train, since we could see that the route ahead would be continually punctuated by roads and settlements. Better to quit while there was still grandeur behind, not suburbia.

> **Useful information, addresses and bibliography**
>
> *Maps IGN Randonnées Pyrenees* 1:50,000 Nos. 8, 9, & 10
>
> *Michelin* 1:400,000 No. 443 and *I.C. Catalunya* 1:50,000 also available for this area
>
> *Topoguias* available for GR7 — all from **Map Shop**, Libreria Quera, Petritxol 2, Barcelona.
>
> *Gran Recorrido: a summary guide to long-distance footpaths in Spain*
>
> *Catalunya Step by Step: booklet on walking in Catalonia*
>
> Centre d'Excursionisme de Catalunya, Rambla 61, Barcelona: for topoguias and books.
>
> **Youth Hostels**, Parc de la Pépinière, Ave de Grande Bretagne, 66000 **Perpignan** Tel.04 68 34 63 32
>
> Mare de Deu de les Nues, Ctra. de Font Canaleta, **La Molina.** Tel.(972) 89 20 12
>
> Mare de Deu de Montserrat, Pg. Ntra. Sra. del Coll, 41-51, 08023 **Barcelona** Tel.(93) 210 51 51
>
> **Train Station** at **Perpignan** for trains to Villefranche, Le Train Jaune, Villefranche to Mont Louis. **Monistrol** for trains to Barcelona.
>
> **Airports** at Perpignan and Barcelona.
>
> **Tourist Offices**: Palais de Congress, Place Armand Lanoux, BP 215 - 66002 **Perpignan.** Tel.04 68 66 30 26.
>
> Rue de Marche, 66210 **Mont Louis.** Tel.04 68 04 21 97.
>
> GranVia de las Cortes Catalanas, 658, 08010 **Barcelona** Tel.(93) 301 74 43.

The Pyrenees and into Spain

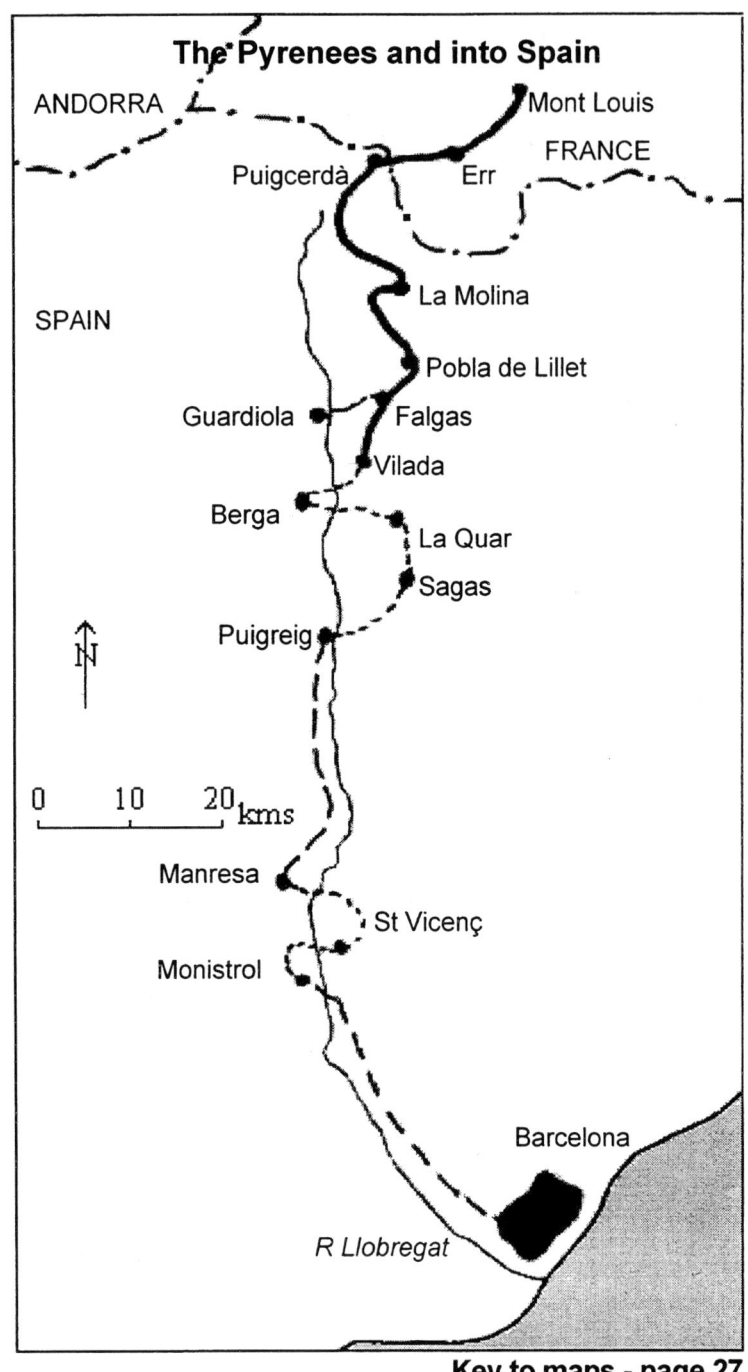

Key to maps - page 27

Down the East Coast of Spain

Barcelona, the capital of Catalonia, was by far the biggest city that we encountered in our travels. Its history can be said to encapsulate the fortunes of Catalonia as a whole. In the mid 14th century, it grew to be the head of a maritime empire, which included the south of France, Sardinia, Naples, Sicily and Athens. But by 1492, with the discovery of the New World, its fortunes ebbed in favour of Seville and Cadiz, on Spain's Atlantic coast. By the late 19th century, Barcelona had once again become a prosperous port, with the development of industrialisation. In order to accommodate the large houses of the prosperous new merchant class, a grid of spacious streets, known as L'Eixample (the widening) was laid out. These new houses of the wealthy were built to the designs of architects, such as Antoni Gaudi, whose unfinished cathedral, Sagra Familia, was an inspiration to visit. The wide Rambla, with its broad pedestrian walk was constructed at this time and soon copied in a number of Spanish towns. Barcelona, once more one of Spain's busiest ports, hosted the 1992 Olympic Games.

We got off to a bad start in this big city. Whilst waiting for a bus out to the Youth Hostel in Plaza Catalunya, Betty took off her pack and put it on one of the fantastic art nouveau wrought-iron seats, whose design was inspired by an interlace of climbing foliage. We became aware of a small, smartly-dressed couple, who we took to be fellow tourists, since they carried a camera. The woman greeted us and asked if we knew where she could find a telephone, but when I indicated one immediately in front of her, she did not seem to be interested, and the focus of their attention transferred to my backpack. They both urged Betty to examine something on my pack, which they were suggesting had dropped down from the trees above. Both were pointing upwards and muttering something about 'danger'. Ostensibly to make it easier for Betty to examine this nauseating stuff, the little man took hold of me and turned me round. When I wanted to turn back, his grip tightened on my neck and at this point I reacted swiftly by swinging him forcefully round, nearly lifting the little chap off his feet. I could now see that his partner had pulled Betty's jumper up from behind and was fiddling with the strap of her bum-bag, looking for the clip. Realising that they had been rumbled, the couple melted away into the crowd, leaving us to wonder at the smoothness of their operation. There certainly was some disgusting stuff on my backpack, which, on examination was chocolate sauce, of the sort sold in squeezy dispensers for putting on ice-cream. So we concluded that the squirting of this stuff was the first stage of their thankfully unsuccessful plan to relieve us of our money.

The Youth Hostel was out of town, on a little hilltop of its own, in a merchant's house of about 1900, which was a fantastic pastiche of different architectural styles — Moorish arches, grand marble staircases, brightly coloured tiled walls and floors and big rooms. As usual there was a splendid mixture of people of different nationalities, coming and going at the Youth Hostel. The staff must view all us transients as walk-on parts in a constant world drama. There was a huge Negro, some six foot six, from California — a real eccentric and show-off. He kept talking about 'working-out' and 'getting showers' without seeming to do either, and was accompanied by a small and adoring Spanish man. He arrived at breakfast with the hood of his jog-suit up and shambled amiably about greeting everyone. In the washroom, which he nearly filled, he stood gazing at himself in the mirror, making faces, flexing his muscles and sighing at the wonder of it all. A real gem! Then there was the Australian who manoeuvred his hand-built customised wheel-chair with panache, making the tyres squeal, as he skilfully negotiated corners and reached his destination always with absolute accuracy. He'd been in the States where he had hired a car to drive around and had been told by the police in one small town in Georgia, that if he was staying more than three days, he would have to buy a gun. Everyone over 14 had to have one. A young, very hirsute Brazilian, who spoke really excellent English, had learnt it in Lowestoft of all places! To judge from his rather upper class diction, it must have been at a language school.

Leaving Barcelona, we climbed up into the Garraf National Park, a wasteland of prickly scrub or bare rock. Abundant vegetation grew only in the beds of the *barrancas*, the now dry ravines which would carry sudden torrents of water during storms.

The G.R.92 was rewarding walking and we made our way down to Tarragona, capital of one of the Roman provinces of Spain. We glimpsed the Roman amphitheatre as we arrived at this seaside town with a long and important history. There were plentiful traces of Roman building — the amphitheatre being the most spectacular and complete. Part of the colonnade of the forum survived and remains of the Roman town walls and towers. After the Roman period, the Visigoths had an important political and religious presence at Tarragona, until the city was virtually destroyed in the Moslem invasion of 716. It remained uninhabited and abandoned in the midst of the no-man's land between the Moslem and Christian domains, until the 11th to 12th centuries, when it once more began to flourish.

Though the city was relatively small, it had a cosmopolitan air and a calmer atmosphere than the hectic traffic and pace of Barcelona. There was a flourishing port, a university, a music conservatory, and side by side, the old town and the late 19th century expansion, with its old and new Ramblas. Tarragona also had a large fishing fleet and in the fisherman's quarter, Serrallo, were a number of restaurants specialising in fish dishes. We had a memorable meal out at one of these, La Puda, which specialised in *romescos*. These are dishes using a particularly delicious local sauce, which is made from almonds, hazelnuts, olive oil, onion, garlic, sweet red pepper and tomato. This was not a cheap eating house, so in order to get a meal that didn't bust our budget wide open, but sampled this local speciality, we had decided to have a paella and a crayfish romesco. But our waiter, who cottoned on to our scheme straight away, advised against the crayfish dish, making a gesture with his hands to a hollow stomach and recommended a dish with several fish in the sauce. His advice was taken and we shared our two dishes and it was a fantastic meal, the sauce being a real taste experience. At one point the waiter saw that our glasses were empty, wagged his finger and came across to fill them up. *In Spain*, he said, *there is a saying that if your glass is empty, the light goes out* (said pointing upwards, using the Catalan word *llum* for light — like the Latin *lumen*). He was one of those experienced old waiters whose manner was grave, but humorous, and he certainly made a memorable meal that much more pleasurable, by putting us at our ease straight away.

Our route took us close to the impressive Roman aqueduct across a tributary of the Francoli. This must have brought water from the north to the Roman city of Tarragona. Close by, in the Francoli river valley, the Centcelles Roman villa had a room converted in the mid-fourth century into a vaulted mausoleum, the cupola of which had some fine mosaics, featuring, amongst other things, a deer-hunt. This mausoleum may have been to commemorate the Roman Emperor, Constans, son of Constantine the Great, who was killed in Gaul in 350 AD.

Further down the coast near Cambrils, we passed an elderly couple picking their olives. They had laid a piece of green plastic net on the ground round the base of the tree, and were combing off the small black olives, with handled metal combs. They were quite ready to stop and chat, and told us that the harvest that year was sparse but the price for these olives, which were prized for their oil, was very high.

Along the attractive, rocky Costa Dorada coast, the G.R.92, though well waymarked, kept being marginalised by the expansion of seaside villa-land. In spite of this, it was a beautiful walk, with low cliffs of honey-coloured sandstone, which by turns was a darker, reddy-brown colour. The sun on these cliffs and on the sea made an idyllic coastline, which was punctuated by frequent little bays, created by the egress of mini torrents beds into the sea.

We left the G.R.92 after L'Ampolla in order to visit the Ebro Delta, unique in Spain for all sorts of reasons, the most important being its populations of resident and migratory birds, amongst the most   varied in the world. On the long straight road out into the delta, we immediately felt at home. We were back in the fenlands of south Lincolnshire. Though the difference in levels was slight, between the shore we had been following and this delta region, which we had seen as a long low line jutting out into the sea for a couple of days, the change in the landscape was dramatic. Its special qualities lie in the reflection of the huge skies in the water of the rice fields and in the convergence of the linear irrigation channels stretching away to the distant horizon. We soon became aware of the abundance of birdlife, herons of different sorts, seagulls, egrets, wading birds and a variety of ducks. There was a powerful wind off the sea, so we sheltered in the lee of a small building by the roadside for our picnic. Someone on a motorbike stopped to ask us the time. He had been shooting and showed us part of his catch, two miserably small snipe, which he said were good to eat.

As this was such a special area, we felt we must have a little time to explore it. The delta was highly cultivated, rice being the main crop. Its fertile soil also grew abundant vegetables, particularly, though not exclusively, along the river banks. One of the local problems was succinctly summarised in a graffito on a derelict building: LA CAVA VOL AIGUA NO SAL (La Cava [part of Deltebre], wants water not salt). All the intensive rice cultivation depends on an irrigation system which, at the delta itself, is controlled by a complex arrangement of water channels and drains, with large or small, adjustable sluices, which regulate the flow. The fresh water supply, upon which the irrigation depends, is brought from 50 kilometres upstream, in canals to either side of the Ebro. The origin of this system was a dam of Arabic construction, near the towns of Tivenys and Xerta, to either side of the river. Though nothing much is known of this phase of settlement in the delta, the Arabic word *ullals* is still used for the fresh water pools at the margin of the high ground, which are fed from subterranean water. They have their own special flora and fauna.

We realised, whilst at Deltebre, that we had completed six months of our journey, so we celebrated with a bottle of excellent Conte Bravo *vino espumoso*; a delicious Spanish bubbly and a meal at Hosteleria Faro, a cheap, cheerful and lively bar with loud television, largely ignored as usual. There we met an Englishman, who turned out to be a judge. In his time, he had been a keen walker, but now was reduced to a few kilometres only, as he had arthritis of the hip. In a deliberate avoidance of sentimentality, he told us that it would have been no use bringing his wife with him, as she was even more crippled with arthritis than he was. We spent a sociable hour or so chatting, and he it was who introduced us to *carajillo*, coffee with brandy. When he heard we were going to Calpe for Christmas, our travelling judge said; *Oh you mean where all the criminals go!* We hadn't heard that one before, but then who are we to argue with a judge, even when off duty.

On our way from Deltebre to Poble Nou, through absolutely flat, fenland-like country, we walked past huge fields of celery, which gave off a wonderful smell. Way out beyond sound, we could see the workers to either side of a large, trundling machine. Then we saw ahead of us a large pinky-white smudge in one of the flooded rice fields. As we came closer, this smudge resolved itself gradually into a mass of several hundred flamingos moving about, with the water coming halfway up their long pink legs. Slowly progressing, backwards and forwards, and gradually advancing towards us, they occasionally stretched and flapped their wings a little, to reveal a wonderful combination of black and scarlet under-feathers. We sat on our packs, picnicked and watched. They kept on going with their slow measured promenade, first one way and then the other, with their heads held high on long necks, and with a quiet, but continuous conversation going on amongst themselves. As if at a given signal, they put their heads down all together and started to feed.

Poble Nou was founded in 1947, as a 'new' village under Franco's regime of re-housing people. We were told that Franco had given land out there in the Ebro delta, to 'people who had nothing', so many hectares each. It was a small planned, rectangular, settlement, all white-washed and with a white church tower at its centre. In marked contrast to the straggling untidy layout of Deltebre, there were ordered avenues of palm trees, date palms and banana trees and courtyards full of lush, dark green foliage, big red trumpet-like flowers, climbing plants, and the clashing reds and purples of bougainvillaea. From here we walked out along the Barra del Trabacador, a narrow spit of sand, to visit the enormous salt evaporation plant on the southern wing of the Ebro Delta. As we walked back in the setting sun, between the rice fields with their little one-storey houses, we saw the unforgettable sight of a hundred or so flamingos, flying into the sunset. Their long necks and legs formed one continuous line, and as they went, they called to one another. With inadequate language, I tried to share my appreciation of this sight with an old lady, who was hobbling along the street. *Flamencs!* I said, pointing to the sky, but she shrugged her shoulders and muttered something, that sounded like; *No se* (I don't know) and shuffled on.

From Poble Nou, we headed north to La Casa Verde, the Ornithological Museum. This was a green timber building with a wide veranda, which had originally been bought from Canada in the 1920s by a hunting syndicate. Now it no longer served its original purpose as a hunting lodge, but hunting had not altogether ceased. That Saturday many vans and four by fours were parked up and shooting had already begun by the time we arrived. It was restricted to certain specified dates, in the compromise reached between the hunters and the environmentalists.

As we continued our walk down the coastline alongside the ever expanding new development, we also encountered many half finished or abandoned buildings. Some ugly, new rectangular blocks of flats, close to the shore and partly inhabited, were already starting to fall apart; concrete facades splitting; verandas flowing with wild vegetation, and sides heavily stained with the rundown of water from unrepaired drains. We came across much of this random and ugly development, interspersed amongst superb coastal scenery. Coming from a small overcrowded island, this squandering of space is hard to get used to.

Great fans of sunlight kept bursting through the clouds out at sea, as we set off from Peñiscola. Past the tower of Torreon Badun, we saw a rare sight ahead, another walker! Through the field-glasses, I could make out some details of a faltering, and shambling figure. The bright green on his back, was a plastic watering can, and he carried several plastic bags, some of them hooked over the end of a wrecking bar, which he rested on his shoulder. Every so often he stopped, to look down, as if searching for something on the ground, or to rearrange his luggage. Yet, his overall progress was purposeful. After some while, we passed him, as he made one of his many pauses, this time at the edge of the track, where he was inspecting something. As we passed we said *Hola!*, and he turned his gaunt old face to acknowledge us, then went back to the business in hand. His clothes were quite smart, with a cap, a dark blue jacket with large yellow buttons, trousers and fairly new trainers.

Later when we stopped to make coffee, our companion of the road passed us, turning this way and that, but keeping up a slow, steady progress. He knew where he was going, because he turned off towards an empty house at the far end of the bay, collected a white bucket from a stone well-head, moved towards the house and thereafter disappeared from view.

As we reached Sagunto at dusk one evening, we dropped in at a busy bar for a drink. Inside, the noise was deafening. The woman behind the bar was cooking squares of *sepia* (squid) on a hotplate, and serving them to customers at the bar or at their tables. A little lad of about 10 was helping to serve drinks. The old men whose glasses he filled to the top, started to protest, but stifled their comments before they were out when they saw what good measure they were getting. An empty, bleak bar is transformed by the great energy and hubbub of the clustered drinkers, who talk or shout without pause, except occasionally to swallow a mouthful of food or drink.

Historically always important, Sagunto has more recently suffered a particularly heavy pounding during the various wars of the 18th and 19th centuries. At the beginning of the 20th century, steel production made it prosperous and only collapsed in the 1980s, after which industry diversified, so that it is now one of the most important economic centres in Valencia.

We were now on the Costa Azahar, the Orange Blossom Coast where orange fruit and dark green shiny leaves looked unreal, like a Rousseau painting or a child's illustration. The air was full of the smell of the fruit. By the time we got to the coast, the mono-culture had changed from citrus fruit to acres of artichokes.

On into the wind we trudged southwards, along a shore of near-black rock with lots of iron nodules in it. There was rubbish everywhere along this stretch of coast. What with cold wind, rubbish and the approaching high-rise blocks, this coastline was going to get less and less fun to walk, so we decided to head up to Pujol to catch the train into Valencia where we arrived in an amazing art nouveau station, with a huge polished stone floor with a tiled design of orange trees and grapevines. My father, a great aficionado of art nouveau, would have loved it.

A warren of little streets and squares, the old town, was a delight to get lost in. The Central Market was particularly impressive with specialist stalls devoted to salt cod, olives, peas and beans of various sorts, onions and garlics, citrus fruits and the superb fish stalls. There were hat shops, shirt shops, knife shops, shops selling fans and brightly coloured, embroidered and fringed shawls. There were specialist jewellery shops selling nothing but gaudy costume jewellery and combs, shops and stalls selling the distinctive, brightly decorated Valencian pottery. Since Valencia is **the** place for *paella*, there were shops devoted to all the equipment required, ranging from the big two-handled shallow metal pans, which are sold in various sizes, the calor-gas rings for cooking it, and the ubiquitous reddy-brown glazed earthenware cooking pots. There were music shops with all the instruments but especially guitars and castanets.

The City museum was a first-rate guide to the long and troubled history of this major Mediterranean city and port. It set the scene, showing how the old course of the river Turia had divided to either side of the higher ground, on which the city was founded with its successive Roman, Visigothic, Arabic and medieval phases.

It was a cool and windy morning, with massed clouds, promising rain, as we caught the bus out of Valencia. Walking out of El Palmar to the south of the great lake of Albufera and into the flat fen-like rice fields, we caught the full force of the rain. It was driven by a cold wind, but there was nowhere to shelter in the flat lands, so we pressed on, accompanied by reed-warblers, flittering in and out of the reeds on the edge of the rice fields, beside the road ahead of us. Egrets rose, white and elegant from their stations in the paddy-fields. The weather cleared little by little so that we could eventually make out the higher ground of the Little Mountain of the Saints. We passed an *ullal*, one of the fresh water lagoons such as we had come across in the Ebro delta. This one was a small round pond with stands of trees around it. The Arabs, not only named these distinctive fresh water sources, but also had a special name for the luminous water in the middle of the lake, which they called *lluent*. Recent drainage of the

Albufera has meant that the lake is now 30,000 hectares, only one tenth of the size it was when recorded by Strabo and Avienus in Roman times. At the top of the little mountain, there was a church and hermitage, guarded by a group of barking dogs. No hermit was visible, but a car left the hilltop as we approached. These days, perhaps, hermits have transport and can escape their isolation, but if so they must lose most of the special quality of 'otherness' and holiness which made the local population support them in their lonely spiritual quest. Northwards over the vast reaches of flat lands, we could see the mountains beyond.

We trekked on via Tavernes de la Valdigne (taverns of the noble valley), named by King James I on his travels. Since there was no local information about footpaths over the mountains from Pedreguer to Jalon, we pressed on by road, through wild hills. As we approached Jalon we saw a lot of activity centred on a *bodega* whose decor made it appear more like an English pub. It had dark woodwork, subdued lighting and a bar in one corner with festive decorations. The place was packed with people, who had arrived by car to get their supplies of wine for Christmas. Over the general hubbub it was possible to pick out several English accents, amongst them Cockney, Geordie and Brummie. On hearing that the local wine was very good, we got our plastic bottle filled up. We stayed overnight at a bed and breakfast run by an English couple who had retired there. It was like a little slice of England transported to Spain. We got a good welcome with the offer of a cuppa straight away. There was an electric kettle and teabags, hat and coat stand in the hall, Hall's Bicycles and Bovril advertisements on the wall, little bowls of dried rose petals, general cosy and whimsy frumpery, nostalgic but inhibiting after the rough and ready establishments of our travels.

Our steps were light and springy with the anticipation of journey's end for our Christmas break at Calpe. We would dearly like to have reached Calpe by mountain tracks, but didn't have enough local information, so we stuck to the road up out of the valley to Benissa, then gritted our teeth for the descent by the main road to Calpe. The first part, climbing out of the Jalon valley, with its ring of mountains, was beautiful. Going up gently through vineyards on to the bare rocky tops, we then dropped slightly to terraces of almonds and olives. It was all limestone country round about, and though the tops were largely bare of vegetation, the lower slopes were intensively terraced and cultivated. For once all the terraces were in use and new ones were in the process of being constructed. The almond trees presented a network of black branches, devoid of their leaves and the foliage on the vines had begun to turn crimson. Three times over as we walked the busy main road, we got wet and dry again. Between the storms, what bore us up was the amazing view of the immortal mountains around. From time to time the views below opened up to reveal that particularly striking lump of rock, the Peñon de Ifach, jutting up out of the sea. From this we knew that we had not far to go, as it is both Calpe's symbol and that of the Costa Blanca.

In the town, we dove into a bar, where we were directed to the Hostal Centrico close by. But it was not open for another two and a half hours, so we shouldered our packs again and wandered down to the beach. It was then that the let-down set in for me. On the promenade were many of our fellow countrymen, and for that matter other foreign nationals, who looked askance at this couple of rain-soaked, scruffy backpackers, with indifference or hostility. I experienced an acute culture-shock and a sense of total alienation and deflation. This was hard to explain, given our knowledge of high-rise holiday land, gained as we had travelled down the east coast, but real nonetheless.

All this passed though, when we were let into the Hostal Centrico by a pleasant and welcoming London manageress. Later, we had an excellent and cheap meal at a Chinese Restaurant. A friendly and courteous Philipino made the occasion more than just a meal, with his unhurried and genuinely interested converse. He had learnt English as his second language and spoke it with complete command. When he heard of our journey, he said, in measured tones, almost like an oracle; "That will give you many memories and many stories to tell when you get back". How better could it be put? A spirit journey for yourselves and a saga to share with others. I was beginning to feel at home in Calpe.

Useful information, addresses and bibliography

Maps I.C. Catalunya 1:50,000 Nos. 07, 08, 09, 11, 12, 17, 22 & 36 and *Michelin* 1:400,000 Nos. 443 & 445

Map Shops: Libreria Quera, Petrixol 2, **Barcelona**

Papeleria Regolf, Calle Mar 22, 46003 **Valencia**

Youth Hostel, Mare de Deu de Monserrat, Pg. Ntra. Sra. del Coll, 41-51, 08023 **Barcelona** Tel.(93) 210 51 51

Tourist Offices: Gran Via de las Cortes Catalanas, 658, 08010 **Barcelona**. Tel.(93) 301 74 43

Fortuny, 4-bajos, 43001 **Tarragona** Tel.(977) 24 50 64

Calle de la Paz, 48, 46003 **Valencia** Tel.(96) 394 22 22

CALPE INTERLUDE

Passing from the blameless but dishonoured state of vagrancy for a while, into one of temporary respectability, we settled in with Pauline and Peter into a fifth floor flat. It had great views of the sea, the Peñon and the mountains. To the southwest, we could see the flat top of Toix, separated from the rolling higher flanks of the Sierra de Bernia by the Col de Mascarat, beyond whose oval depression appeared the more distant, majestic pointed summit of Puig Campaña. To the north lay Olta, behind which the ample ridge of Lloma Larga rose to the rounded summit of Sella del Cau. And this magnificent ring of mountains was completed north eastward by the Sierra de Pedramala. We felt there, more part of these, than of the ground below us. Each day brought a different and fantastic dawn over the sea, and sunsets behind the mountains. One dawn, on a particularly clear day, we saw the Balearic Islands, 100 kilometres to the north east. One sunset, the flamingos circled round and round the shallow water of the *salinas* (old salt-pans), before settling for the night.

One night before Christmas, there was a tremendous storm, with hailstones as big as thumbnails which set all the windows rattling and woke us up. There were piles of them up against the building the next morning. We heard that 13 of the flamingos had died and for a few days they seemed to have deserted the *salinas*.

Over the last 30 years, Calpe has grown a seaside adjunct, many times the size of the original hill-top town. The high-rise blocks of flats, lining the seashore reminded me of nothing so much as grounded ocean liners, waiting for higher water to float them out to sea. They are rumoured, some of them, to have been built with Mafia money, perhaps hence the comments of our travelling judge, about the criminal fraternity in Calpe. The block next to ours, a tug-boat compared with our ocean liner, had been empty and derelict for 17 years, we were told, because of an unresolved argument between its owners, one a Spaniard, the other Italian. Behind these seaside giants, there is a suburban hinterland of white-washed, pantiled villas, stretching up the mountain sides. The modern town centres on a main shopping street called after Gabriel Miro, a poet from Alicante, with gift shops and cafe-bars, to cater for tourists. One learns to look around and beyond these modern developments to appreciate the grandeur of the surrounding coastal scenery, with the terraced hillsides close by, and the extraordinary shapes of the bare mountains behind, made even more dramatic by the constantly changing weather patterns during this winter period. With the sun on it, the limestone of the Peñon and the surrounding mountains, is a warm yellow, which changes to a dull grey as rain approaches. And then of course there are the ever-changing colours of the sea, blue, turquoise or grey and the constant sound of the waves.

For our winter stay we joined an international community of elderly people from all over northern Europe, escaping the rigours of their colder climates. These national groups tended to gather together in restaurants and bars, catering for their particular tastes in food and drink, often run by their own nationals. One or two places tried to recreate the atmosphere of the English pub and offered fish and chips, draught Tetley's and Saturday night singalongs.

There are German and English language Costa Blanca newspapers and clubs of all sorts. The bowling green along the front looks as if it comes straight from an English seaside resort, with the players all dressed in their whites and taking their game very seriously. The big difference is that they play on blue-painted composition surface rather than grass. One night a week the cinema in the old town, puts on a showing of a film in English.

Calpe was, until 30 years ago, a small fortified town on a low hill overlooking the sea, separated by a couple of kilometres from its good natural harbour under the lee of the Peñon de Ifach. The Romans made use of Calpe's position on the coast, with rock cut tanks for a live fish farm, decorated at one point with relief sculptures of mermaids, and salterns alongside to preserve its produce for export. A villa with mosaic floors, close to the sea, was being excavated. It is said that the big *amphorae* used to store and transport wine, olive oil and fish sauce were made close by.

Calpe's medieval fortunes were uneven, with the usual history of sackings and rebuildings. On a bad day for Calpe in 1636, pirates captured almost its entire population and took them away to slavery in North Africa. They were only returned years later on payment of a large ransom. Some of the old hilltop town still exists, with its narrow streets and parts of its defensive wall. This still retains its Spanish character and is largely unchanged, at least out of season, by the enormous influx of visitors.

Christmas Eve brought some of our family, Phil, Becky, Sam, Fania, Sue and Pete to join us. Ben, Peter's son, and partner Joan, arrived on Boxing Day. Two more flats in the same building had been booked to accommodate them all. Christmas Day itself was a real slap-stick spectacular. We had three ovens cooking away on three different floors. The lifts were going non-stop, with people passing one another carrying turkeys, dishes of roast potatoes and other goodies. Pauline and Betty masterminded the show, and after a few glasses of champagne it was miraculous that all this cooking came together in the second storey flat, where ten of us regaled ourselves. While in England they were enduring below zero temperatures, we were sitting out on the balcony in shorts and tee-shirts. Some of the younger members of the party were even reckless enough to plunge into the sea, and of course the Peñon had to be climbed. From the balcony we saw the assault party appear on the top of this great lump of bare rock, tiny, but visibly waving.

We were invited for New Year by our old friends, Peg and Geoff, who have settled at Oliva, 50 kilometres from Calpe. Though they have English friends at Oliva, they have rejected the 'Brit' community with all its snobbery, cliquishness and quasi-colonial attitudes. The house they live in is at the top of the old medieval town, a network of narrow streets with their whitewashed houses, winding up the hillside. After nine years they were obviously accepted by, and very much part of, the Spanish community in their street and of the town generally. Everywhere we went on New Year's Day, there were greetings of *Feliz Año Nuevo* (Happy New Year) with the response, *Igualmente* (The same to you). We were introduced to the Spanish way of seeing the New Year in. Each of us was presented with a wine glass containing twelve grapes to be eaten when the first stroke of midnight sounded. Every grape consumed before the last strike of twelve, ensured a happy month for the coming year. It was not as easy as it sounds, with a growing number of pips to contend with, but we managed about half of them in the given time.

On New Year's Day, in a scenario very different from England, we walked down through orange groves, to eat at a little restaurant near the beach, where Peg and Geoff were well known. It is a popular custom to eat out for lunch on New Year's Day and the restaurant was packed with Spanish families and very noisy. Various kinds of cold fish were set out on the tables for the first course. This was followed by the Spanish *ensalada mixta,* a great plateful of mixed salad, then came beautifully fresh fried soles with chips. Geoff had chosen a lovely local wine to accompany the meal. It was as well that we had the walk right up to the top of the town afterwards, to walk off the effects.

Another celebration in the local calendar is that of the Moors and Christians. A version of this festival is to be found extensively in Spain. Though now a pageant, it reflects the real conflicts that continued between the two faiths in Spain for centuries. At Oliva, Peg told us that they have a mock battle down at the beach, which the Moors win. Then they come into town for another battle, which the Christians win. Everyone dresses up for their respective part in the pageant and enters into the spirit of the thing. After the battles, there is a week of festivities, fireworks and drinking.

For us, as walkers, the advert in the Calpe paper that appealed most, was a walk organised by the Costa Blanca Mountain Walkers. We went along to join in this and found that about 50 people turned up. Though most of these were English, there were some French and Belgians and the club welcomed all comers. The day's hike took us up the cultivated valleys of the near mountains, with their terraces and on to the rough tops; a round trek of about 13 kilometres. The multiplicity of farm tracks we met that day, made us realise that, with local knowledge, we could certainly have walked off-road from Jalon to Calpe.

Some of the most remarkable of the mountain paths are the trails known as Mozarabic by the Spanish. The term *'mozárabe'* (almost Arab) referred to Christians living under Moorish rule. They are well-made stone pathways, carefully revetted and zig-zagging up and down ravines, constructed on gradients gentle enough to be easily manageable by man or beast. Sometimes they can clearly be seen to give access to improbably steep series of terraces; elsewhere they connect one settlement over the tops with another in the next valley. In their way, they are just as impressive as examples of constructional engineering, as the more widely known Roman roads, bridges and aqueducts, and have often stood the test of time and neglect. Other footpaths lead to *ermitas*, remote chapels, where a particular saint's day might be celebrated once a year, and still others lead to *fuentes* (springs), sometimes long since dry. But these and other aspects of a country way of life, now largely gone, still leave their traces in the countryside.

A similar process to that which has been underway for sometime in the UK, is also taking place in Spain. Country footpaths, once in everyday use, to take people to and from their workplace, have often been completely lost and are now being rediscovered for recreational use. Walking clubs of different foreign nationals, drawn to explore the beautiful mountain interior, are enthusiastically relocating the old country ways, unused by farmers and villagers for a generation or two, sometimes far longer.

Useful information, addresses and bibliography

Maps: *Michelin* 1:400,000 No. 445 and IGN 1:25,000 Nos. 822-III, 822-IV, 848-I, 848-II

Mountain Walks on the Costa Blanca by Bob Stansfield Cicerone Press.

More Mountain Walks on the Costa Blanca, Locally produced

Map & Book Shops, Papeleria Regolf, Calle Mar 22, 46003 **Valencia**

Libreria International, Altmir 6, **Alicante**

Airport at Alicante.

Autobuses UBESA from Alicante to Calpe.

GRAN RECORRIDO G.R.7
THROUGH ALICANTE & MURCIA PROVINCES

The thought of walking amongst more holiday homes and developed sea-fronts, didn't appeal. It had been all right to navigate our way down to Calpe, but now we felt a decided need to walk in the mountains again. We were due, in six weeks, to spend a fortnight at the Sunseed Desert Project near Almeria. This was the next major objective in our travels, so now was the time to explore the mountain region as we made our way southwards.

At Calpe station, while waiting for the train to Alicante, we could not help but hear the loud English voice of a man shouting down a mobile phone. With his wife and retinue, he came over to talk to us. They both wanted to walk the Pilgrims' Way across northern Spain, when their children grew up. He was a jolly, burly, red-faced farmer from Cambridgeshire who had a villa just above the station, on the slopes of the Olta, and had been out walking there. The burly one and his wife asked us with genuine interest about our travels. When they heard how long we had been walking, he said with great profundity, *Yes, you can walk a long way in a long time.* And so pleased was he with this pearl of wisdom, that he repeated it, at intervals, a couple of times, obviously feeling that his audience hadn't paid it due attention, *As I say, you can walk a long way....*

The girls in Alicante Tourist Office wanted to be helpful, but had no information about footpaths. Not an unusual occurrence but just as we were going out of the door, one of them suddenly remembered something, and said, *Momento!*. She fished around below the counter and came up with just what we wanted, the newly-printed guide for the section of the G.R.7, which lies within Alicante province, from Alcoy to Pinoso. Having decided that we would start at Elda, the closest it came to Alicante, we then needed to know whether it was possible to carry on into Murcia province. We returned from a trip to the Mountaineering Club at Murcia armed with an A4 sheet for the Murcia section of the G.R.7 from Pinoso to Cañada de la Cruz.

We hoped that, with good waymarking on the ground, and the 1:50,000 army maps as back up, we would be able to find our way. Once back in our room, we set about attempting to plot the G.R.7 route on the maps. All we could really do, was underline place names mentioned on the A4 sheet and hope that the waymarking and the paths were good in between!

Before leaving Alicante, we climbed up to the Castle of Santa Barbara, whose history reflects the importance of Alicante. The French bombarded the city for seven days non-stop in 1691, then immediately afterwards it was involved in the War of Spanish Succession (1701-1714), in which the castle was nearly destroyed by English troops. In the War of Independence (1804-1814), Alicante became the provisional capital of Valencia.

Table of Distances

1. Elda - Monóvar	12.0km
2. Monóvar - Pinoso	19.0km
3. Pinoso - Jumilla (bus)	30.0km
4. Jumilla - Calasparra (28km by bus)	52.0km
5. Calasparra - Moratalla	19.0km
6. Moratalla - Caravaca	13.0km

Day 1: Elda — Monóvar

We travelled to Elda on the bus and, crossing the river Vinalopo, picked up the red and white markers of the G.R.7 without any difficulty. The weather was cold and grey with a chill wind, but it was great to be walking again. We were soon off the tarmac and out into countryside with bare rocky hills and cultivation terraces. Almond trees predominated as a crop and were just starting to bloom. Our stint for the day was just over nine kilometres on tracks, with another three kilometres down the road to get to Monóvar, for a night's lodging. We made good progress and reached a little wayside *Ermita* (Chapel), our halfway point by mid-morning. A peep inside the unlocked door, showed a well-tended shrine, with candles and flowers on the altar.

The sun came out as we walked on and we decided to stop for lunch before reaching the tarmac road at Chinorla. Once in Monóvar, we had difficulty finding the Restaurante Remus, where an uncaring barman shook his head at our enquiries about rooms. This was a blow, as we had been told over the phone that we would find accommodation there. When we enquired at the *Ajuntamiento* (Town Hall), it became obvious that we were talking to the source of this dud information, to judge by the blushes of the girl concerned, when she learned that we had had no success. She told us, without actually admitting her mistake, that the nearest place to stay would be Elda, right back where we had been that morning!

Day 2: Monóvar — Pinoso

As we stood waiting in the dark for the 7.45am bus back to Monóvar, we noticed a lad with Down's Syndrome, sitting in the park across the street, having an animated conversation with his bag of sandwiches, which was next to him on the seat. He had a folded umbrella, which was used to make a number of forcible points and then expansively waved in the air. We thought he might have been rehearsing some tellings off that he'd had at home or work. He was a useful guide to the eventual arrival of the bus, as, a few minutes before it came, he crossed the street to join us and greeted a middle-aged man by patting him on the stomach. Both were obviously regulars on this route.

Having walked the three kilometres back to Chinorla, we got off the busy road and rejoined the G.R.7, which led us by a rough track up a beautiful valley. To either side of us, there were terraces of almond trees, with white or pink blossom beginning to open patchily. From the Collado de Victoriano at the top of the valley, we could look down on the huge expanse of cultivated terraces and fields that lay ahead of us. We descended by a track to the dead straight Carretera de la Romana, which you could well believe was Roman, as it forged its way across the plain. Fortunately we crossed straight over it, and rose gradually by farm tracks to Casas del Señor. Here we took shelter from the cold wind, sitting at the edge of a wide, concreted water channel which ran through the centre of the village. There was a supermarket of sorts and even a bank, but no bar, as our guide said there was, in this remote place *dotado de bar y comestibles* (bar and food available). From there we climbed up to the next col, Collado Encebras, and then made a long but pleasant descent, through enormous almond and olive terraces, round to the north of Cerro de la Sal, the Salt Mountain, to arrive at the windy 'frontier town' of Pinoso.

Before we had got inside the door at the Bar Mercedes, the woman wanted our money off us. Rather to her surprise, we insisted on seeing the room first, and though it was cold and gaunt, we knew that the only other place to stay was much more expensive. So, unenthusiastically, we parted with our money. After dumping our packs and fleeing the frigid bedroom, we came down to a large unheated bar, where we hoped to get some food. When we finally got through to Madame Mercedes, as Betty had dubbed her, that we were frozen, she produced a circular electric heater, of the kind sometimes used as bed-warmers in England. This was placed underneath the table, which was covered with a heavy cloth reaching the floor. We removed our shoes and gratefully soaked up the wonderful warmth. This rather grasping woman redeemed herself in our eyes, by producing some of her own, home-preserved green olives, deliciously flavoured with fennel, and a bottle of wine. She then went up further in our estimation by serving us a good meal, after which we were well able to face the rigours of our room.

Day 3: Pinoso — Jumilla

Our first job was to enquire at the Casa Consistorial for any local information about the next two places along the line of the G.R.7, Torre del Rico (Rich Man's Tower) and Venta Roman (Roman Inn). In our Gran Recorrido book, it said that you could *pernoctar* (overnight), *comer* (eat) *y avituallarse* (and stock up) at these two places, but we knew already that such statements needed checking locally, and, if they could not be confirmed, then they had to be rejected We also needed to find out the times of any buses running from Pinoso. On all these queries, the officials of the Casa Consistorial were completely useless. When they mentioned the time of a bus to Jumilla, the women sitting waiting their turn, immediately contradicted them, but there was no consensus. The clerk said there was no bus until

6.30pm, the women said there was one in the afternoon, someone else at the lottery booth told us there was one at 1.45pm and our timetable said 3.45pm! We went to the Police Station to see if they could help. But though the places we wanted to visit were only a few kilometres away, the policeman knew nothing about them. Without any advance information, it didn't seem feasible to embark on a two-day stretch of the G.R.7. In summer you could at least camp out at night, but in winter you were instantly cold when you stopped walking, and it was dark by 6:00pm.

We set off to walk round the almost circular Salt Mountain. Though we never reached the quarries themselves, we understood that the salt from there went down to Torrevieja on the coast for processing along with the sea salt. Our walk gave us magnificent views out over the vast, highly cultivated, plateau-lands, ringed with mountains, which characterised this area. Pinoso, a windy, one-horse place, of no great beauty in itself, was on the edge of one of these plateaux. Its industries, wine production, and the quarrying of salt and marble, produced enough wealth, to support a sports centre, a public library, a Casa de Cultura, a riding school and a magnificent stadium, all in a village of only 5,800 inhabitants, as the publicity leaflet proudly relates. As we returned towards the village, we could see below us wagons constantly trundling up and down the main road, loaded with huge square blocks of the creamy, off-white marble, characteristic of the local quarries. At the edge of the village was the *bodega*, where we stopped to get a fill of the really excellent red wine. It was 1993 Crianza Tinto and you could taste a sort of smoky oak flavour which is what the Crianza label implies. This wine is kept in oak barrels for two to three years. While we walked, we had discussed what to do next. As we could find out nothing about Torre del Rico, we decided to make a detour to Jumilla, if indeed a bus actually turned up, and then rejoin the G.R.7 at Venta Roman. We waited hopefully for the bus, sheltered from the chill wind and it turned up at 2.15pm, a time that no one had predicted.

The bus took us across the huge plateau, with vineyards stretching into the distance on either side, past enormous *bodegas*, placed along the main roads, and into the brand new bus station at Jumilla. There, we immediately established that there were buses to Venta Roman early next day.

The 13th century castle, dramatically overlooking the town, was in the process of being restored. The Spaniards go in for the use of large scale concrete reconstruction of their monuments; we had seen it before, unsuccessfully done at the Roman theatre of Sagunto. At Jumilla it worked. There was no mistaking new and old fabric, and the old would certainly have fallen down without being propped up by the new. We returned at sunset by the old medieval route from the castle, which zigzagged steeply down the hill into the centre of the old town.

That night at Hostal Pipa, we all sat down to dinner at 9.0pm. There were two large parties of workmen, and a few other couples like us, who, all told, filled the dining room. We were waited on by a single, plump but sprightly waiter, who moved between the tables in a sort of ballet, swaying and pausing and continuing deftly. He seemed to have no difficulty remembering the long and complicated orders from the two big groups, and shouted the orders through the hatch. Being fascinated by these sorts of things, we watched with admiration, but agreed that his virtuoso performance would not have been possible without a very efficient kitchen regime to back it up.

We phoned Peg and Geoff at Oliva, to let them know that we would arrive in Granada in a few days. When we told Geoff where we were, he exclaimed indignantly; *What are you doing **there**? Do you know you are in the place that produces the best wine in Spain?*. We didn't, but assured him that we had sampled it and enjoyed it greatly, though I have to say that the wine of 'the great little village' of Pinoso was actually better still.

Day 4: Jumilla — Calasparra

The bus left us beside a dead straight road, marching south-westwards down a wide valley, between ranges of rocky tops. So this was Venta Roman — just a small bar and a filling station in the middle of nowhere. We were reassured to find the red and white markers and set off up a long gradual climb through almond terraces, where there were gangs of three or four men, working together, busy pruning the trees. They used three-pronged, wooden step ladders to reach the upper branches. At this early hour, the aromatic smoke from little piles of smouldering prunings went straight up into the still air. As we walked, I kept seeing blocks of stone lying on the surface of the cultivated ground, particularly the characteristic, triangular, Roman facing stones, which suggested that this was where the Roman settlement lay, that had given its name to Venta Roman on the main road.

Our path took us between the narrow and secret folds of the Sierra de Bonís and on to walk down its western flank. On a new bridge, there was a rare combination of waymarks, the red and white markers, accompanied by 'G.R.7' **and** 'E4'. We kept wondering about these European routes, such as the E4, who knows about them, plans them and has any details? All we have, is a German-produced map of Europe, that gives very sketchy written routes, and even more imprecise lines on maps. Where they have difficulty establishing and publishing their long-distance routes, as the walking clubs do in Spain, one wonders whether these well meaning, but extremely rare European waymarkings are of much practical use. We travelled on beside the Sierra de Ascoy, all a fine upland walk with extensive views, mostly of badlands, planted recently with pines, in an attempt to arrest the erosion of the soil.

When we reached Creza, we caught a bus to Calasparra, to avoid a long stretch without accommodation. It was dark when the bus drew in. At the Hostal La Posada we received a warm welcome, though a stone cold bedroom. We are beginning to get hardened to this lack of heat in the cheap *hostales*. They are quite adequate so long as you can get a meal and some wine to warm you up before going to bed. They are still better if you can get hot water for a bath or shower as well, but though the *hostaleros* would always tell you that the water was hot, it very seldom was.

That night we were set to eat on a sort of minstrels gallery, from where we could see telly, football as usual, and the activities of the crowded bar below. We were waited on very efficiently, by the son of the house, who didn't look much more than 14. When language became a problem with the menu, he was persuaded to write the Spanish names of the dishes down, something it is almost impossible to get waiters to do as a rule, when there is no printed menu. We had as much as we could eat and drink and more, and retired to bed positively radiating heat.

Day 5: Calasparra — Moratalla

We strode off confidently down the C3314 towards Caravaca, with the clear instruction to turn off between the 17th and 18th kilometre markers on to the old road to Moratalla. But our confidence was misplaced. There were no waymarkers and it was not at all obvious where to turn. Eventually, having gone way past and returned, we made our own choice of turning, without really knowing, and asked someone we met, for the *camino viejo* (old road). They signed us round the side of the unnamed hill, west of Calasparra, towards the hill of San Miguel. There were several tracks, so we kept following our noses. After about one and a half kilometres, lo and behold, a red and white marker painted on a bench. Expansive views of mountains unfolded as we bowled along at the upper margin of cultivable land. We didn't see any signs of the cultivation of rice for which Calasparra is known. Part of the time, we were on rolling upland scrub, which would have been impossible to find our way across without waymarks, since there was a maze of tracks.

We picniced early at the Casas de la Carrasca, a group of ruined houses on a ridge, where sheep and goats would have been the main livelihood as there was not enough soil to grow crops. We descended to cross the Arroyo de Ulea and followed the Rio Benanor crossing the road at Casa de Garrido. After travelling along the south flank of the hill, called Moratalla la Vieja, we eventually came down to an old ruined medieval bridge with a humped back, just about passable on foot. From there, it seemed an endless ascent through almond and olive terraces. Several family groups were out picking olives by cutting the branches off and pulling the olives off on to sheets laid out on the ground. At the Hostal Alemeida, in Moratalla, our hostess seemed anxious to impress us with her fair prices and her good cooking.

Day 6: Moratalla — Caravaca
Reluctantly, we decided we couldn't continue the trail of the G.R.7 westwards to El Sabinar and Cañada de la Cruz, since we could find out nothing about either shops or accommodation at these places, and anyway the stints were too long, some 30 or more kilometres each. There was no bus until afternoon, so we set off to walk the 13 kilometres by road to Caravaca, as we'd decided to get to Granada as quickly as possible.

Early next morning, we caught the bus to Lorca. It was an ancient bus, dead cold and rattley and seemed in danger of falling to pieces when it gathered speed on the straights. Suddenly, we were unceremoniously bundled out without explanation, onto the still-dark streets of a village. The connection for Granada would arrive in about half an hour. Desperately cold, we crossed the street to get a *carajillo* (coffee with brandy) in a brightly lit bar. Our connection was a reassuringly new coach, with some heating on. As we travelled on, we became aware in the half-light, of writhing couples all around us. It was the young brains of Spain, indulging in a spot of rumpy-pumpy, on their way to school. We felt amused and a little staid as we smiled at one another, aboard this mobile 'knocking shop'.

The journey from Lorca through the *alto plano* (high plain) was spectacular. Distant snowy mountain summits flanked our view as we neared Guadix with its semi-troglodyte dwellings built into the hillside round the town. Their white-washed chimneys protruded as if out of the rock. The clear air and sun gave us a brilliant view of the snowy sides of the Sierra Nevada.

Tramping the streets of Granada, we nosed our way more by instinct than knowledge, into an old part of town, and found some lodgings in an old Moorish house, now Hostal Roma. We had a bedroom with sloping floors, a casement window, a heater and disapproving heraldic lions on fluted wooden columns to either side of the bed, holding swags, one each, saying LAUS DEO. Praise be, indeed, for another good landfall!

Useful information, addresses and bibliography

Topoguia GR7, Rebollar - Venta Boquilla.

Maps: *Michelin* 1:400,000 No. 445

Spanish Army Maps, SGE series 1:50,000 available from *Cartografia de Sur*, Valle Inclán, Granada

Map & Book Shop, Libreria International, Altmir 6, Alicante

Club Universitario de Montaña, Apdo Correos 4.193, 30.080 Murcia.(for info on GR7 in Murcia)

Airports at Alicante, and Granada

Autobuses between Alicante and Granada

Tourist Offices: Esplanada de España, 2, 03002 **Alicante** Tel.(96) 520 00 00.

Corral del Carbón, 18009 **Granada** Tel.(958) 22 59 90.

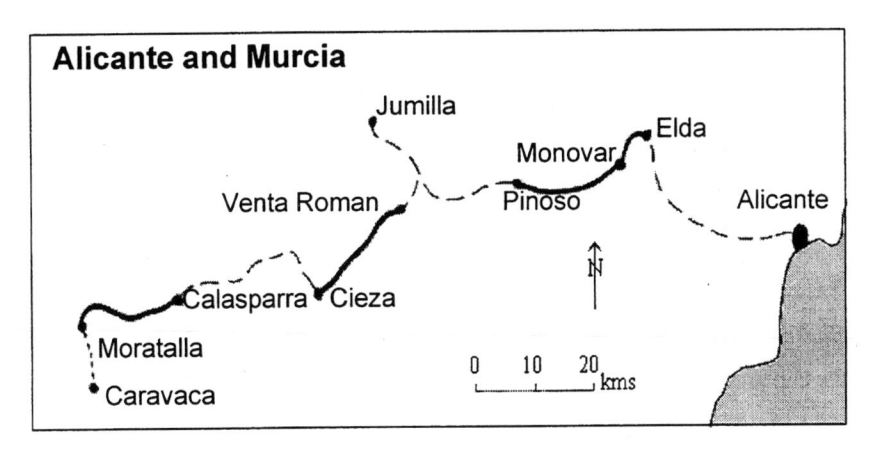

Alicante and Murcia

Key to maps - page 27

GRANADA & THE ALPUJARRAS

Granada was the height of sophistication after our walking in the mountains and we took a little time to explore. Started in 1238 under the Nasrid dynasty, the Arabic phase of the city's history reached its zenith with the construction of the defended palaces and gardens which make up the Alhambra. This followed a period when the Almoravids, a sect of warrior monks, whose purpose was to defend Muslim Spain, made Granada their capital in 1148. With the Christian reconquest of Spain, complete in 1492, the Alhambra saw a new phase of activity. King Carlos V (1516-1556) planted a palace in the Alhambra, a grand and ugly symbol of the new order. He also made a number of embellishments, such as gardens and fountains, both there and in the town. With Columbus's discovery of America in 1492, and all the new wealth coming into Spain, it was significant that he established a seat in the centre of the most potent symbol of Arabic power, the Alhambra. At this time Seville held the monopoly of trade with South America, and Cortes conquered Mexico in 1519. But all this new power and wealth, was soon challenged and reduced. By the 17th century, the Alhambra was the haunt of beggars and thieves, and in 1812, Napoleon's troops ransacked the Alhambra and nearly blew it up, as they retreated. It was the 19th century Romantic Movement, with visits from Gautier, Byron and other luminaries, which led to its rediscovery and reinstatement as one of **the** great monuments of past civilisation.

Carlos V's grandiose fountain stands beside the huge Moorish keyhole arch which forms the main entrance to the Alhambra. Wandering around the Generalife and its gardens you could imagine that in the hot summer months, the elaborate stone open-work decoration of the Moorish screens would allow maximum breeze and filtered light to enter the buildings. This summer palace was approached through a series of wonderful ascending gardens. Water, channelled through them, with fountains and ponds at intervals, displayed Arabic skills in water engineering, in a highly imaginative and decorative fashion.

The other palaces, with their courtyards with fountains and with formal flower beds, were overwhelming in the sheer abundance of their intricate stone decoration and the detailed scalloped vaults of their ceilings. For us, brought up on the austere grandeur of Norman architecture, or even the relative exuberance of the Decorated style, all this Moorish detail is hard to read — and 'read' seems to be the right word, since a major part of the decoration is made up of writings from the Koran. The main part of the Alhambra was built from the 13th century onwards, but the oldest part, the fort called Alcazabra, came before. From one of its lookout towers, Torre de la Vela, there was a fascinating view over the old Moorish town, Albaicín, and its defensive wall. As it was brilliantly clear, we could see the snowy summits of the Sierra Nevada to the east and far out over the fertile *vega* (horticultural land) to the south.

Memorials and monuments to former famous men of letters were everywhere in the city. Our wanderings took us to the house of one of Spain's greatest poets, Frederico Garcia Lorca. This house, in the *huerta* de San Vicente, on the edge of the fruit and vegetable-growing plain, was maintained as a memorial. He was shot in 1936, at the beginning of the Spanish Civil War, when he had already established his reputation, and had been over to South America to meet the Argentinean poet, Neruda. The very simply furnished house had been preserved more or less as he left it. Lorca was a good friend of the composer De Falla, whose house was also preserved in another part of the city.

Ceramic tiles are used everywhere for the street signs, with the writing in blue on a white background. Tiles of this kind were used in the Plaza del Poeta, to commemorate the poet Luis Rosales, whose poem, *Autobiografía* is quoted on one of them:

> *Como el naufragio metódico*
> *Que contarse las olas que*
> *Las bastan para morir . . .*

Like the methodical shipwreck which counts the waves, that are sufficient for death . . .

Granada is perhaps **the** great place for flamenco. We went to a concert in honour of a nationally famous flamenco guitarist from Granada, Juan 'Habichuela'. His nickname means 'red kidney bean', and was given to him because he was a snappy dresser. The big new sports hall where the concert was held, was packed to hear five hours of flamenco, performed by this famous guitarist and other members of his talented family. The highlight for us, and I suspect for many of the audience, came towards the end, when Ketama, a group I had long admired, also part of the family, who have achieved international fame, played some splendid rock-flamenco. They had everyone dancing in the aisles — old or young, got up to do their own thing where they stood. There wasn't room to move from your seat.

We sat next to Steve, an engineer from Belfast, who had settled in Madrid, and was being taught guitar by one of the 'Habichuela' family. It was interesting to get a Belfast man's view of his own city. He reckoned it had changed greatly since the IRA cease-fire of 1994. The city centre had opened up. There were bars and restaurants open and people were enjoying the unfamiliar sense of what a city should be like — full of life. He'd worked all over Europe, and reckoned that, contrary to their reputation in England, the Spaniards were the hardest and most efficient workers that he had come across. Though he loved Madrid for its night life and its carefree spirit, he thought that he might move somewhere like Granada, where the pace was a little less hectic.

From time to time during our stay, we pestered the ever-helpful staff at the Tourist Office, in order to work out our plans. We had heard that the Alpujarras, the foothills on the southern flank of the Sierra Nevada, were worth exploring, and gradually formulated the idea of walking through at least part of them, to reach our next objective, Almeria, some 100 kilometres, as the crow flies, to the south east. There was an extremely useful tourist map of the Alpujarras, which showed where there was accommodation and bus routes. So our next step was to go to the bus station and obtain all the relevant time tables, so that we had some sort of life line if the stints or the weather proved unmanageable.

As we were about to leave Granada, we managed to get BBC World Service again after a long time of bad, or no, reception. But the news was not good. The IRA had broken the cease fire in impatience at the British Government's lack of progress with the peace talks. They had exploded a bomb in the Island of Dogs, and another one was defused in Shaftesbury Avenue after a phone call. We thought of Steve and his optimism for Belfast. Whatever happened, it was doubtful that he would ever go back, except to visit, and eventually bury, his parents. He was one of the new Europeans, in there earning his living, regardless of what happens about British participation in the European Union or the single currency.

Table of Distances

1. Granada - Orgiva (45km bus)	56.0km
2. Orgiva - Pampaneira (6.5km bus)	16.5km
3. Pampaneira - Trevélez (9km bus)	27.0km
4. Trevélez - Cádiar	22.0km
5. Cádiar - Ugíjar	18.0km
6. Ugíjar - Almeria (bus)	75.0km

Day 1: Granada — Orgiva

We caught the bus to Lanjarón, about 40 km to the south. After two weeks in this great city, much enjoyed, we were ready for off, with our plans for our walking through the Alpujarras as well advanced as we could make them. As always there was a thrill of anticipation as we shouldered our packs.

The Alpujarras, form a still quite remote area, tucked in between the high peaks of the Sierra Nevada and the coastal ranges to the south. They have a special micro-climate which nowadays makes it possible to grow a rich and varied range of fruit and vegetables, and under Moorish rule was ideal for the growing of mulberry bushes and hence the production of silk, for which Almería was at one time famous. The geology has produced some extraordinary landscape as it is trapped between higher ground which formed a lake in geological times, on to whose bed the rains washed down Triassic limestone and red marls, to form a deposit several hundred metres thick. When the lake dried out, it left these compacted silts exposed to the force of later weather patterns. Just as they had been formed by rain action on the higher slopes, so their later history was defined by the action of water upon them. This led to the formation of deep straight sided gorges, where the water had forced its way through. Where the lake deposits were less deep, the water action led to the creation of shallower *barrancos* and conical mini-peaks, such as we saw on our way to Ugíjar.

Under Moorish rule, the region was colonised by Berbers from Northern Algeria, who brought their distinctive tradition of flat topped houses with them. These were proof against occasional extreme weather conditions, in the form of tornadoes, and have survived to this day. In the Reconquest by the Christians, when the Moorish kingdom of Granada was ended, the Alpujarras were given to the Moors and their king Boabdil. Progressively, harsher persecution of the Moors, led to a last revolt in 1568, when the Moorish settlers in the Alpujarras rose against intolerable conditions. It took two years for Christian forces to quell the revolt, after which all the Moorish inhabitants of the Alpujarras were deported as labourers to north west Spain. To fill the vacuum, a huge influx of families from Asturia and Galicia were given land there. This was one of the many cases of forced movement and resettlement of local populations in Spain's turbulent history.

Our bus journey took us across the intensively cultivated *vega*, south of Granada, and then started to climb on a very twisty road round huge folds in the mountains' flanks and *barrancos*, to reach Lanjarón. It is the foremost spa town in Spain, which gives its name to a bottled mineral water on sale everywhere. Since it has been in operation since 1795, it is provided with a number of fairly expensive looking hotels.

It doesn't take long in the Alpujarras, to appreciate just how deeply fissured the landscape is, with the courses of roads entirely determined by the negotiation of innumerable *barrancos*. Therefore our hopes of being able to use some of the footpaths marked on our newly acquired maps receded somewhat. As we tramped along the road, our attention was mostly taken up by this extraordinary scenery where roads and villages clung tenuously to the mountainside. We were keen not to have to walk all the following day on roads, and Betty had spotted a track from Orgiva, marked on the map, which set off from the cemetery outside the village and we decided to try it. At Orgiva we first encountered the lovely scented white flowers of the orange trees, which were coming out on the branches, alongside the previous year's ripe fruit.

Day 2: Orgiva — Pampaneira
Dawn was distinctly unpromising with massed grey clouds moving purposefully up from the south west. Undecided as to what to do, we bought supplies and breakfasted in a cafe, watching the rain set in. Our alternatives were to wait for a bus in about two hours, or to set off and risk a soaking. We chose the latter, and climbed up to our first landmark, the cemetery. By the time we got down to the river, it was raining steadily and what had been a harmless trickle, as we approached Orgiva the day before, was swollen to a strong torrent. It wasn't safe to try and cross to a track, which would bring us more quickly to the road, so we trudged up the east bank of the river, trying and rejecting various tracks which would get us up out of the *barranco,* which by this time had become quite steep. The rain was coming in sheets as we neared the road bridge to Carataunas and we scrambled very steeply up through some almond terraces, to emerge on to the road.

We were chilling off rapidly, so decided to walk up the road to Carataunas and catch the bus. From a vantage point outside a roadside cafe, we could at last see the bus, making its way with infinite slowness round the interminable bends in the road. By the time we got on to it, we were not only soaked but cold as well. The old country folk turned to look at us briefly, without interest, as we found our seats. The bus went wiggling and twisting its way up the mountains and at one point had to stop to negotiate carefully around a fallen boulder, which took up half the road.

In the village shop, we met somebody *profundamente borracho* (absolutely blotto), who insisted that we went back to his house, which he said was *'Arabi'* (Arabic). He jumped up on a roof, swaying over a considerable drop to point out the great snowy summit of Mulhacén to the north west. Inside, his house was very Spartan - table, chair and telly, with a fine fireplace, whitened for display, not used. For heat he had one of those under-table lifesavers, with long drapes to the floor, which we had experienced at Madame Mercedes'. Having got us there and sat us down, he didn't really know what to do with us. He opened a tin of anchovies and started scoffing these, offering them to us half-heartedly, as an after thought. But together with some bread, and a refill of white wine from the shop, that looked like being his dinner. He kept referring to Hitler and doing a salute, and to Mussolini, apparently with approval, though it wasn't easy to be sure what he meant, what with his befuddled state and our limited Spanish. It was fairly clear anyway, that he didn't think much of *Juan Maior* (John Major). His wife and two children were in London. She earned *mucho dinero (*lots of money) and came back for holidays. He liked it in the Alpujarras, it was *mas tranquilo* (more peaceful), perhaps a bit too *tranquilo* for his own good.

Day 3: Pampaneira — Trevélez

By morning the weather had cleared to a perfect day — lovely in the sun, but really cold in the shade. It wasn't too surprising that it was cold out of the sun, since we were at 1059m. at Pampaneira and not far off the snow line. You could see that the higher farms, above the village were all just below the lowest dusting of snow. As we climbed up by road, the view unfolded before us. Something that is special to the Alpujarras are the linear clusters of white houses, seen from afar, nestling against the vast folds of the mountains. In the village square of Portugos, groups of gnarled men standing or sitting at its edges, stared at us expressionlessly, without hostility or curiosity. We had been looking for a baker, and eventually a helpful soul actually led us to the door of the house where you could buy fresh bread, but it had no sign or indication outside.

We strode on until we came to a rusty coloured stream, where our leaflet said 'you must pause and drink the health-giving waters'. We did pause, but it was because there were picnic tables there, a very rare occurrence and also they were in the sun. There was a little chapel to Nuestra Señora de las Angustias (Our Lady of the Anguishes/ or perhaps griefs or more likely aches and pains, since drinking the iron-rich water was thought to be curative). We tramped on to Busquistar and as we were not far off the time that the bus for Trevélez was due, we waited for it. As we got on, I noticed again, the craggy, creased and deeply-tanned faces. These were not people to whom a living came easy, and they looked at us from another world. It was as if, in their eyes we did not exist.

Trevélez has two claims to fame. It is the highest village in Spain at 1476m. and it produces highly prized hams, which owe their special quality to being cured in the snow. It is the only village at the end of its valley and is about 10 kilometres from the nearest settlement in either direction. Though it is in a beautiful spot below snow capped summits, it seemed pretty cheerless to us on that cold day, in spite of its wonderful setting. We looked around and all we could see were shop windows stuffed full of hams. A cold wind blew, nobody was about. We wished we'd stayed on the bus. Two places advertised *habitaciones con baño y con calefacción* (rooms with baths and central heating). No wonder, it was bitterly cold, even in bright sun. The place we chose was possibly the only one open. Though we had a radiator in our room, it remained as cold as a tomb even after a couple of hours with the heating on.

Though we felt desperately cold in the Alpujarras, the actual temperatures were nowhere near as low as we are used to in England in winter. One reason for this, is that the periods of cold are much briefer in Spain, just a few hours in the day, for just a few weeks in the year. So buildings are not really warmed, and as the accommodation we were using was not in much demand during that period, very little or no attention was paid to warming it. The other reason that we were feeling the cold so much, was part of the continual difficulty of being round-the-year backpackers and providing for all eventualities. When we were walking in the summer months in shorts and tee shirts, we had to carry **all** the rest of our clothing. Therefore the warm weather gear was kept to a minimum. We would never dream of dressing in thin cotton trousers in February at home and yet that was our usual attire, so it was not surprising that we were feeling cold during the night hours, even as we packed on all available garments. Once the sun took over again we felt quite adequately dressed.

Day 4: Trevélez — Cádiar

The man at the grocery store asked us if we were walking up into the snow, an idea that had no appeal whatsoever, but that is apparently what people come there to do. To warm ourselves up, we set off at a good pace round the eastern side of the valley, which was not yet in the sun. As we strode out, we wondered where all the pigs were that were destined to be turned into hams. In the village we had heard no sound of them, but looking across and down the long steep slope of the valley opposite, we could see isolated farm buildings, with their accompanying terraces, scattered over the hillside. Presumably these housed pigs.

The day before had definitely been the nadir of our Alpujarras venture but with the sunshine we warmed up and our spirits rose. As we rounded the corner out of the Trevélez valley, a wonderful panorama of mountains opened up in front of us to the east. Bit by bit, the country softened and the valleys expanded in more ample folds, so that you could at last believe in the special micro-climate that made these valleys famous for their high productivity in fruit and vegetables. Again we saw the thin lines of white buildings set high up on the mountain sides, and we could see Cádiar for a long, long time, far below us, before we reached it. We wriggled endlessly round the innumerable folds and crevices of these water worn mountains, so unsuited for modern day traffic, with the roads in constant danger of being swept away down the steep slopes. On this stretch, we often saw mules being used for transport. In many places they were the only way to get produce and equipment up and down the terraces.

At the Cádiar junction, we saw that our goal for the following day, Ugíjar (pronounced Ooh-**hee**-harr) was 26 kilometres by the main road. As we watched, the Cádiar bus glided by us, and footsore as we were, we had an urge to flag it down for the last four kilometres into the town, but we were mid-cuppa. As it turned out, we managed one of those unforgettable finishes to a day, by taking an earth track by La Huerta Granja, a short cut that led us down to the little village of Narila and on in warm low sun, through a froth of almond groves in full bloom, to Cádiar.

Day 5: Cádiar — Ugíjar

On our map, there was a track marked, that looked as if it would keep us off the road and take us a considerable distance towards Ugíjar but we found that, after four kilometres, it petered out at a series of steep *barrancos*. This left us to scramble down the loose and treacherous side of the mountain to regain the road. Fortunately we did this at the junction of the minor road for Yator, so that at least we knew where we were. We then followed the road wriggling in unbelievable contortions round the badlands (rocky and shaly corrugated hills on which virtually nothing grows) to Yator, which was set in an idyllic valley with its river and fertile fields to either side, where many different vegetable crops were growing. Above, the mountain slopes were lit up with almond blossom. We picniced by the one ruined building of Venta Guita, at the junction of two river valleys. As a change from our usual tinned fish or cheese, we had a superb mushroom scrambled egg, which, with good fresh bread and the lovely local *rosado* wine, purchased in Cádiar, made a wonderful picnic.

We journeyed on by a high route, with an astonishing panorama below us, following for some kilometres the line of the Rambla Seca, a dry river bed, with boulders in it. You couldn't see how this landscape was any use to man or beast, yet interspersed amongst it were some isolated but highly productive lands.

At the junction where a branch road led south to Yorairátar, we stopped to make tea beside the badly slumped bridge over the dry river bed. This was a symptomatic feature of these badlands. Everything was on the move, ready to slide and subside when the rain came. According to our calculation we felt we should be nearing Ugíjar but could see no sign of it. We climbed steadily after crossing the river, but could get no views in the fissured landscape. Suddenly and unexpectedly the town appeared before us, set in this curious jigsaw of little valleys and totally hidden from view until we were practically there. Arriving out of the hills, it seemed strange to come into a normal little town with a bustling bar and people still finishing their Sunday lunch at 5:00pm.

The place we stayed seemed the ultimate in sophistication. It had a remote-controlled air conditioner, which gave us heat when asked to, after first testing with a sensor and thereafter puffing the welcome warmth out at intervals, presumably when its sensitive little soul felt the temperature drop. We had an *en suite* bathroom with soap and towels, and even hot water. This was a great joy. When we went down to eat at about 8.30pm, the place was quiet, all the earlier customers having gone home. Only grandma, endlessly patient, was left with the grandchildren.

Day 6: Ugíjar — Almeria

Ugíjar was idyllic the next morning — it was a brilliantly clear, sunny day, for once without any wind. We had to decide what to do next. Our information about places to stay had been obtained in Granada and because we couldn't get any information about the eastern Alpujarras, which falls within Almeria Province, we were unable to explore the Rio Andarax and its settlements. We thought we might go on to Berja and walk on towards Almeria from there. But then we discovered that the bus went all the way to Almeria, so this time we stayed on it.

Useful information, addresses and bibliography

Maps: *Michelin* 1:400,000 No. 446

Spanish Army Maps, SGE series 1:50,000: from Cartografia de Sur, Valle Inclán, Granada

Books: *South from Granada* by Gerald Brennan

Walking in the Sierra Nevada by Andy Walmsley. Cicerone Press 1996

Youth Hostels: Calle Ramon y Cajal,2, 18003 **Granada** Tel.(958) 27 26 38

Isla Fuenteventura,04007 Zapillo (**Almeria**) Tel (950) 26 97 88

Airports at Granada and Almeria

Autobus: Granada to Lanjarón

Almeria to Ugíjar

Tourist Offices: Corral del Carbón, 18009 **Granada**
Tel.(958) 22 59 90

Parque Nicolás Salmerón, 04002 **Almeria**
Tel.(950) 27 43 60.

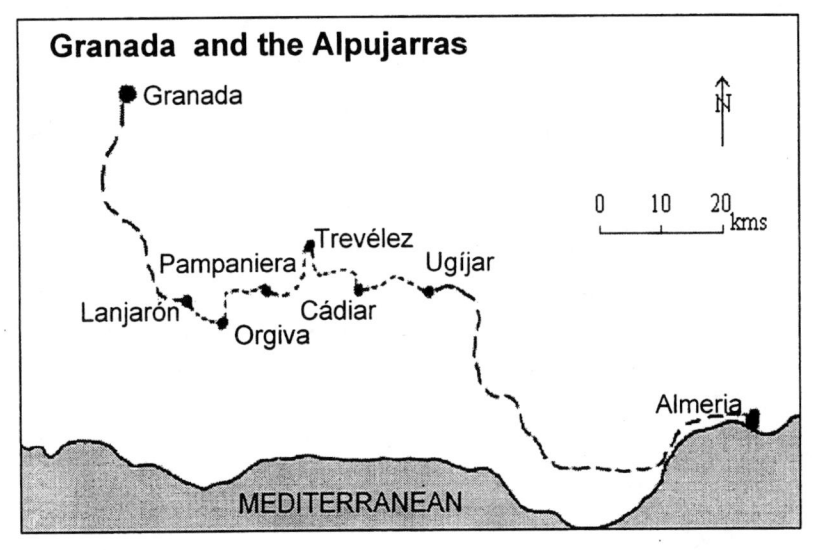

Granada and the Alpujarras

Key to maps - page 27

Granada & Alpujarras 169

SUNSEED AND ALMERIA

On a hot sunny afternoon, we caught the bus out to Sorbas from Almeria, excited at the prospect of realising at last a long-held ambition, but feeling like raw recruits not knowing what would be expected of us. The Sunseed Desert Project had been set up to look for practical solutions to the problems which are causing deserts, like the one through which we were travelling, to spread worldwide. South east Spain was chosen as having similar climatic problems to Africa, yet being accessible enough from England to attract volunteer workers.

After being dropped by the bus, we walked the last seven kilometres out to the project. For us, it was right to arrive, on foot. Rounding the final bend in the road, we looked down on a deep valley of chaotic rock tumbles and beyond that to the lunar landscape of the gypsum plateau of the Karst. At first sight this uncompromisingly harsh landscape looked an impossible place for any project to flourish. When we spotted a cluster of wind generators and solar panels, we knew we must have arrived and a steeply descending mule track brought us to the old main earth roadway of the village, with its line of white washed houses. There was no one about but we wandered along till we came to a cottage with a blackboard hanging outside saying; *Welcome to Ben and Betty*. Someone poked their head out of the door, said *Hola*, and offered us a cup of tea. This was Pili, a Spanish girl from Galicia.

We were allocated a small room with two beds, which had the simplicity of a monastic cell, with its white-washed walls and beams holding the roof. The spaces between the beams were filled with tightly packed bamboos. The two window spaces through the thick walls had no frames, but layers of plastic had been pinned over them to keep out the cold. Two hanging shelves made from bamboos and two upended fruit boxes as bedside tables, completed the furniture. It soon became a bit more like home, with our familiar litter of packs, tea-making equipment, radio and maps. In the early hours, Betty woke with the familiar, unwelcome symptoms of a migraine, which refused to budge and kept her in bed until late afternoon. She felt some despair at falling ill in a place where all the simple toiletry needs were so complex. But, after a pre-dawn stagger to the compost toilet down the garden, all she needed was to lie still and wait for it to go away.

While Betty was laid low with migraine, I went out to explore our surroundings. The setting of the village makes it a very special place. Seen from above, you look down on a valley, whose northern end appears to be totally choked with a fall of massive boulders that have split away from the tall cliffs on either side, coming to rest on the valley floor, leaning against one another at drunken angles, or shattered into hundreds of pieces, as if dropped from a great height. The most remarkable feature of this valley is that the river has constantly running water, which rises from a spring just to the north of the rock tumble. Rio de Aguas, is special, as it is the only river in the whole region to have year-round water.

A village, *Los Molinos,* grew up here with several water driven mills. But the water was hard won. It was conveyed from the spring at the base of the cliffs, along a rock cut channel, with manifolds at intervals, in the shape of archways in the rock face. These were cut at different heights so as to control the intake of water and to allow the surplus to return to the river, if the water in the channel went above the required height. It was then taken a kilometre or two along the valley side, in an open channel, to feed the village garden terraces. The mills along its course had their own leats, fed from the irrigation channel. They were the *raison d'être* of the village, and in former times were used to grind the flour, produced on the broad lands of the river valley as it opens up northwards and westwards towards Sorbas.

It is said that in its heyday, the village had about 400 inhabitants. One of the contributary causes to the decrease in population, was that the impurities contained in the drinking water of the village, led to fatal kidney complaints. When the Sunseed Project came to Los Molinos, about ten years before, it had been deserted by its original inhabitants, but had started to attract settlement by foreign nationals. Water for drinking had to be brought in.

Early on our first working day, we were sitting on our beds

enjoying our morning cup of tea, when down below, the door opened noisily and we could hear a voice chanting in a loud tuneless monotone. Heavy footsteps climbed the stairs and the chant was repeated at much closer quarters, so that we could make out the words; *Thank you for the sunshine, thank you for the rain, thank you Lord...* But the singer, the tall, hatchet-faced Tony, the household manager, was stopped in his tracks as Sylvia, a newly arrived recruit, woke with a start and dissolved into helpless laughter at this morning's version of the wake-up routine. Each morning it was different, sometimes we were roused by drums, a didgeridoo, a gong and even comb and paper!

Our first day's work brought us directly into contact with one of the main activities of the project — the tree nursery. Betty and her group were shown how to pot-up the tiny seedling trees, which had germinated in trays. They were native species of saltbush and carob, quick growing species of pine and eucalyptus, and brooms for nitrogen-fixing. Meanwhile, Gordon, a quietly spoken Scotsman, showed me how to construct the shade areas, to protect the tender young seedling trees from the fierce heat of the summer sun. Eucalyptus poles were used for the uprights, and bamboo canes with black netting stretched over them, formed the roof. Gordon was a forestry student from Bangor University, who would soon be off back, to investigate a planting project in the Scottish Islands. *Trees are it*, he said.

A second cook was needed to work alongside Rachel, the young redhead, who was working at the project for a year, as part of a geography degree and Betty rather rashly volunteered. Rachel had worked in a *ferme auberge* in the Pyrenees the previous summer, as a cook. She was calm, well organised, coped with a rather primitive kitchen and played classical music on the tape player as she worked. They cooked homity pie, houmous and a stir-fry of courgettes and tomatoes for 35 people — an almost totally vegan diet, which had been adopted, partly for reasons of economy and partly from principle. When asked by well-meaning Westerners, what they can best do to alleviate suffering in developing countries, Third World representatives reply, *Change your own lifestyle*. So the community at Los Molinos, have deliberately chosen this low-impact lifestyle, to reduce its demands on world resources, with the goal in mind of becoming as self reliant as possible.

Sitting outside relaxing after work waiting for the meal, I watched a game of chess in progress, which was part of an on-going tournament. The participants were sharply contrasted. On one side sat Paco, the quiet Spanish guy from Madrid, who had been on the staff for over a year. Beside him on the wooden bench, closely watching his face for the slightest change of expression, was Carmencita, a small black dog, his constant shadow. Paco made his moves without flourish and without saying a word. Justin, on the other hand, his recently arrived opponent, was full of bravado and badinage, trying to shake Paco's calm with his continual chatter. The light was beginning to fade as the game progressed at the wooden tables outside the kitchen door. Appetising smells were making us aware of our hunger. Over the sitting area the bare branches of the pruned back vine were tied to wooden poles and would give a canopy of green shade, by the time the heat of summer made it necessary. Looking down over the terraced gardens it was still just possible to make out the river in the valley bottom as the dusk deepened. At last the gong sounded to call us to the meal. Paco had quietly won his game of chess and everyone rushed to queue up at the kitchen door, ravenous after a long day out of doors.

We had been warned the previous evening to be ready for a trip out to Aguarico, in the project Landrover, for a morning of tree planting. It was a tight squeeze to get everyone in, including Graham and Shirley, the project managers, who were going shopping for supplies in Sorbas. They dropped us off and we hefted the tools to climb up the mountain side. The land at Aguarico belonged to a landowner in Sorbas, who was allowing Sunseed to plant on 170 hectares, where vegetation had been destroyed a few years earlier by fires. They'd had groups of local school children out to help with the planting. Chris, a young and dedicated forestry student, was in charge. He showed us how to hack the deep holes in the parched, rocky hillside, necessary to give the seedlings a good start. It was hard, back-breaking work. After spending half the morning making holes, the planting procedures were explained, which gave the little trees the maximum chance of survival. On this particular occasion, pines were being planted, but other species of trees and shrubs were being tested experimentally for their soil retention and regeneration properties on these denuded hillsides. It was inspiring to wander over the mountain side and see some of the small trees that had been planted a year or two earlier, that were now making growth and transforming the landscape. There was no shelter when it came on to rain and the job had to be completed. So we were wet and muddy by the time the Landrover returned to pick us up.

Since our trousers were caked with mud, we had to set about getting them clean and dry. Betty thought she had encountered every kind of primitive gadget for washing clothes but had only previously seen a washboard used as a musical instrument. As the patio where the laundry was done was also being used for drum-making, she thought maybe that was its purpose. But in fact the wash board was very effective for removing the mud. While the washing and scrubbing of many trouser knees was being carried out, the drum-makers, Duncan and Shaun, arrived to ask if anyone had seen the goatskins which they had been preparing. The drums were made out of the boles of agave trees and covered with the skins. The chief suspect of the theft was Wriggly, a big black amiable dog with a smooth glossy coat. He was an exceedingly energetic animal, who liked nothing better than to join in a tour round the project, or accompany people walking into Sorbas. I firmly believed in Wriggly's innocence because I had observed him pass by the goatskins without showing the least interest.

'Household duties' was an unpopular part of the rota for which we were expected to volunteer. It soon became obvious why it was unpopular, since it involved emptying four brimful containers of urine from the ablutions block and one from the compost toilet. On unscrewing the tops of the massive plastic bidons, where I was supposed to deposit this lot, a truly awesome aroma greeted me, as these too were already full. Frustrated in my menial task, I went to look for Paco to ask what to do with all this stuff. Having previously found Paco rather reserved and remote, his enthusiasm became obvious as he explained how he would use the diluted urine to water the garden terraces. Now, knowing how my humble chore fitted into the scheme of things, I went about my duties, happy that our waste products would in turn enrich the gardens. Very satisfying!

The most important part of the household duty, then, revolved around ensuring that the sanitary arrangements were cleaned, emptied and materials for the compost toilet, such as loo paper, water for hand-washing and organic matter, such as dry leaves and grass, to throw in after use, were replaced. Once you knew how all these arrangements, at first sight so cumbersome and uncomfortable, were part of the process of recycling waste for productive use, you could see that the whole system fitted together in a wonderful closed loop. Nevertheless it was easy to understand with what joy the news was received, when towards the end of our stay, it was announced that the pipework was complete, which would enable the urine to be piped directly into the bidons and nobody would have to empty the containers by hand anymore.

The work at Sunseed had a satisfying quality seldom found in the regular work of the 9 to 5 sort. You could see it fitting into the overall purpose of the community. Because there were well-defined and admirable aims, the low-impact lifestyle made complete sense. Betty and I felt a little part of something of real value.

As our supplies, particularly of cash and booze, were running low, we made a trip into Sorbas for replenishments. We had been told that it was a good walk to follow the river bed upstream into town. The tricky bit was negotiating the rock tumble a couple of kilometres from the village, following the irrigation channel and scrambling over, round and under the tumble of boulders. Once we were clear of the rubble we came to the source of the river, an idyllic spot of green growth and then we followed the dry river bed beyond that into the centre of the town. The houses were spectacularly perched on a flat topped piece of rock, and abruptly ended at precipitous cliffs. In a wonderful old shop, with sacks of flour, crates of vegetables, hay forks and a muddled collection of other items, we found loose wine. It felt almost sinful sitting eating a three-course *Menu del Día* in a restaurant, after the spartan conditions at Los Molinos, but it did taste good. We bumped into two other volunteers in the supermarket and we all acted like naughty truants, as we compared our indulgent purchases. Dobbo showed us a glimpse of the enormous *chorizo* sausage, that he was packing away into his bag. Sadly, he didn't get a look in, as he fell victim to 'Montezuma's Revenge' and while he slept between visits to the compost toilet, the cats devoured the sausage.

After we had been there for a week and had a turn at most of the chores, we felt enough confidence to put our names down to prepare lunch, which also entailed making the next batch of fresh wholemeal bread. It was quite a responsibility and there had been one terrible day, when the dough had not risen and the bread had turned out hard and inedible. Poor Paul, a recently arrived volunteer, who had made it, was not allowed to live it down and became known as Paul 'the brick'. Although Betty had often made bread, it was quite a different proposition turning out 16 large loaves in a temperamental gas stove, to baking a couple of small loaves at home. With some trepidation we assembled the enormous heap of flour and other ingredients. We asked advice from David, whose dance-like action when kneading dough, had produced a very good batch of bread. The system was to cook enough bread each morning to last for 24 hours and it was around for breakfast and snacks during the day with various spreads or left-overs on a help-yourself basis. Some of the dough was saved each day and used to leaven the next batch. As soon as the loaves came out of the oven, the smell of freshly baked bread brought one after another into the kitchen to sample it.

One of the houses was in need of some urgent repairs, and I helped in the task of rebuilding a wall and making a chimney stack, using the local *yeso* (gypsum). We had to be very quick using this building material because it dried in four minutes. The rubble was laid out in a line, then the *yeso* was slapped on it and roughly finished on the outside. A smoother skin would be added to the interior later. We were rebuilding a tumbledown lean-to to provide further accommodation. Ian was much older than most of the volunteers and had worked on a number of overseas aid projects. Though at first he seemed to be rather a know-all, giving the impression that his skills were being under valued, he was in his element there, a really good teacher and work mate. Young Paul, 'the brick', was the other member of the team and his energy and good humour helped the job along wonderfully. It was a messy job and you could identify the people who had been working on it by the fact that they all ended up with white dollops of dried *yeso* from the top of their heads down to their boots.

In the evenings it turned quite chilly and the wood burning stove was lit in the long low dining room. Supper was an occasion for leisurely talk, followed by the allocation of the next day's work, and progress reports on the different work going on, the tree planting, the gardens, the building work or the alternative technology projects. New arrivals were welcomed and departures were thanked and cheered. The reports were delivered in a light-hearted way. Even Duncan's announcement about the loss of the goat skins, he managed to make hilarious. When his girl friend Yvonne, who'd had a frustrating day, reported about not being able to make the computer do what she wanted, she decided to talk instead about the letter she had just received from her former boyfriend, to tell her how well he was getting on without her; but in spite of everything it had been a wonderful day, because she had at long last worked out how to wash her hair in a bucket!

Anyone was welcome to lob in their twopennyworth, by way of announcements, comments or jokes, and the important business was done in a humorous, though effective way, so different from the usual leaden and unspeakable staff meetings. We enjoyed sharing a bottle of wine with Graham, Shirley and their visitors who had previously worked on the project. They reminisced about the early days, when they had helped to clear the irrigation channel — dangerous and heroic work. It involved a three person team working underground in the dark, one person hacking out the rubble fill of the choked channel and pushing it back to the next in line, who scooped the debris through their legs to the one at the back, who put it into a basket for disposal. When this work was complete, not only were they able to irrigate the garden terraces once again but also there was a supply nearer to hand for washing and domestic needs, a tremendous step forward for the project.

That night was Nick's birthday and as so often on the slightest pretext, the younger ones, and a few who were not so young, took themselves off to one of the houses to celebrate. One young lass of around nineteen, nicknamed Miss Waffy, had come out to the project as a short term volunteer. She was a slightly built girl with long fair hair and didn't look the kind to be drawn to physical hard work. She had confided in us that she thought that she would be able to have a cheap holiday in Spain and spend all her afternoons sunbathing. She must have been a bit disappointed but to be fair she had put in a good stint on the tree planting. The idea of a party was obviously more in her line and off she went with all the others.

The next morning I was due to go out on a grass collecting foray. Nick, the birthday boy, appeared ready for work the same as ever, but Dobbo, one of the not so young partygoers, who was supposed to be in charge of our group, was totally unable to get himself together. After many urgings, with me carrying food and drink for a mid-morning snack, sacks and sickles, we set off — an ill-assorted group if ever there was one, Miss Waffy, much as ever and a hungover, short-back-and-sides Ian. Dobbo was clearly having difficulty coordinating his feet and needed numerous smoke breaks along the way. Nevertheless, he showed us the particular grass needed and beyond the rock tumble we found a good area, where we lightened my load by consuming the food and drink and cut the grass and filled our sacks for the return journey. The grass was needed for the cavity insulation between the outer and inner walls of the experimental adobe solar ovens, being built and tried out by the project. 'Short-back-and-sides' Ian was a Development Studies student who had finished his course and, being unable to get a job, had worked in a hotel as a commi-chef to get the money together to come out to Sunseed. He was hoping to go to Tanzania, where some of the experimental solar ovens, developed at Sunseed, were being tried out for real.

This expedition was part of Dobbo's continual search for the grass needed in the construction of the solar ovens. He was one of several working on different models at Sunseed. By using the heat of the sun for cooking, there would be less need to collect firewood and hence aggravate the process of desertification. Research into appropriate technology was supervised by Pete, who was frustrated much of the time by being diverted from the work on ovens, solar stills, channel-hearths, solar collectors and other such important experimental work, to do repairs on the generator and the ram-pump, to supply day-to-day needs.

The ram-pump was a prototype, presented to the project by Warwick University. It was used to pump water almost vertically up the side of the valley, into a storage tank at the top of the village. The only energy used was that provided by the force of gravity. The water was for the use of property owners of the village generally, and they, in their turn, were supposed to ensure that the Sunseed houses were supplied by means of a gravity-fed pipeline. Whilst we were there, we got no water for the showers in the ablutions block from this supply. The politics and disputes about the supply of water were complex and mirrored the kind of problems encountered frequently in the African countries that Sunseed was setting out to help.

The irrigation channels for the vegetable plots needed to be cleared of weeds and re-cut ahead of the growing season. We were instructed in this work by Paul from Hornsea, East Yorkshire, a man of few words who was in charge of growing supplies for the kitchen. One of his great strengths, was that he was a fluent Spanish speaker, so that he was able to talk to a few of the old men around, who had expertise in how the garden terraces were cultivated. Of all the people at Sunseed, he was the most involved, at a personal level, in the local community. He played football for a local team and when the General Election was held, he was employed as a teller. When Paul discovered that Betty had experience of raising seedlings, he set her on sowing trays of tomato, basil and onion seeds, to be germinated in the underground greenhouse. This was a wonderful structure, dug about two metres below ground level and covered with a framework of bamboo covered with clear polythene. It provided a more even temperature for germination than outdoors, where the nights were pretty cold and the days sometimes quite hot.

Because of the long-term nature of so many of the projects we worked on at Sunseed, we promised ourselves that we would return someday. We were especially keen to see how the trees we had planted would progress. It was easy to see how people got drawn in and found themselves staying on, or returning year after year. But, for the moment, we had a walk to continue and get out of our systems. Departing on foot, as we had arrived, we felt that we left a little bit of ourselves there at Sunseed. Wriggly appeared, sensing that there was a good walk in it. There certainly would have been, hundreds of kilometres of it, but giving him a pat and a stroke, we strode off, with David calling him back.

At Almeria, we found lodgings in one of many high-rise blocks close to the seaside, mostly occupied by Spanish families. From our cheap bed-sit, we could just get a glimpse of a vertical strip of the Mediterranean, gleaming between the high buildings and watched the comings and goings of the ferry boats plying between the port and Africa. Our onward journey was to be a series of bus hops, so that we could see Cordoba and Sevilla *en route* to Portugal, where our next major chunk of walking would take us north to Santiago de Compostela.

Fragments of several periods of Moorish defences, belonging to the tenth century heyday of Almeria, survive. For a brief while, it was a prosperous trading centre, specialising in the production of fine silk. The later ascendancy of the Christians over the Moors was celebrated in a huge statue with its arms raised in blessing of the city below. But under Christian domination, the city fell into decline, from which it only really recovered in the 19th century with the development of the port. Iron and marble from inland quarries was brought to the coast by rail for export. Now the new growth industry around Almeria is the intensive horticultural growing under vast seas of polythene, which stretch for many kilometres. One day, we saw some activity at the huge rust coloured, triangular shaped sheds by the station in Almeria, which intrigued us, and were beckoned in by two workmen. This was a rail terminal for iron ore brought down from Linares, which was unloaded, wagon by wagon, and moved by an underground conveyor belt, to ships in the port. At that very moment, there was a huge, Limassol registered tanker, called Indomitable, which was loading iron ore bound for Rotterdam. At dusk that evening, it was towed out by tug to begin its journey north. It was an impressive sight to see it slowly edge its way out to sea.

While we were there we saw some wonderful sunsets. A particularly collectable one flooded the sea with changing colour, shades of mauve and pink, different minute by minute. The last of the sun caught the undersides of strung out clouds, streaking them with vivid fire for a few moments. It was a great cosmic show. People stood around on the seaside *paseo* watching, and we took to joining them each evening. Every time it was different. The Spaniards, much as they love their towns and their bars, were obviously just as impressed as we were. There was a long moment's silence as the colours reached a climax, then their animated conversations would start up again as the sun disappeared.

Useful information, address and bibliography

Sunseed Desert Project, Apdo.9, 04270 Sorbas, Almeria. (details for prospective Working Visitors)

Country Living by Bob Harrington. Available from Sunseed. (describes local way of life in English)

Youth Hostel, Isla Fuenteventura, 04007 Zapillo, Almeria.

Airport at Almeria.

Autobuses from Almeria or Alicante to Sorbas.

Tourist Office: Parque Nicolás Salmerón, 04002 Almeria. Tel.(950) 27 43 60.

THE COAST OF PORTUGAL

The weather, whilst we were in Lisboa was typical of April in England, but about ten degrees warmer. Bright sunshine kept tempting us to sally forth without macs, only to find that the weather turned quickly to showers. Easter Sunday morning was bright and the grass of the park was an unbelievably vivid green. It sloped down to give panoramic views of the city, built on a series of hills and, beyond that, to the broad river Tejo. We were drawn to the quayside, and wandered along observing the shipping and the fishermen. The river was full of boats, large and small, and ferries were plying across its great expanse. The city was a pleasant, relaxed and slightly seedy place to wander. The pavements made striking use of small white and black stone sets, often arranged in floral or geometric patterns, and everywhere interspersed with the city's emblem, a galleon, rendered in black stone.

What we thought was Russian we discovered was the guttural sound of Portuguese. My attempts at communication in Spanish were understood, but when the rapid reply came, I was completely unable to make anything out. All we had been able to find in the way of an aid to learning the language, was a miserable phrase book, which spent most of its time telling you how to complain, and very little about how to enjoy yourself! On the positive side, Betty extracted from it, a very useful vocabulary for food.

The Velha Goa restaurant offered the chance to have some Indian food. Being totally ignorant about Goa, we asked the friendly waiter, who explained that it was a former Portuguese colony on the west coast of India, which had recently become part of 'the big India'. This colony had been noted for its trade in Indian spices, and its cuisine reflected a subtle blend of influences and a distinctive mix of spices.

As we were returning across the little park near our lodgings, where the old boys slept out amongst the shrubbery, and assembled tables and chairs for their drinking parties, we passed the Lycée do Camoes, named after Portugal's national poet, with a statue of him in front. He was declaiming, with his hand outstretched and fingers spread, just waiting for a fat, contemplative cigar to be provided. But I am sure that, if some kindly soul furnished the poet with this aid to inspiration, the old boys in the park would have it off him in no time. *No use wasting a good smoke on him*, they might say; *Best to give it to us, who keep his name and fame alive.* While happily taking it in turns to suck on the great rolled tube of tobacco, they would, no doubt, quote fluently from the dead poet's verses:

Let us hear no more of Ulysses and Aeneas,
My theme is the daring and renown of the Portuguese,
The heroes and poets of old have had their day,
Another and loftier conception of valour has arisen,
Nymphs of the Tejo, you have inspired in me
   a new and burning zeal.

At the 'Ar Libre', which acts as an umbrella organisation for all outdoor activities, we finally discovered that the staff were all about to set off on an excursion to Spain and no one was available to give us advice about walking in Portugal! We felt somewhat pissed off, but had by that time more or less decided anyway that we would have to work out our own route, as we had got used to doing. Nevertheless it was disappointing as we would have liked to find out if any long-distance, waymarked footpaths at all existed in Portugal. Without these or decent maps, we didn't feel able to explore the mountains of the interior. We later discovered that Portugal has 20 National Parks, in only one of which are there waymarked paths.

The man at the Tourist Office showed us a copy of an out-of-print leaflet on the pilgrim routes in Portugal, heading for Santiago. It looked as if they started from Porto, one going up the coast and the other heading north east, some way inland from Vila do Conde. The Société des Amis de St. Jacques in Paris had sent us details of other routes from further south, but it looked as if these were now no longer footpaths, having become tarmacked roads, of little interest to the walker. From what we could gather the coast north of Lisboa was not nearly as built up as the south facing coasts of Algarve or the Sintra coast, west of Lisboa. Some years earlier a young English walker, who we had met in the Pyrenees, enthused about his walk down the Portuguese coast, so we decided to give that a go. The next port of call was, therefore, the Geographical Institute, where we bought the necessary 1:50,000 maps to get us as far as Porto. With these and the Michelin 1.400,000 motorists' map, we caught the bus to Sao Martinho do Porto on the coast north of Lisboa to start our walking.

We edged our way round and to the north of Sao Martinho on to a track through the sand dunes. *The bay at Sao Martinho is like a shell*, our friendly waiter at the Velha Goa had said, cupping his hands to demonstrate, and so it was. Following our track, we rejoiced at being on the trail again, smelling the lovely sweet smell of new growth and flowers everywhere. It was a very bright and sunny day, with warm wind — ideal for walking. Pale yellow daisies took over from the yellow oxalis which had been everywhere in southern Spain. Masses of bright pink or cream Livingstone daisies, with succulent pointed leaves, just grew out of the sand. There were scarlet pelargoniums, growing to the size of small trees, particularly near ruined cottages. The most delightful, were little yellow daffodils, with fine, wisp-like fronds, sweeping back from the trumpets, growing out of patches of bare earth. Sweet peas were already flowering brightly in the gardens, and we saw again the beautiful swallow-tail butterfly sitting with its wings spread wide soaking up the sun. Portugal had just had a spell of some of the worst weather in living memory, and it looked as if the seasons were now trying to catch up, with everything blooming at once.

It was nice to be free of the cities, much as we had enjoyed them. This was where we really felt at home, in the countryside, walking again on soft earth. We could see sandy beaches ahead of us, disappearing to the north in a salt sea haze. We asked ourselves, *Would we have known that this was the Atlantic, if we didn't know?* (Sounds like a question for our Cambridgeshire sophist.) I think the answer would be *yes*, because of the white horses going far out to sea, and the mighty breakers pounding along the shore. The Mediterranean certainly had its waves and its choppy seas. But this Atlantic coast had an ancestral familiarity about it, going back way beyond childhood memories to an ancient kinship which made us feel instantly at home.

It quickly became apparent that our new Portuguese maps were really only any good as a general and approximate idea of what was happening on the ground, as we followed a series of sandy, seaside tracks. At the approach to Nazaré, our map showed a bridge over the river and a way we could avoid the main road, so we confidently strode through some gates into what turned out to be a new harbour. Our bridge over the river had disappeared years before. Even our Michelin motoring map had the new harbour on. Our 'new' map was dated 1969! Their lack of local topographical detail and the way they are issued as flat sheets, not folded handily for use, makes you wonder who these maps are aimed at. They are certainly not of much use to walkers. Nevertheless they have an antique charm about them!

Nazaré was a real seaside holiday place, just recovering from an influx of Spanish visitors, who had come out for Holy Week. All along the front, people were touting for business, trying to sell thick woolly jumpers and socks, which it was not difficult to refuse on this lovely warm afternoon. They were also trying to sell overnight accommodation in German, French and English! And it was someone who spoke to us in English who got our business, even as an old crone in a chair was desperately trying to attract our attention in a mixture of Spanish and German. ¿ *Quiere zimmer?* We went down the shelving beach and dipped our toes in the Atlantic, while kids all around us were plunging in and out of the water. The older women of the village mostly dressed in black with knee length skirts, full petticoats and ankle socks. They usually had coloured pinafores over the skirts and big black head scarves. Quite a few of the women carried heavy loads on their heads with a tightly rolled ring of fabric to cushion and support the weight.

We were able to walk on firm wet sand for the last few kilometres to Praia de Vieira, as the tide was going out. This area was quite remote, and the absolutely fabulous sandy beach had just an occasional way through from the road some distance inland. It was beautiful, but boring and hard walking. We could see our objective for an hour or two before we reached it. The wind was strong, the sun intense and we were getting quite burnt. To the north Perdigao kept appearing and disappearing like a mirage in the intense sunlight, wind and salt sea haze. We thought we were beginning to hallucinate.

That night we had an excellent meal — *bacalhau a brás*, salt cod chunks with onion and egg. The woman who owned the place, had worked for many years in Paris, but her husband, a local, wanted to come back home. She was a warm and friendly individual and listened with interest to our tale. When we got up to go, she asked Betty how old she was, and when she heard, kissed her on both cheeks in a spontaneous gesture of support and female solidarity.

At Figuera da Foz, Betty arrived back exhausted but triumphant after visiting the market. Although it was a dull morning, the light inside the market hall was decidedly dimmer, filtered through small windows high up at the ends of the rounded roof. Immediately the noise and bustle engulfed her. At a bread stall, she had stiff competition from some local women who were almost coming to blows over cakes. These were a local Easter speciality of sweet yeast dough. Whole eggs with their shells on were baked in the centre and crisscrossed with glazed dough. There was the two egg model and some larger four egg versions which were the most sought after. One woman, who had been waiting patiently for one of these bigger cakes, became hysterical when she saw the last one sold to someone else who pushed her way in and grabbed it first. Betty stood her ground and eventually got bread buns and two samosa-like pasties.

We made our way on sandy paths through the pine woods by a series of lakes, two or three kilometres inland from the coast. Near the first of them, Lagoa dos Braços (Lake of the Arms), we paused to eat the delicious strawberries we had bought for our breakfast and realised what botanical riches there were around us. At the edges of the woods were white orchids. Pinky brown water avens hung their bellshaped flowers over the edges of the dykes. The bright blue and pink flowers of vigorous, hairy viper's bugloss were everywhere, growing out of the sandy soil. Spikes of glowing, golden lupins stood out against the white and blue periwinkle with its shiny leaves covering the ground. Yellow cups of marsh marigold and pale pink water lilies crowded the shallow water of the lake margins. It was like walking through a continuous wild flower garden, and in the cultivated cottage gardens, there were the long trails of sweet smelling mauve wisteria on the walls and stands of white arum lilies.

Before we left Tocha, we wandered round the busy Sunday Market, which had transformed the huge space around the church, completely deserted the previous night. They were selling farm tools and equipment, fruit and vegetables, bric-a-brac and second-hand clothes. People were eating portions of yellow soaked beans, out of paper, as a snack. But the main activity of the market centred round a series of huge black spits, with chickens being roasted over beds of charcoal, which were periodically fanned with bellows. The spits were turned by women who were so tanned, they were almost black — no doubt helped by the clouds of dense smoke from the fires. I paused to get one of these chickens, they looked and smelt so good. Every so often, they were sprinkled with salt and basted with a piquant sauce. As I waited my turn, I saw that the tents behind these spits were packed with men, women and children, sitting on benches at long trestle tables, noshing away. They had chicken, salad and bread and the talk and the wine were flowing freely. The whole scene was like the subject of a Brueghel painting, transported to warmer climes. At the bar adjoining, I was offered a drink by a bloke who very much wanted to communicate, but what with the language problem and the drink, it was a bit difficult. He introduced me to his good friend, who was swaying around. As he talked to me, he kept hold of his friend's jacket to stop him crashing to the floor.

At Sao Jacinto we watched all the kids, soldiers, assorted dogs and other passengers, waiting for the 8.0am ferry. It left absolutely stuffed full of people, and with some hanging on the outside. We thought that walking down the road, along this isthmus of land, from a one-horse place like Sao Jacinto, would be really peaceful. But we reckoned without the wagons which were incessantly trundling back and forth, fetching sand and taking it somewhere north. As we left, we passed by some docks where small craft were being made for the Portuguese navy. When we could enjoy it, in the rare moments between the wagon traffic, the view out over the large, enclosed, watery expanse of the Ria, was superb, with small fishing craft near at hand and further off the settlements on its far side, and way beyond them, the mountains. A group of cocklers on a rapidly disappearing sand bank, were anxiously awaiting their lift home, as the tide rose. Scanning the water, we couldn't see any boats approaching, but, as if from nowhere, one appeared just in time to collect them. In another minute or two their island had completely disappeared.

We liked Porto, so we stayed for a while. It is Portugal's second city, but it has a more human scale for walkers than Lisboa. Who was it who said, that no city should be so big that you couldn't walk clear out of it in half a day? Anyway, that was Porto. It is built on the high rocky north bank of the river Douro, and has given its name to its main product, port wine, which is also a major tourist attraction. It can be sampled and studied in various 18th century warehouses, built along the south side of the river in the new town, Vila Nova de Gaia, which probably owed its origin to trade in this blended and fortified wine. We duly did our sampling by tagging on to a coach load of French. The warehouses contained rows of enormous oak barrels and lock up stores with stacked bottles of different vintages of ruby, tawny and white port. The whole operation was slickly presented by a young lady, in the traditional Sandeman, broad brimmed black hat and cloak. The French said that in France they prefer port as an *aperitif*, whereas in Portugal as in England, it is usually drunk after a meal or on its own.

We took a 100 kilometre trip upstream by train to Régua, where the grapes for the port are grown, through countryside cultivated in small plots, with vines on concrete supports, below which other crops such as broad beans or potatoes were growing in the shade. The last half of the journey was close to the steep rocky banks of the river, with wild, wooded slopes reaching right down to the river's edge. At Régua, the landscape opened up to reveal the hills around, covered in vine terraces right up to their tops. By the river the white blooms and sweet scent of dog roses were all around us. Plastic debris high up in the trees, showed the level the water reaches when the river is swollen with rains. Work was proceeding on enormous concrete pillars to carry a new motorway over the river gorge. These pillars were so lofty that it was a long time before we could detect the movement of the tiny-looking tower cranes, transporting their loads up and down. On the south bank of the river, a vast ugly scar showed where the vine terraces had been cleared to make way for the new road. The giant, black effigy on the hilltop amongst the vineyards, with its cloak and sombrero, advertising Sandeman's Port, by contrast seemed puny.

On the return journey a voice suddenly said, *Are you guys touring around here?* It belonged to Luis, a Canadian Portuguese, visiting his parents, who had returned for good to their farm near Régua. His loyalties were obviously somewhat divided between the two countries. He was critical of the Portuguese for joining the Spanish fishing fleet in Canadian waters, and censorious of Portuguese shopkeepers for taking two hour lunch breaks. But worse than that was the bus driver who hadn't allowed his grandmother time to get on the bus, and shut the doors on her. When Luis had criticised him, the bus driver simply said, *She should have hurried up. I love my people*, Luis said, *But*...

As far as we could make out, no actual pilgrim footpaths survive. There was therefore nothing to be gained by turning inland at Vila do Conde, just to walk on roads. From Póvoa de Varzim, about 30 kilometres to the north of Porto, we walked north along the coast. Past old, one-storey cottages on the edge of the shore, in front of which stood circular, thatched, stacks of seaweed, we walked on through a series of coastal 'improvements' and were quickly out into real country again on a track between stone and earth walls. To either side were enclosed small grass fields, rather reminiscent of the landscape of the west of Ireland. This later gave way to a different farming regime, where the sand dunes had been rearranged to provide level fields, with evenly sloping sides to them, on which vines were growing. The levelled areas were given over to onions, in all stages, from the seedling plants to the mature bulbs ready for harvesting.

As we were passing through a little village, an old man in a pony and trap offered us a lift. We stowed our packs in the back and clambered up to sit beside him, feeling rather guilty at increasing the load for the diminutive pony. The old man kept up a continuous monologue, talking to us or the pony, and I don't know who understood least. He was from the village we had just come through and was on his way to his fields. Up ahead we could see a group of people carrying on an animated discussion in the road. Their carts and tractors were parked higgledy-piggledy. On the verge, close by, two young lads were laid out side by side, with the wreck of a motor-cycle beside them. They were very still, and one had his face partly covered with pulled grass. Either they were unconscious or dead, and as we passed the old man muttered something about *ambulancia*.

He pointed directly ahead to show us our path for Apúlia, the next village north along the coast, before he turned off to his fields. If it had not been for him we wouldn't have found this quiet track, which led us between one after another of the sunken sandy fields, where whole families were busy planting out onions. There were greetings and cheery calls to us, as we passed each family group. We made a welcome break for a moment or two from their hard work.

At Apúlia everything looked closed. In the small formal park, on one side of the main road, there was an obsequious plaque saying that the park had been opened by His Greatness the Under Minister for Rural Development. But on the other side of the road, a bronze statue of an emaciated and haggard-looking fisherman, dragging the net draped over his shoulder like a heavy burden, seemed to tell the real story. Between the little villages, everyone was out in the fields, planting onions or cabbages, picking potatoes by hand, cutting grass with sickles and collecting it into bundles, and leading manure to the fields. There were some small tractors about, but also carts with almost solid wooden wheels, pulled by donkeys.

Back on a major road, the traffic became intolerable and we were fortunate to be able to catch a bus into Viana do Castello. Viana was founded by King Alfonso III in 1258, to provide a trading and fishing centre on this good estuary. Following the Great Discoveries, its fishermen fished for cod off Newfoundland. It grew prosperous and, in the 17th century, the wealth produced by trade in Brazilian sugar and gold, accounted for the building of fine town houses and churches, which made Viana the most architecturally sophisticated place that we saw in Portugal with styles right down to 20th century 'art-deco'. Clearly it escaped the earthquakes which destroyed so much fine building in Lisboa. There were many Portuguese visitors, and Viana's obvious prosperity and sophistication were in marked contrast to the relative poverty of the seaside towns we had seen further south.

At Valença, the lass that cut Betty's hair, had, like Luis, returned from Canada. But she had come back to Portugal for good, because she hated the long winters in Canada and wanted to get away from the highly competitive lifestyle to a more free and easy way. Her family had a farm near Valença. She said, *Some years the grapes or the potatoes fail completely, and there is no help from the government.* Government statistics for unemployment were low, because many of the people working on the land, though classed as employed, worked almost for nothing.

Leaving Portugal behind us, we recrossed the bridge over the Minho. ¡*Adiós Portugál, hola España*! We had really enjoyed our month's stay amongst the friendly outgoing people of Portugal, not yet bored with foreigners. Dutifully following our directions for the pilgrim route out of Tui, we climbed up to the cathedral and with great excitement, found the first of the yellow arrows we were to follow all the way now to Santiago de Compostela. These led us down hill and along a wide street of stone houses, parallel to the river. There we got briefly entangled in a party of chattering and giggling schoolgirls on their way to their gym lesson.

On a wet Mayday Fiesta morning in Redondela, there were groups of kids struggling to carry heavy wooden crosses, decorated with pine branches and garlands of yellow marsh marigolds, which we had been seeing everywhere in the countryside. A procession was in the offing and the kids were roping in any of their mates who tried to pass without taking a turn. We left the town in a thin curtain of rain, following the arrows. The curtains turned to sheets and back again to thin veils, through which a group of bedraggled youths were struggling to carry another decorated cross, down into the town. There were eight or so carrying and about the same giving them spells, all with much shouting and joking.

In Pontevedra, whenever you hesitated, someone was always ready to show you the way. We followed the old medieval streets, which had once been the principal streets of the town, and were now bypassed, but thankfully not destroyed. The walking of this route is still a live and actively continuing tradition. We were on our own walking and had not seen anyone heading for Santiago, and yet we felt we were not alone. People greeted us as we passed in town and country, smiled or waved and pointed ahead saying, *A Santiago de Compestela, si*, as people must have done to generations of pilgrims. We are not religious pilgrims, yet the whole of our travels could be said to be a sort of pilgrimage — two vagrants in search of the world. It made a pleasant change to feel that we were part of a tradition of walking there, whereas in Portugal we sometimes felt like freaks, since nobody walks there if they don't have to.

Alternately in woodland or rolling green farmland, we journeyed happily on. After walking out of Caldes on the old high street, we came across two women who were ploughing a field with oxen, one led and the other guided the plough behind. Then the walking wasn't so good, with our path continually crossing and recrossing main roads, but at least it was keeping us off them. With our attention distracted by the traffic, we must have missed the point where the yellow arrows turned off the main road again. Betty later said that we should have returned to find them. I felt that to turn back through the traffic, and perhaps even then not find our proper route, was worse than continuing. I'd got myself into a grim and stubborn mood and was all for pressing on and getting this awful five kilometres or so into Padrón over. The heavy traffic put an unexpectedly heavy and immediate stress upon us both. For suddenly Betty stamped her foot and yelled against the din of the traffic, that she was not going to walk the rest of the way into Padrón, with me in that mood. She abruptly turned off the road down a track to a bridge over a stream, and found by it an idyllic spot to rest, brew up and regroup. We watched in silence for some time, the water-boatmen on the surface of the stream, with the sunlight casting for each, six oval pads of shadow on the stream bed. Little fish rushed back and forth in shoals and then disappeared. On the bank there was lush foliage with young alder trees. Dark blue-green dragonflies hovered over the water margins and were suddenly away. I was tempted by the hot sun and the clear water to strip off for a dip. We talked ourselves out of this little break in our usual harmony, in the peace provided by this haven, and marvelled that nature so quickly reasserted herself outside these linear strips of hellish modern interference. If there is a deity, it has to be the old Greek goddess Gaia.

On the final stretch to Santiago the path led us through back lanes and villages, where all the dogs barked us through the entire length of the winding alleys, and out into the farmland and the woods beyond. One of the features of those Galician villages, was the *horreos*. These were small barns standing on little pillars, all entirely built of granite. They had pitched roofs, often with crosses at either end, and slatted sides. They were for storing the maize. We dozed after eating, on the mossy floor of a disused quarry and woke up, half wondering if we were dreaming, to see a party of pilgrims with their pilgrim hats and staves tied with yellow ribbons, coming into the clearing. They were real alright, and came from Tui. After pausing briefly to chat, they passed on towards Santiago. The last few kilometres into Santiago were a bit tantalising, as we twisted and turned on our path, with distant views of the city, appearing, then disappearing behind wooded hills, without coming nearer. But that path was a good one; it got us nearly into the centre before we got onto the roads.

We had reached Santiago at last and the end of another major stage of our journey.

Useful information, addresses and bibliography

Maps: *Portuguese Army Maps* from Instituto Geografico, A Cadastral, Lisboa

Clube de Actividades Ar Libre, Centro Associativo du Calhau, Tartue Florestal de Monsant, 1.600 Lisboa

Societé des Amis de St. Jacques de France, B.P. 368.16, 75768 Paris.(for info on pilgrim routes)

Walking in Portugal by B.Davies & B.Cole. Footprint Guides, 1994

Youth Hostel: Monte de Gozo, Carretera Santiago Aeropuerto, 15820 Santiago (3km from city) Tel.981 56 28 42.

Airports at Lisboa and Santiago.

SANTIAGO
AND THE FIRST PART OF THE PILGRIM ROUTE

In spite of the shops full of pilgrim tatt, the old town of Santiago wasn't spoilt, in the way that Lourdes is, with its rows of shops, selling awful junk, like plastic Virgin water-bottles and anything to fleece the tourists. Santiago has undergone many transformations since 813, when the hermit Pelayo had a dream, showing him the whereabouts of the tomb of St. James. The news of this miraculous discovery echoed across Christendom and led to a thousand years and more of pilgrimage from all over Europe. Pilgrimages were an important part of the medieval church and after Jerusalem and Rome, Santiago became the favourite shrine. It got the backing of the monarchs of Europe and the wealthy monastic orders. The abbey of Cluny was particularly important in providing hostels and safe passage for the pilgrims. While no doubt fulfilling an important ecclesiastical function, in offering absolution of sins to those who did the long and arduous pilgrimage, the fame of the place in Christian Europe, was a useful way of ensuring that Islamic power was curtailed. After only 40 years of supremacy in northern Spain, Islam was never able to re-establish its hold there. To have the Infidel far away in Jerusalem was bad enough, but when he had conquered most of Christian Spain and threatened France too, that was too much!

After many alterations and rebuildings, the present layout of the huge cathedral and the other churches and streets of the old town took shape in the 17th century, giving the place an air of ample baroque splendour. The streets were provided with covered colonnaded walkways and the area around the cathedral, with huge stone stairways leading to vast paved squares, to its west and east. These were planned for the reception of hordes of pilgrims, and must have provided a great contrast to the earlier huddle of wooden houses around the cathedral, described by a pilgrim who had visited before the great rebuilding.

There are three strands of musical tradition special to the place — church music, plainsong and choral; troubadour music brought by the pilgrims of old; and Celtic music, originating in pre-historic Galicia. The latter went back beyond Romanisation and Christianisation, but had survived them with its beautiful lilting melodies and its fiddles and bagpipes, reminiscent of Scottish and Irish music. Galicia is proud of its Celtic heritage.

Table of Distances

1. Santiago de Compostela - Arca	21.0km
2. Arca - Arzúa	20.0km
3. Arzúa - Melide	16.0km
4. Melide - Palas de Rei	14.0km
5. Palas de Rei - Portomarín	24.0km
6. Portomarín - Sarria	23.0km
7. Sarria - Triacastelo	20.0km
8. Triacastelo - Alto de Poyo	12.0km
9. Alto de Poyo - Vega de Valcarce	25.0km
10. Vega de Valcarce - Villafranca del Bierzo	16.0km
11. Villafranca del Bierzo - Ponferrada	22.0km
12. Ponferrada - León (bus)	104km
13. León - Mansilla de las Mulas	20.0km
14. Mansilla de las Mulas - El Burgo Ranero	19.0km
15. El Burgo Ranero - Sahagún	18.0km
16. Sahagún - Calzadilla de la Cueza	23.0km
17. Calzadilla - Carrión de los Condes	17.0km
18. Carrión de los Condes - Frómista	20.0km
19. Frómista - Castrojeríz	25.0km
20. Castrojeríz - Burgos (bus)	39.0km

Day 1: Santiago de Compostela — Arca

It was at this point, turning east to walk across northern Spain, on this classic European pilgrim route, the Camino Francés, that we started our homeward journey. Good though our French topoguide *Le Chemin de Saint Jacques en Espagne* was, we quickly realised just what a mind-bending experience it is, to follow a guide backwards **and** in a foreign language. What is more, all the yellow arrows point to Santiago and are not designed to help the return-pilgrim, so you are constantly having to swivel your head round to search them out on the back of telegraph poles or the blind sides of buildings, high or low.

Past the chapel of San Marcos, ever upwards, we started to meet a trickle of pilgrims, travelling towards Santiago. By paths and tracks we crossed and recrossed the main road to Lugo. The surfaces that we were walking on had frequently been levelled by laying down gravel. At road crossings, strips of white granite sets marked our way. Round the western end of Santiago airfield, the path was kept separate from the road by providing steps and a rolled sand strip for the walkers. At every half kilometre, there was a stone marking the distance from Santiago. Never before had we had this 'red carpet' treatment as foot travellers.

The refuge at Arca was quite like the French *gîtes d'étape*, providing kitchen, showers and dormitories. We cooked in the sunny kitchen and Detleff, a tall German, joined us to eat. He told us that he had started walking with a loose group of about 15, who would sometimes walk together, or meet up in the evening at the next refuge. But he had now lost touch with his 'family', and would do the last stint into Santiago the next day on his own.

Day 2: Arca — Arzúa

Country lanes took us through little hamlets, whose names marked the old pilgrim route — Rua (road), Brea (path), Calzado (street), Tabernella (little tavern). Before Tabernella there was a bridge, Puente de Ladrón (Bridge of the Robber), named after a robber who had no doubt preyed on unwary pilgrims, perhaps centuries ago. He had also given the stream a bad name for it was called Rio Ladrón.

A memorial plaque was placed beside the path for Guillelmo Watts, a pilgrim of 69 years, who had died on a hot day in August 1993, only two days from his goal. At least Guillelmo Watts from Paris would be remembered, but it brought back to mind the memorable biblical phrase, 'and some there be who have no memorial'; for how many over the centuries must have perished along this well-trodden route and received summary and unmarked burial by the wayside?

As we struggled up the steep hill to Arzúa, an old man asked us where we had come from. When we said we had walked up to Santiago from Portugal and were now walking home, he said, ¿Por qué?. Why indeed? I was able to say without hesitation, *Porque nos gusta mucho caminar* (Because we like walking very much). *Muy bien* (very good), he replied, and smiling, patted each of us on the shoulder. If you do anything because you enjoy it, that's OK by the Spanish.

After an excellent meal at the Fonda Frade, our hostess placed a bottle of home-made brandy on the table for us to help ourselves to a glass. Two cyclists came and sat at the next table. We overheard from their conversation that they were English and turned to chat. When we said where we were from, one of them called John, who had a broad Yorkshire accent said, *You may know my brother, he lives in the next village to you.* We didn't need to be told who his brother was, because the accent and looks were so familiar, we realised his brother was someone we knew well. John and his friend Jim from Glasgow, had almost completed the pilgrim route on mountain bikes. We had a friendly natter and in the near dark, they peddled off to their *refugio* at Ribadiso, three kilometres away.

Day 3: Arzúa — Melide

The Ribadiso refuge consisted of a group of fine stone buildings, recently refurbished, which had served as a pilgrim hostel since the 15th century. Beside it, a little stone footbridge crossed the Iso and set us off on our route. At a point where we thought we were lost, some Santiago bound pilgrims emerged to reveal the path ahead. We passed on through beautiful country, woodland and farmland. In the bright sunlight we saw lizards with vivid phosphorescent green and black spotted skins. A family of young swallows were learning to fly. One flew down and through the water of a trough and then sat preening its lovely sleek, glossy, blue-black feathers, showing us the reddy-brown around its beak. Though there were still many people working by hand, tilling, spreading muck and planting, we noticed more signs of mechanisation than before, tractors and the unwelcome sight and smell of intensive units for cattle and pigs.

Day 4: Melide — Palas de Rei

Another brilliant day of strong sun with high cloud, produced a wonderful light amongst these wide hilly horizons. The countryside changed to open moors, the lower slopes of which were cultivated, but the tops left wild with gorse, white and yellow broom and bell heather. Over the open heath, we passed some ponds where the din of frogs croaking was very loud. They stopped as we came level, but most of them stayed visible, with their heads above water, their bodies supported by the water weeds. Their green skins had darker stripes and spots in rows. These last few days there had been masses of apple blossom and the classic spring combination of bluebells, white stitchwort and vivid green grass. Entering the woods at one point, a woman greeted us as we passed her cottage. A little further on, we had taken a wrong turning, and she whistled to attract our attention, and pointed us in the right direction, and then when we were on the right path she raised her arm vertically and waved us farewell.

Near Palas de Rei, there was a painted sign, addressing pilgrims on the way to Santiago, ¡*Animo peregrinos os falta poco*! (Cheer up pilgrims, not far now). We could take it as meant for us, as we had only about two kilometres to go to our resting place. At the top of a flight of steps in Palas de Rei, there was the *refugio* in front of us. Having got ourselves installed, we were washing out a few essential garments, when a party of four, three English and a German, trooped through. Tony seemed determined to go into the complicated details of their party's arrangements to meet up and walk together. Rosie appeared, pleased with her newly acquired sun hat, and was dismayed to hear that the forecast was for rain. Meanwhile, whilst Betty was hanging out our washing, Judith was explaining to her, that she and Tony were both married but not to one another. The fourth member of this troupe of actors had a non-speaking part. The young German, Dieter, had a dreamy romantic look, enhanced by his curly locks and his long flowing coat. Somehow, our first meeting with this group, had the air of a scene from a play of the J. B. Priestley era.

The second act took place in the interior of a rather gloomy eating house, where we had been the only customers. Suddenly the troupe came in and joined us to eat there. The atmosphere was immediately transformed to party time. We all had a good evening, with the wine and the chat flowing. Dieter's beam broadened, the more so when two young Swiss girls, also pilgrims, turned up to eat at the next table.

Day 5: Palas de Rei — Portomarín
In the visitors' book at the refuge, was the following heartfelt pilgrim's entry, *Nada. No sale nada de una cabeza vacua, las piernas me han consumido el cerebro. ¡ULTREYA!*. (Nothing. From an empty head nothing comes out, my legs have consumed my brain. ONWARD.).

We halted for coffee at an upland crossroads. As we sat waiting for the water to boil, with the rain coming on, Mariet, a Dutch woman, stopped to talk to us. She sat on her pack and offered us chocolate. The previous year she had walked from Holland to Santiago, and on to Finisterre, which she had liked so much that she had returned. There was no mistaking a world wanderer from the far off look when she described her travels. She had the legs for it, real billiard table legs. Betty reckoned that talking with us for ten minutes, gave her the excuse to really let rip to catch up with the others she was walking with. Though not tall like a lot of the other Dutch walkers, she was full of energy and strength. You could easily believe that she could do 40 kilometres a day and keep it up. What is it with these Dutch, that makes them such phenomenal walkers? They seem such mile-eaters, as if they must walk to the ends of the earth while there is still time!

As we made our way down to the river Miño to cross to Portomarín, the rain came on heavily and we got absolutely soaked. Quite a few drowned rats like us had already arrived at the small refuge there, where as usual we had a good welcome.

Day 6: Portomarín — Sarria

We crossed the dam, then wound steeply uphill and lost our way at a junction of tracks, where, as so often, there was no marker to guide us. It was a day of getting lost and getting wet, several times over. There was one sudden heavy shower, which we were able to avoid by diving into a disused wayside chapel, but the next time the heavens opened, there was no shelter but a group of oak trees, through which the heavy rain and hail found their way to us, without any problem. Soaked to the skin, we reached the main road and as luck would have it, were able to get a bus into Sarria.

At Hostal Londres that evening, we sat next to two other English walkers, husband and wife. She was small, wide eyed and a bit gushing, and spoke of her backpack as 'her sins'. So I asked her, *Will you leave them behind at Santiago?* Unaccountably she did not reply. He had a thatch-like beard which he kept on fingering. When I told him about the brandy being put on our table in Arzúa, for us to help ourselves, he said sanctimoniously; *Yes, but we must remember that these people are very generous and not abuse their hospitality.* He was a lecturer on a sabbatical, and had a caravan parked somewhere close to the Mediterranean. When they had finished the pilgrim route, this would be their base for their children to visit and for him to do his work. It sounded like nice work if you could get it. He said he liked meeting people along the way, but was glad that he didn't have to walk with them and sleep with them as well. The feeling was mutual! They seemed to have stepped right out of a Posy Symmonds cartoon.

Sarria had the feel, with its rich reddy brown sandstone castle walls and houses, of the old border towns between England and Wales, particularly because of the similar quality of light when the rain stops and the cloud lifts, to give those vistas of blue-green hills — like Houseman's *'blue remembered hills'*. Even the smell of fresh rainy air, with its hints of bracken and moorland, was similar. It was at Sarria that we celebrated one year on the trail, with a bottle of 'bubbly'. This had now become our way of life, and we had ceased to count the distance we had travelled. Our enthusiasm for the vagrant life was still as great as ever.

Day 7: Sarria — Triacastelo

By the time we stopped at Fuentearcuda, the rain was coming down steadily again and we ate standing up in the shelter provided by the porch of a little lock-up store. An old woman came down some steps from the house opposite, picked her way through the mud across to a barn, and tottered back up; chickens came hopefully out to scavenge our food remains, but returned disconsolately to shelter. The last few kilometres, through wooded valleys, should have been a delight, but in pouring rain it was just sheer slog.

Day 8: Triacastelo — Alto do Poyo

There were patches of sunlight high above us, making the fields on the mountainside, just below the snow line, glow with brilliant green. Several pilgrims were setting off towards Santiago. Rain set in again as we braced ourselves for 15 kilometres of uphill to O Cebreiro. We arrived soaked at Alto do Poyo at 1337m, a col with a restaurant on one side and a *hostal* on the other, and called a halt there. Feeling much restored after hot baths, we went down to the bar, where our *hostelero* served us drinks, brought wood for the fire and urged us to write in the visitors' book. From this we saw that there was a steady flow of pilgrims, apart from December and January, when the entries dried up. Snow was still lingering from a heavy fall two days before, and this was May! Bull fighting was on television. It was the first, and we hoped the last time, that we would see it, since it was a nauseating spectacle. Basically, one bull after another was brought out, taunted, tortured and killed. Our host, wanted us to join in the fun, as the bull charged and pushed over a blindfolded horse, protected with body armour, whose rider got off at the critical moment. This was all part of the fun and had our man in stitches. The bull was allowed two charges and toppled the horse each time, but the third time, a man on another horse stuck his lance deep into the bull and pulled it out dripping with blood. Then the fancily-dressed, posturing *torero* started his routine of taunting again. No doubt there is a lot of skill to it, but the end was not in question. I felt so churned up, that I took my beer outside. The view had briefly opened up to reveal the mountains and distances we had missed as we trudged up in the siling rain. It calmed me to see all that splendour. Betty was not so upset as me at the time, but found that the torment and killing of the bulls came back to her in the night.

Day 9: Alto do Poyo — Vega de Valcarce

We set off at a good clip, to get the circulation going and met a couple of gutsy English girls, for whom the pilgrim route was the first long walk they had ever done. One was thin, orange haired and wore one boot and one plimsole, a combination which told its own tale; the other was of stocky build, dark haired, bespectacled and cheery. They were part of a loose 'family' of 15 or so, of assorted nationalities, that met up at night in the next *refugio* along the trail. With all their aches and pains, they were still full of the magnificent views from O Cebreiro the previous night. We wished them well, they needed it.

By the time we reached O Cebreiro the sky was blue and the sun was hot. We were aware that this was a tourist honeypot, because we had already seen photographs in tourist literature of the thatched huts called *pallozas*. These rare survivals of an ancient building tradition, possibly going back to the Bronze Age, were squat, one storey stone structures, thatched with rye stalks and broom. This was an important stage in the pilgrims' journey to Santiago as it was the highest point after the Pyrenees. From there on, having had a long haul up, their journey would be less arduous.

Descending steeply down through woods of oak and beech, we met lots of pilgrims toiling up. The mountain villages didn't have much in the way of gardens but by the time we got down to the valley settlements of Los Herrerias, they had gardens again and the buildings were of slabs of shale or schist. We had done with the typical Galician villages, each house with their own *horreo*, and were into another geology and another building tradition.

In Vega de Valcarce, we sought out the Bar Charly, to get the key for the *refugio*. When we got up there, we met Ruud, a Dutch cyclist, who was laying out full length on a bench in the sun. This was about the most basic refuge we encountered. There was only cold water for the showers, one large dormitory and no cooking facilities but they only wanted 100 pesetas (50p) for an overnight stay. Ruud was riding a road bike, which meant that he was confined to roads with a decent surface, and doing 100 kilometres a day. He seemed a bit lost and hadn't really got into the spirit of the pilgrim route, which is essentially for walkers. He had heard about John and Jim, struggling to stick to the walking route with their mountain bikes, joining forces to manhandle one bike at a time, on uphill slopes in difficult terrain. No wonder they only did 27 kilometres or so a day. Much of the route we'd followed had been strewn with large boulders, or negotiated rocky stream beds. Ruud clearly could not see the point of all this effort.

Horreos in Galicia

Day 10: Vega de Valcarce — Villafranca del Bierzo

At Trabadelo, about seven kilometres down the steepsided valley, we were looking for the alternative route, which our French guide gave us, rather than slogging on down the valley on the main road. We had got into the middle of this little village, with its cattle, cow shit, dogs, cats, chickens, sheep, sheep droppings, crewyards and its glorious earthy, animal smell, before we realised that we had come too far. With help from the village postman, we retraced our steps to the steep ascent, which started our alternative route. As we picnicked under the chestnut trees at the top, a cart came lumbering by, with solid wooden wheels, pulled by two cows, on a one-piece wooden yoke. A man stood in the cart with the reins and a woman walked behind with two dogs. They stopped to chat and he said it would take us about two hours to Villafranca. On our high ridge, we had a little breeze, as we wound and undulated amongst masses of white, yellow and violet broom, mixed with gorse, bell heather, ragged robin, rampion and prickly scrub. Our path began to wind downward, flanked by rock rose (*Cistus ladaniferus*) bushes with their large floppy white flowers and characteristic dark purple-brown blotched centres. We rounded a corner and suddenly Villafranca was in view below us, dominated by its sturdy four-square castle. Beyond it across the plain in the far distance, were what looked like the sandstone battlements of a huge castle, glowing reddy-brown in the evening sun. This was the area of fantastic sandstone pinnacles called Las Médullas, where the Romans mined for gold. We can certainly count this as one of our best days walking.

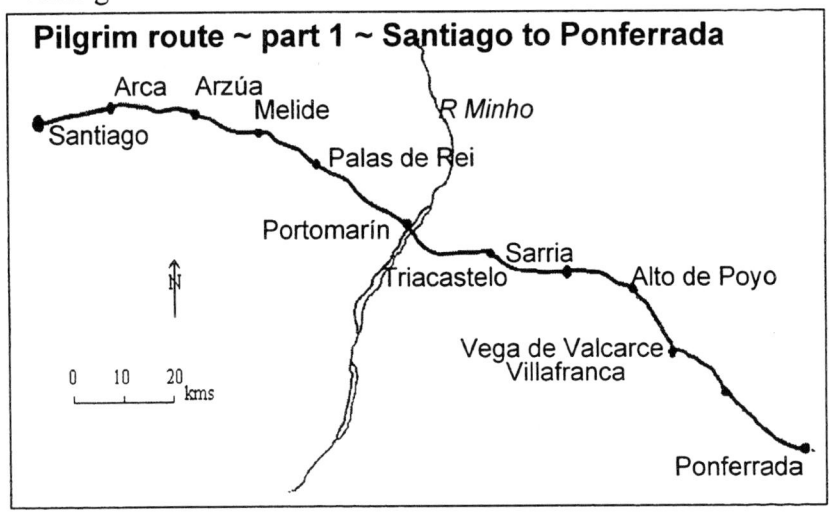

Pilgrim route ~ part 1 ~ Santiago to Ponferrada

Key to maps - page 27

Day 11: Villafranca del Bierzo — Ponferrada

Climbing up through narrow cobbled streets, lined with old wood-framed houses, we left Villafranca. If ever there was a place to return to, this was it, with all the beautiful hills and mountains around to explore. From the refuge an ancient track, with deep ruts worn into the sandstone, took us straight into the countryside. Its high hedges were full of pink dog roses, scented honeysuckle and yellow broom. Our views were over the rolling vineyards of the Bierza, and eastwards to the snow-capped tops of the Montes de León. Storks were nesting in a church belfry, the parents clearly visible, standing in the huge untidy mass of sticks that formed their nest, with their two young. We met a Frenchman, *en route* for Santiago, leading two donkeys, who paused briefly to chat. He had a tent and camped out at night.

Day 12: Ponferrada — León

The next day's stint to Rabanal, was too long for us, so we decided to bus on from here to Leon. This allowed time before leaving to walk up to the old town across the river Sil, and visit the castle with its fairy tale battlements. The bus wound in and out of coal-mining valleys, with little settlements, and dense scrub oak cover between the many scattered small-scale mines. Some sort of treatment works at Ponferrada, must have accounted for the enormous slag heaps just north of the town, by which the *camino* goes. Then we were up and over the mountains, and down to Astorga, with its Roman battlements and Gothic cathedral. As we glided on in our air conditioned bus, through the hot afternoon, we could see pilgrims toiling along the path across the plain. The sight of them produced a mixture of feelings — part envy, part guilt at missing out a chunk, and part a wicked luxurious feeling of wellbeing as we were transported in cool comfort, for a little while letting up on our long walk.

We dozed off and came to as we entered León. Retribution swiftly followed for skipping the route in comfort. We felt absolutely dreadful when we got off the bus, dopey and disoriented. With our senses dulled, we needed to find a spot by the river to brew up a cure-all cup of tea. We found a resting place at Hostal Reino de León. I felt a little shamefaced laying the pilgrim patter on the landlady, to get her to lower the price, since we'd arrived by bus, but only a little, mostly I was pleased to get the room at a price we could afford.

We visited the San Marcos Museum, in an old convent and pilgrim *hostal* by the river. This houses, not only the museum, but a church and the luxury Parador hotel. No room for the humble pilgrim now. We moved on to see the remarkable wall and ceiling paintings of the 11th and 12th century church of San Isidore. The most remarkable of these old paintings, formed a calendar depicting the agricultural activity appropriate for each month of the year, such as the ploughing, the planting, and the harvesting of the grapes. I briefly visited the cathedral and was bowled over by the glowing colours from the fabulous stained glass windows, so deep and rich.

Day 13: León — Mansilla de las Mulas
We met a 'family' of young pilgrims, in good spirits — Swiss, French and German, walking together. When they heard of our plan to walk back to England, one of them said, *And what about the Channel?* I said, we would be walking on water of course. He replied doubtfully, *Well, its been done once, but a second time, I don't know . . .*

The landscape had changed. We were now walking through the vast tablelands of the *meseta*. Huge fields of barley alternated with big pastures for cows and sheep. We found mushrooms, which we collected and carried on with us to cook later. Mansilla had once boasted town walls, mostly constructed of layers of cobbles in *adobe*, now ruinous, but reconstructed on their west side. The name Mansilla de las Mulas, sounds like 'Stables of the Mules', *mansilla* being a diminutive of the Latin *mansio*, which, in the Roman Empire meant a road station, where horses were changed and accommodation provided. The *refugio* was in an old house in a back street of this small village, composed partly of *adobe*, sun-dried clay, and partly of fired bricks. In the stone flagged courtyard of the refuge, we chatted to the other overnighters, sitting in the dense shade of an enormous fig tree.

Day 14: Mansilla de las Mulas — El Burgo Ranero
Breakfast of fried eggs and mushrooms, was a real treat. Elsa, a lone Dutch woman, was quite envious, but when we offered her some, she declined, having already eaten a far more healthy breakfast of yoghurt and cereal. Elsa had undertaken this journey, from Holland to Santiago, on her bicycle after her marriage broke up. She was using this spell on her own, to have time to think and re-evaluate her life. She was full of admiration for us, for doing the journey on foot, but Betty said that no way would she have been able to do it on a bike.

That pleased her, because she had found that some of the walkers tended to look down on cyclists.

Once clear of the village, we joined a specially created pilgrim track, gravelled and planted with young poplar trees, running alongside a broad farm road, which gave access to big fields, mainly arable, with wheat, barley and rye. This planting was part of the plans for 1999 Holy Year, by which time the trees will have grown to give effective shade. At intervals, wide shallow valleys broke up the monotony of these long stretches. They had been supplied with white concrete tables and benches, under mature poplars, which stood amongst the lush grass beside the streams, and lent a surreal quality to this silent land. The Cordillera Cantabrica, with its snow-capped summits, marched with us, some 70 kilometres away to the north. Though it changed little as we travelled on, there was a grandeur about this scenery which stopped it becoming boring.

At one of the surreal picnic spots we ate and snoozed in the heat of the day. As we woke, we became aware of masses of reed warblers flitting about in the reeds by the stream. Amongst the tall lush grass, the white, star-shaped flowers of *ornithigalum* stood out. Refreshed, we set off for El Burgo Ranero, which was like a town out of the Wild West. There were a few outlying, ruinous *adobe* houses, well on their way to returning to the parent earth from which they had been fashioned. The village was mainly built of *adobe*, of a rich, glowing red-brown colour, sometimes with brick frontages added. The refuge was a brand-new building made of *adobe*, well-appointed with dormitories upstairs, and downstairs, a kitchen, eating area and ablutions. We went out into the calm of a beautiful sunset and wandered by the village pond with its croaking frogs. Our room was full to capacity, with a party of Spanish walking to Santiago. They insisted on having the window closed, but in the wee small hours, I opened it, to look out on a three-quarter moon and a sky full of stars.

Day 15: El Burgo Ranero — Sahagún
To beat the heat, we set off at 6.30am. Even so, others were off before us, slipping out in the half-dark to continue their journey. Dawn over the Cordillera Cantabrica was a superb sight. At Bercianos del Real

Camino, another *adobe* village, more or less halfway on our day's stint, we tried to find the bar mentioned in our book, but saw no sign of it. We trundled on through great fields with huge skies, and reached Sahagún soon after midday.

Day 16: Sahagún — Calzadilla de la Cueza

We were away early again at the start of another scorcher. As we climbed up out of the town, we passed the remains of a Visigothic monastery, founded by Sanctus Facundus, from whom the name Sahagún was derived. This had been sacked with monotonous regularity by the *musulmanes* (soldiers of Islam), and reconstructed after each sacking. Thereafter the lands were given to the Benedictines of Cluny, who built a great new monastery there. This in turn was ransacked by the local population and, after *Desamortización* (sale of church lands) in 1835, it sank into desertion and ruin.

Through a sea of barley, the Ermita de la Virgen del Fuente could be seen from afar amongst a group of poplars. The windows of the church were bricked up, but picnic tables and chairs were set out under the trees. Every year in April people gathered there to picnic and dance. Pilgrims of old will have welcomed this shady spot as a place to quench their thirst and rest after travelling across the hot empty spaces. Only part of the old stone bridge across the river survived.

The villages were in the valley bottoms, with streams and stands of poplars, whose shade was in marked contrast to the searing heat of the uplands. At Terradillos de los Templarios there was a pilgrim *hostal* which had formerly been run by the Knights Hospitallers. We ate and rested on a shady green. As we had our sights set on Calzadilla to overnight, we pressed on up a silent valley, through more barley and eventually dropped down through oak woods to reach it.

There was no sight nor sound of anyone, and there were no cars on the street, as we walked into the village. We thought it was a 'ghost' town until we came to a large sign painted on the road which said BAR, with an arrow. This we followed with our hopes rising. There was a hotel at the very edge of the village. We could hear the usual hubbub of conversation and television blaring away. As I approached the bar, a man in shorts came across the room to greet us.

We joined a jolly group of Americans and Dutch for a drink. Greta, the American wife, was one of those bouncy, energetic blond females — vice president of something in California. She and her husband, Hank, were keen cyclists, and were biking to Santiago. Hank kept buying the beer, which she refused, because she was on a diet. But as she was talking away, non-stop, her arm would snake out behind her, find his glass and transport it to her mouth, almost as if it had a life of its own. With only the slightest pause, she would swallow two enormous swigs, and the arm would dutifully return the glass, while she continued talking.

Day 17: Calzadilla de la Cueza — Carrión de los Condes

The weather had changed to cool, cloudy and windy as we strode along a dead straight track through undulating farmland. We got out of the wind to breakfast beside the old mill canal of the Abbey of Benevivere, now a large farmhouse. This abbey used to have a dependent hermitage on the route that we had walked, but this had completely disappeared in the intensive barley cultivation.

At the refuge at Carrión, one bloke was already installed, a Spaniard from Madrid, who was having trouble with the tendons in one of his feet. *I speak only American now*, he said, *I used to speak English, when I lived in Potters Bar, a small place outside London.* He now worked as a fire chief on an American airbase and had saved up the time to do this walk to Santiago by taking on extra shifts. The pilgrimage to Santiago was something he had wanted to do for himself, to plan his own route and timetable. But now he had this bad foot, and knew that if he went to the doctor, he would be told not to go on.

A party of Italian walkers arrived, then an Austrian, a Dutch cyclist and two Germans. The Italians were most sorry for themselves, hobbling around, painting their feet with red stuff, which made them look as if they were rubbed raw. Doing their washing, talking amongst themselves, they didn't communicate with the other nationalities. Whether they were religious we didn't discover, but they were certainly into punishing themselves with 30-40 kilometres a day. The *refugio* was next to Santa Maria church and had a lovely enclosed garden at the back — quite its nicest feature. I wrote up some of the diary sitting out there in the sunshine and Betty wandered around it, missing her own garden.

Day 18: Carrión de los Condes — Frómista

I had made tea before the lights went on at 6.0am. The Austrian was off first, and much to the surprise and chagrin of the Italian party, us two old hands were off next around 6.30am, glad to be out in the fresh air again after a night in this small cramped refuge. After so many months on the road, our morning routine, getting our breakfast and packing up, ran pretty smoothly.

The morning was chilly and overcast and we had to stop and put on an extra layer. We were again in open rolling arable countryside. Our topoguide's diversion took us by the Ermita del Virgen del Rio, a church with a hermit's house attached which had grown piecemeal, with patches of old stone, brick and tile used indiscriminately. The whole effect, though a hotchpotch, was pleasing and the romantic aura of the place was increased by the rambler roses tumbling around the door. Then there were several kilometres along the river Ucieza, where considerable effort had been taken to make this path a viable alternative to walking on the road.

Day 19: Frómista — Castrojeríz

Frómista took its name from the Latin *frumentum* meaning barley, for which it has long been important. There were three churches, but the gem was certainly the earliest, the 11th to 12th century, church of San Martín. The church was built of a wonderful warm yellow limestone, cut in small blocks. Its special feature, both inside and out, was the rich array of lively relief sculptures at roof level and round the semicircular arches. Amongst the variety of subjects portrayed, there was a profusion of acrobats, animals, mother and child pairs, tongue-stickers and a variety of devils, enthusiastically devouring humans. The exterior was further decorated with horizontal bands of cabling and the roofs were pantiled. Perhaps the restoration had been somewhat over zealous, because the church presents an unbelievably perfect appearance.

The first pilgrim was just arriving in Frómista as we were leaving about 10.0am. It was a beautiful day's walking, first of all along the bank of the Canal de Castilla. One of many pilgrims we met that day was Cornelius Bull of Boston, Massachusetts. A lively and enthusiastic Christian, he told us of his plans to go on after Santiago to visit Ireland and do the pilgrimage of St. Patrick in Donegal. After Boadilla del Camino, we had a distant view of four, flat-topped hills, in a row on the horizon. It seemed to take us for ever to reach them and we eventually realised that our path would climb to pass through the middle cleft. As we climbed we met a Belgian couple, Thérèse and Joseph, of about our age. They had walked from their home, 25 kilometres north of Brussels, in 50 days. Though we only exchanged a few words, we felt a bond with them. They gestured to their feet and ours and Thérèse said; *Goot feet ja?* In this high plateau land of the *meseta*, the footpath ahead could be seen snaking its way through the fields into the far distance. Though the going was easy, there was always enough diversity to make this walking deeply satisfying.

Near Itero de Vega, we downed our packs and sat outside a little concrete shelter to eat. It was looking as if it might rain anytime. A group of Brazilians stopped to talk to us. They were doing the pilgrim route as a good walk, rather than for any religious reasons. After Santiago they planned to walk down the coast of Portugal and were keen to hear from us what it was like. From the edge of the broad flat top of Mostelares, we could see Castrojeríz in the valley, nestling against the flank of another hill slope, crowned with the remains of a castle. It started to drizzle and our objective was still an hour's walk away. The refuge was run by a welcoming Belgian couple, who offered us coffee when we arrived. They were running the refuge for a month and would hand over to another Belgian couple at the end of their stint.

Day 20: Castrojeríz — Burgos

We caught a bus into Burgos. A bakery was open, so were able to eat fresh bread and marmalade while we stood waiting. On the bus we travelled over more plateaux and could look down on the massed waving heads of barley, and see amongst them the heaps of stone, upon which tufts of gnarled hawthorn had taken root. That terrain where so little soil had formed over the rock, seemed at the limits of cultivable land, and yet the crops were vigorous and unblemished. As we came down the valley of the river Arlanzón, we could see ahead of us the great open-work towers of Burgos cathedral and closer in, saw, across the river, the medieval town gate of stone which led to it. By one of the many bridges we entered Burgos, through the 14th century Arco de Santa María, the main gate into the walled city. Pension Peña, on Calle de la Puebla, one of the narrow streets running through the old town, was a cheap and congenial place to stay.

Useful information, addresses and bibliography

Maps: *Michelin* 1:400,000 Nos. 441 & 442

Guide(in French) *Chemin de St. Jacques* from FFRP

Confraternity of Saint James, 1 Talbot Yard, Borough High St. London SE1 1YP for *Guides to Pilgrim Route* in English

Youth Hostels: Monte de Gozo, Carretera Santiago Aeropuerto, 15820 **Santiago** (3km from city) Tel.981 56 28 92

Consejo de Europa R.J, Pso. del Parque 2, 24005 **León** Tel.987 20 02 06

Gil de Siloe R.J, Avda.General Vigón, 09006 **Burgos** Tel.947 22 03 62

Airport at Santiago and **Train** and **Autobus Stations** at Burgos

Tourist Offices: Rúa del Villar, 43, 15705 **Santiago de Compostela** Tel.(981) 58 40 81

Plaza de la Regla, 3, 24003 **León** Tel.(987) 23 70 82

Plaza de Alonso Martínez,7, 09003 **Burgos** Tel.(947) 20 31 25

Pilgrim route ~ part 2 ~ Leon to Burgos

León
Mansilla de las Mulas
El Burgo Ranero
Sahagún
Calzadilla de la Cueza
Carrión de los Condes
Burgos
Frómista
Castrojeríz

0 10 20 kms

Pilgrim route ~ part 3
~ Burgos to Logroño

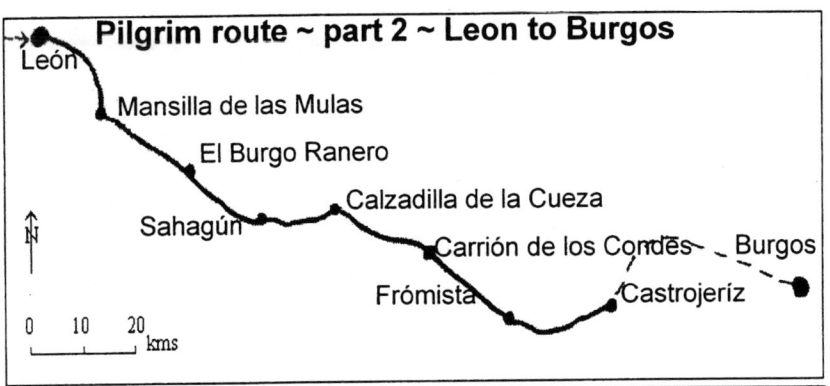

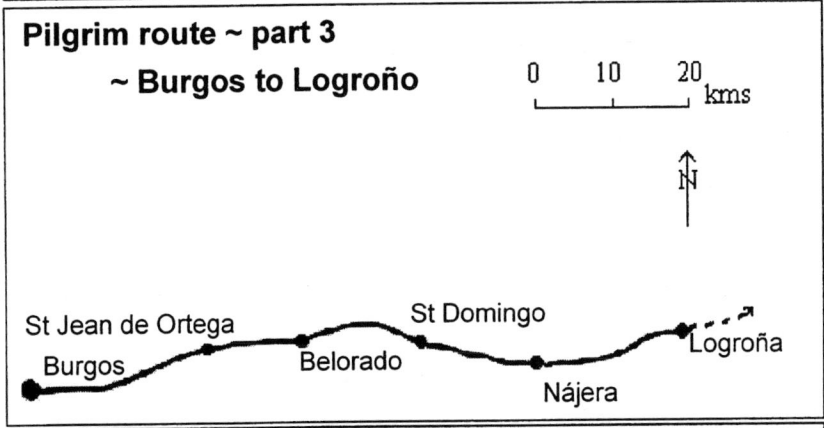

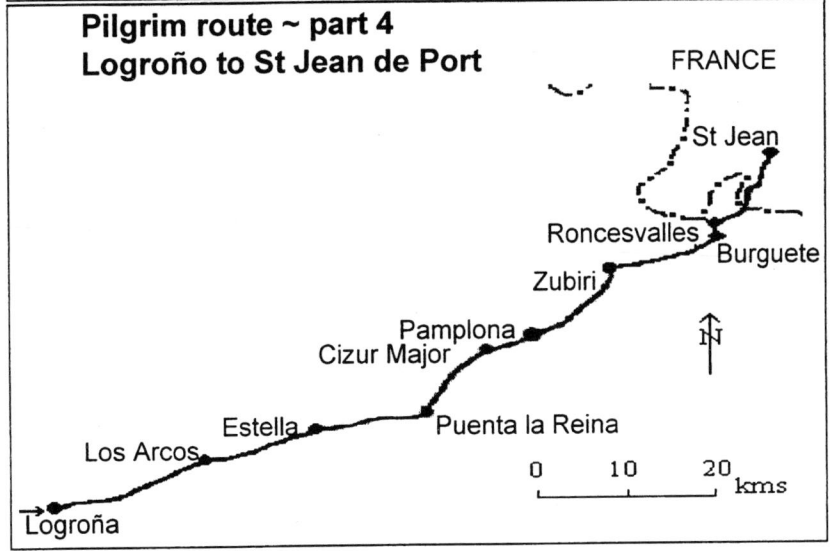

0 10 20 kms

St Jean de Ortega
Burgos
Belorado
St Domingo
Nájera
Logroña

Pilgrim route ~ part 4
Logroño to St Jean de Port

FRANCE
St Jean
Roncesvalles
Burguete
Zubiri
Pamplona
Cizur Major
Estella
Puenta la Reina
Los Arcos
Logroña

0 10 20 kms

Key to maps - page 27

The Pilgrim route 215

THE PILGRIM ROUTE
— PART TWO

It was pleasant to spend a few days looking round Burgos where they were celebrating Corpus Christi. There was a great assembly outside the cathedral, with the huge, brightly painted processional statues, many times life size, on the square. They represented the King and Queen, a Princess, two black-a-moors and one that looked Chinese, with a strip of goatee beard. As we watched, a silver casket on a bier was brought in procession, through the town gate and up to the cathedral steps, with its escort of soldiers having to thread their way through the dense crowds. The officiating priest had a pair of step-ladders placed for him to mount up on to the bier. Silver crosses of complex designs, with multiple cross-pieces, were carried through the crowds. Children were all done up in their Sunday best, if they were not in costumes of mob-caps and pinafores, obviously part of the ceremonial. In an adjoining square, dancers in black heavy dresses and short coats decorated with bead embroidery and head dresses, began a slow statuesque dance as we passed. In such hot weather and with so much clothing on, anything more lively would have been out of the question. Large crowds were watching and participating, and you felt that the citizens were justly proud, and, religious or not, they all had a stake in the ceremonial. There were, no doubt, a few of us tourists about, but this grand spectacle was part of city life. It is interesting that many of the Spanish there, would be newcomers to the city, who arrived in the 50s and 60s with the expansion of industry around Burgos. For this reason, the city's history needs constantly to be re-enacted, so that it stays in the collective memory.

Burgos was a Visigothic settlement, hence the Germanic name — *burg*. The city was founded by King Alphonso III of León in 882. Later, it was the city of El Cid, who was born of one of the great families of Burgos, around 1026. His full name was Rodrigo Díaz de Bivár and his nickname, El Cid, comes from the Arabic, *sidi*, meaning 'lord'. He was exiled because of his independent ways, and carried on his swashbuckling in Zaragossa and Barcelona, before becoming King of Valencia. Hollywood clearly recognised him as a 'goody', carrying on the 'good fight' against the 'baddy' *musulmanes*, and hence suitable material to become a marketable hero in films, though in earlier life he had actually fought on the opposite side! As a symbol of all that is patriotic and in defence of Christianity, he had a splendid equestrian statue erected to him in Burgos in 1956, entitled El Cid Campeador (El Cid the Warrior). This must have been a deliberate act of patriotic historicism, during the time of Franco, who saw himself in much the same role of defending Christianity. In the early days of the Civil War, Burgos was Franco's seat of government before he moved in on Madrid. It is no coincidence that Burgos now is a thriving city, with lots of industry; this happened under Franco.

Table of Distances

1. Burgos - San Juan de Ortega	27.0km
2. San Juan de Ortega - Belorado	25.0km
3. Belorado - Santo Domingo de la Calzada	26.0km
4. Santo Domingo de la Calzada - Nájera	22.0km
5. Nájera - Logroño (bus)	26.0km
6. Logroño - Los Arcos	27.0km
7. Los Arcos - Estella	20.0km
8. Estella - Puente la Reina	20.0km
9. Puente la Reina - Cizur Major	18.0km
10. Cizur Major - Pamplona	05.0km
11. Pamplona - Zubiri	22.0km
12. Zubiri - Roncesvalles (taxi)	21.5km
13. Burguete	(rest day)
14. Burguete - St Jean Pied de Port	26.0km

Day 1: Burgos — San Juan de Ortega
On this misty, dewy morning, we saw masses of paper-white butterflies, clinging to the flowers of the wayside thistles. It looked as if the air would be full of them, once the sun came up. We climbed up and over the Matagrande at 1050m, with large arable fields all the way. It was still very misty as we crossed this featureless flat top, a wide expanse, where stones had been cleared in lines to create growing land. We obviously missed a spectacular view, since there was a large notice board saying, that San Domingo, *looked out from here on the expansive plains of Navarre and had not seen anything so fine.* All **we** could see was just a few metres in front of our boots!

Passing through Atapuerca, we noticed features typical of the houses in these *meseta* villages, which are made of cobble walls, with timber framing above. It is easy to see where the cobbles come from, but, nowadays, there is often not a tree in sight, to provide the timber Our guide sagely said, *this is a reminder, that the countryside hereabouts was formerly well wooded.* Gunfire sounded in the distance — real gunfire this time not celebratory fireworks. We had followed a neglected fence with notices saying; Military Zone, as we descended to Atapuerca, so this must have been an artillery range. In between prolonged bursts of gunfire, were the distant strains of military pipe and drum music. During our picnic the sun broke through, hot and strong. So we moved on to find a shady spot under poplars, by a stream near Ajés, for a siesta. It was beautiful there but it didn't take many minutes to realise that we were in an insect jungle. Looking into the long grasses around us, we could see that they were seething with life. In Ajés nothing stirred, except the occasional dog, but they were too overcome with heat to bark. The weather by this time was thundery, and as we entered old woods of oak and pine, and saw them stretching out ahead of us, slow heavy drops of rain were falling. Amongst that forest, somewhere, was our objective for the night, the monastery of San Juan de Ortega, founded on this stretch of the pilgrim route, which was otherwise devoid of accommodation. This monastery had been highly praised by several people we had met along the route, and by our guide, for the genial priest, his great welcome and his garlic soup.

The monastery was half ruinous, with efforts at modern restoration. A refectory, dormitories and a fine imposing church were in active use. It was set in a clearing in the forest which entirely surrounded it. A bell began to ring, and most of the pilgrims hurried into the church. We realised too late, that this was probably the passport to the famous garlic soup! Instead we had good *tortilla* and salad served with slap happy gusto and good humour by a large, stocky peasant woman at the only bar. Her open and relaxed manner contrasted with the generally rather uptight attitudes of those in the monastery.

Day 2: San Juan de Ortega — Belorado

I was up at half light and made tea on a washstand on the landing. There were already quite a few milling around, even before 6.0am. It was good to be on the trail again, and we quickly put distance between us and the monastery, as we walked up through barley fields into the pines. At a point where we could breakfast in the sun, we stopped right by the track and our spirits lifted with its warmth and some food inside us. We climbed up steadily to reach what our guide called, *a sinister monument*. It was a memorial to those who had been assassinated at that place, in the Spanish Civil War. The inscription on the memorial, we translated as saying; *Their deaths were not in vain, only their assassination.*

Day 3: Belorado — Santo Domingo de la Calzada

We lost the advantage of an early start, struggling to find the right road out of Belorado, with no clear marking to help us, which made a demoralising start to our day. The route was through roller coaster country, with more huge fields of barley, varied occasionally with sugar beet and potatoes being watered with sprinklers. Gradually the mist cleared and the sun broke through, to give an afternoon of searing heat. It was a long and fairly uneventful day of about 26 kilometres.

Day 4: Santo Domingo de la Calzada — Nájera

Arable farmland covered the low, rounded hills and every possible gradient had been cultivated, with only the rough and rocky tops, inaccessible to machinery, left in a wild state of scrubland. It was at the same time a magnificent sight to see all these rolling hills and fields, but salutary to remember that all this has only happened with the advent of large-scale, energy-gobbling farm machinery. What would it have been like before? The size of area farmed from the villages must have increased enormously. Huge garages below the houses accommodated tractors, used to drive to the day's work in the fields around.

By midday the heat was powerful and we reached Azafia, where we were able to buy fresh bread and chilled water. The church had a lovely deep shady porch, where we had our picnic, then stretched ourselves out and dropped off to sleep. We were rudely awakened from our slumbers by the powerful voice of a small, energetic, white haired figure, who entered the cool shade of the porch, already in mid flow. He paused before us, with traces of dinner down his front, and in his deafening tones, proclaimed in a great flow of half understood Spanish, that he was the sacristan of the church and also the warden of the refuge. *It's too hot to walk to Nájera*, he said, adding that he could sell us some very good Rioja wine at only 200 pesetas a bottle. While all this browbeating was going on, we struggled to regain consciousness. Fortunately he didn't seem to require coherent answers. He turned to a hot and weary pilgrim, who had just come in out of the sun and taken his boots off to rest in the shade. In a trice the sacristan had bullied him into staying at the refuge, and dragged him off without giving him time to put his boots on. By the time he returned, we had recovered ourselves and he insisted on showing me his church, in great detail. It was memorable for some beautiful, richly coloured, modern stained glass. In his bluff country manner, the sacristan welcomed all in an open and inclusive way. He was proud of his church and he knew what pilgrims needed. A manner so different from that of the priest at San Juan de Ortega, it was hard to imagine, yet he was undoubtedly a christian too. We didn't dare pause for a cup of tea in case he started on us again.

The thirsty lands around here were watered by massive concrete irrigation channels, proceeding from the vertical shafts of artesian wells from which the water was pumped. The landscape was beginning to change; we were leaving the *meseta* and coming to a region of sandstone. After the rising ground of the vineyards, we came to a mini-canyon of sandstone cliffs and pine woods, through which our path took us over and down to Nájera.

Day 5: Nájera — Logroño

To avoid the prospect of an overlong stint across the plain, on what promised to be another very hot day, we took a bus to Logroño. It was the city of the storks. There were storks' nests on every available tower. On the twin towers of the cathedral there were a dozen or so nests, one above another. Who gets to be top birds, we wondered, shitting on the rest? Is it first come first served, or is there a traditional dynastic pecking order? Do they fight for positions nearest the bells, so that they can blow their minds? Why is it that they have a predilection for old churches and towers, eschewing modern buildings? Another mystery is what they feed on. We saw them floating high up in the sky and coming back to land at their nests, but we never saw them fishing by the rivers or pecking at grain and fruit in the country. Sometimes church builders had tried to dissuade the storks from nesting on their towers, by incorporating large stone birds into the structure. But this sort of unsporting attitude was quite rare and they mostly seemed to be tolerated. We had seen the large untidy nests on many of the church towers of the villages we had passed through since Villafranca del Bierza. In some places, even though we hadn't actually seen the nests and the birds as we had arrived at night, we would hear the characteristic clattering of bills the next morning at dawn.

Day 6: Logroño - Los Arcos

We went to catch the 7.30am bus as far as Viana, a medieval hilltop town, complete with town wall, gates and little squares. There we picked up yellow arrows again and followed them down the hill, where we found the first of our old friends, the French-style, red and white markers of the G.R.65, which is the waymarked pilgrim route from Cahors to Logroño. Our path led us a circuitous route round and over *barrancos*, up into mountains with almond and olive trees for the first time for months. When we had seen these trees in Alicante and Murcia, soon after Christmas, the almonds had been in full bloom. Now they bore fruit and the olive trees were covered with tiny cream flowers.

Day 7: Los Arcos — Estella
We headed eastward out of Los Arcos, up a wide valley, full of the wonderful malty smell of barley. It was like smelling the wort of some cosmic brew of beer. This scent on the air only lasted for the first hour or so, once the sun was up, it disappeared. A shepherd with his flock of sheep and goats, pointed out the track ahead. We followed a little stream lined with vivid green grass and poplars. Looking back, we could see it snaking its way in a dark line through the fields of tawny-brown barley. A series of uncultivated low hills, covered with scrub, stuck up from the surrounding barley fields. They looked, for all the world, like a row of bony fins or plates on the back of some submerged prehistoric creature.

Wild cherries hung invitingly by our track. They were deliciously ripe and we picked a few to eat with our picnic. We toiled up the hill slope to Villa Mayor de Monjardín, where, being wine-less for lunch, it was rather devastating news that the village had no bar. In this desperate situation, I decided to try the imposing looking *bodega*. I entered its cool and airy premises and wandered amongst the huge stainless steel vats, looking for someone. The smartly attired receptionist told me that they only sold their wine by the bottle, when I held out my *plastico* for a refill. However, for some reason, she relented, and took me through to the young chemist who was testing various wine samples in his little laboratory. He led me to one of the mammoth stainless steel cylinders and drew me off one and a half litres of *rosado*. There must have been 30 or so of these steel giants; each of them, he said, held 100,000 litres, though they also had some that held a mere 80,000. I thought I heard Bacchus give a quiet, echoing chuckle amongst those cool, giant containers. When I asked, *How much?* He said; *Nada, hace mucho calor hoy.* (Nothing, it's very hot today). I thanked him profusely and that low chuckle followed me out into the intense light and heat of the day. *Bien viaje* said the young chemist, as he returned to his work. It was only then that I realised what a dishevelled specimen of humanity I was, covered in sweat and with matted hair. They had obviously recognised someone in dire need.

At some little distance from the village, we came across an

elaborate stone-building, set into the hillside, housing a *fuente*, or spring, right beside the pilgrim path. This consisted of a vaulted stone roof and steep stone steps leading down to the clear blue-green water — a most unusual sight in the parched landscape. As we approached Estella, we passed an abbey. Alongside, were the buildings where the wine for the abbey was produced. Set into the side of these buildings, where our pathway went by, there were two taps, one with wine and one with water and a message inviting pilgrims to help themselves to a glass. We could hardly believe our eyes. There had already been one bottle of free wine on that day and now we were being offered more. We tried it out, and very it good it tasted. Though it was good wine, perhaps the cool water was just as acceptable in the heat of that afternoon.

Day 8: Estella — Puente la Reina
Once we had picked the markers up, we were on a splendid track rising steadily to become a contour path, weaving us around the edge of the valley, above the vineyards and cereals. We crossed the Iranzu river by a medieval bridge at Villatuerta, and at Lorca climbed up to the little square, where we headed straight for the fountain and doused our heads in the water. One of a large group of Spanish walkers resting in the shade, came over to talk. When he heard that we were on the return route, he assumed that we had walked to Santiago and were on our way back. Pilgrims have a special admiration for those who return on foot. So we had to declare our hand, that we had come up from Portugal. When the whole story came out, that we had been walking for over a year, he embraced us both and went to tell the others. There were murmurs of *chapeau* all round. The Spanish have adopted this French expression of admiration, literally meaning 'hat' but suggesting 'we raise our hats to you'.

The next village, Ciraugui, was inconsiderately placed on top of a steep hill. When we had climbed to the top in the heat and humidity, we were keen to get into the shade for our lunch and rest up for a while. A rather severe nun dressed in a starched white habit, passed us as we were setting out our picnic on a stone bench and told us we should sit at one of the tables of the nearby bar. The woman at the bar wished us ¡*Buen provecho*! as she passed and obviously had no objections.

Just as we were sorting out our direction at the fourth village of the day, Maneru, the heavy humid weather that had prevailed all that day, turned suddenly to rain. We sheltered under the verandah of a brand new but unoccupied house and when it had let up to fine rain, we made our descent by a dramatic path, twisting in and out of *barrancos* to Puente la Reina. We would have stayed at the refuge there but it was seething with people, and was the only one we saw with triple-tier bunks. There was only one loo each, for male and female, and there must have been at least 40 people already. So we fled in search of an *hostal*.

While we ate, football was blaring out as usual on the telly. The Dutch guy watching it at the next table, was looking a bit glum. We gradually realised that it was the World Cup and that England were playing. What really surprised us, in view of their recent form, was that England were winning. Then it came to me in a flash. I remembered reading that England were due to play against Holland, who were tipped to win, but there we were with England in the lead by three goals to nil. No wonder the Dutchman was looking glum. The waiter, realising that he had English and Dutch sitting at adjoining tables, was watching avidly for reactions. Not being football fans, we must have disappointed him. The game had been almost over before we even registered that England were playing. But the Dutchman was obviously very upset and he could hardly bring himself to speak to us as we left.

Day 9: Puente la Reina — Cizur Major

Puente was a place specially created for pilgrims. It had developed along a narrow, fortified strip of road. The medieval bridge led into the main street of the old town. Our onward route was through the villages of Obanos and Urtega. For the last few days we had noticed that there was a different building style, with doorways and windows made of monolithic blocks, creating in effect the main supports for the front of the houses. Smaller stone was used for infill and a plaster finish added. The doorways usually had semi-circular tops made of radiating stone blocks. Between the villages there was a lovely ridge walk with barley fields on one side and almond trees on the other. There were frequent ant trails across our path, and we observed them climbing up the stalks to get at the heads of the barley. The ants cut the individual grains from the heads, then collected these from the bottom of the stalk, where they fell, and manoeuvred these spiky containers across the path where their orderly columns could be seen, passing backwards and forwards, like a miniature army with their banners.

Ahead of us in the distance we could see a line of huge modern white wind generators along a ridge. This was the Sierra del Perdón, which we started to climb. Our path wove its way through barley fields which extended up the steeper slopes of the mountain side. The view was a great reward when we got to the top. The whole fertile valley of Pamplona was laid out before us, with the foothills of the Pyrenees just visible beyond, in the heat haze. Gazing up at the slender and elegant stems of the white wind generators, made us feel like the ants we had been watching earlier. Though they were not catching enough wind to move them much, at ground level we had a welcome light breeze.

We now began the long descent and, as we reached Cizur, it clouded over and began to rain. So we stayed there, rather than push on the last five kilometres to Pamplona, at a delightful private refuge, set amongst the mature trees of the garden of a large house.

Already installed there were two Spanish bikers, one Spanish walker, and an Irish father and daughter, Willie and Ruth. Ruth had been poorly, so they had just returned from a visit to the hospital, but it seemed to be Willie who had suffered with the walking, nearly crucifying himself on the first leg out from St. Jean Pied de Port, in which there is a 1000m climb. It is a hard start for anyone, especially if they are not used to walking. Willie was great company, and a fluent Spanish speaker too, since he had lived in Ecuador. A discussion got going with the Spanish bikers on the pros and cons of the separatist movements in Spain. We wished we had understood more. When we asked Willie, he was honest enough to admit that he hadn't understood all the subtleties of the arguments. When Willie complained how hard the walking was, one of the Spanish cyclists took him to task. He squeezed Willie's calves which were white, freckled and plump, and then proudly showed off the muscles in his own bronzed legs. *And what age are you?* he asked Willie. When he replied, *I'm 60*, the Spaniard triumphantly countered, *Well, I'm 62*.

Day 10: Cizur Major — Pamplona

The cat was curled up on the chair and Willie and Ruth were still fast asleep, as we left our leafy bower around 7.0am. The route into the city, by the university and the huge 17th century fort, was surprisingly pleasant. Three young American graduates, who we met, were setting out to walk to Santiago in a month! Though they were quite experienced backpackers in the States, they told us they had never encountered walking so hard as the Pyrenees.

Hostal Lambertini, where we stayed in Pamplona, had an eccentric air about it, which immediately appealed to us. It was situated on the fourth floor, up a rather grand staircase in a house that had seen better days, near the centre of the old town. Once inside the *hostal*, we had to make our way gingerly with our packs on, down a long corridor stuffed full with a bizarre collection of 'works of art'. The walls of the corridor were almost covered with glazed and marquetry pictures of a bewildering array of subjects, from evil looking faces to chocolate-boxy cottage scenes. There was even a shop-window bust made of wickerwork, equipped with sunglasses and a straw boater, by an artists' easel. When our host opened the door into our room, we were delighted to find that it had a splendid view right over to the Pyrenees. We found a good local dish for our meal that evening; an excellent bean stew called '*pochas*'.

A local fiesta was being celebrated. We witnessed a demonstration by Basque political ex-prisoners in the street. It took the form of a sort of street theatre, in which each of the prisoners, wearing masks and striped prison uniform, was questioned and briefly revealed their faces. This was watched impassively by the spectators. It would have been good to know more of what was being said, but they were speaking Basque, which is totally different from Spanish. There was music in the streets — mostly very fast and lively music from brass bands, strolling, then stopping in the squares, but playing all the time. People followed them, dancing in the street.

Day 11: Pamplona — Zubiri

After Pamplona, the landscape changed, with wooded valleys taking us ever deeper into the mountains. Gone were the expansive uplands with their huge fields of cereal; we were entering the foothills of the Pyrenees. The afternoon's walking, though much of it through fine wooded country, was spoilt by the sudden appearance of twin chimneys pumping smoke high up into the sky, before it was caught by the wind and spread its pall over the countryside far and wide. These chimneys belonged to a magnesium extraction plant, which we had to walk through. First of all, we encountered a heaving and pulsing pipeline, which was carrying the water of a stream through the quarry. Then we crossed the quarry floor past a huge plant, where a stream of black liquid waste was continuously adding to a conical heap below and forming large lagoons of slurry where nothing grew. It was all dreadfully ugly and made us realise how extremely fortunate we had been to encounter so few such industrial nightmares.

Zubiri was not a pretty place, being strung out along one and a half kilometres of busy road and consisting mainly of identical blocks of flats. The refuge was full, so we camped alongside it in a meadow on a pleasant balmy evening.

Day 12: Zubiri — Roncesvalles

In the morning it was pissing down with rain and I woke with earache. Our tent is absolutely waterproof, so we had an early morning cup of tea and waited, hoping that the rain would stop. It didn't, so we packed up in the rain as quickly as we could, and rushed into the refuge to have breakfast. Everyone was reluctant to move off in the rain, but one by one, they decided to continue their journey to Santiago. We sat on after everyone had gone, but if anything the weather got worse. In view of the earache, we looked for an alternative to walking. It turned out that there were no buses, and, as we were feeling very cold and damp, we resorted to a taxi to get us to Roncesvalles.

Take us to the centre, I said, as the taxi driver pulled up, seemingly in the middle of nowhere. There were just a few buildings with beech-woods stretching up to the shrouded mountains above. *This is it*, he said, parting me from 3,000 pesetas, almost half our day's allowance, before wishing us a cheery *buen viaje,* and leaving us there, bewildered, in the rain. So this was the great Roncesvalles, about which we had heard so much, the first pilgrim staging post in Spain for those who had just crossed over the Pyrenees. We voyaged no further than the *hostal* just in front of us. It really hurt to pay as much as we had to, but it bought us a pleasant, warm, *en suite* room where we could get out of the rain.

Betty went out later when the rain let up a little, to see what the place had to offer and came back rather disgusted. *There's nothing real here*, she said, *Nowhere to buy any food, only visitors' centres and tourist trinket shops.* What is more we couldn't move to cheaper accommodation because she discovered that the Youth Hostel and *refugio* were closed during the day. I guess the sick pilgrim had it pretty tough in the old days, but it's none too easy now if you are on the cheap.

Later in the day, the rain stopped and the earache had receded, so we walked down through the beech-woods the two kilometres back to Burguete, to find a shop and cheaper accommodation for the following night. As we walked there and back, we had wonderful views of red kites, gliding around the valley high up above us, often in loose groups. One time we saw two cavorting together in a spectacular aerial dance.

Day 13: Burguete

An overcast and cloudy day, as well as lingering earache, decided us to delay our crossing of the Pyrenees for another day. Before moving down to Burguete for cheaper accommodation, we made a trip in the swirling fog, up to Col de Ibañete, a couple of kilometres up the road. This was the traditional site of the Battle of Roncesvalles, publicised and romanticised in the twelfth century *Song of Roland* into a contest between Moslem Spain and Christian France. The bare facts are that Charlemagne's nephew Roland and his troops, returning from sacking Pamplona, were ambushed by Basques and butchered there, on the 15th August 778. Right would seem to have been entirely on the side of the Basques, but because it is the aggressor's poem, it is they who are the heroes as well as the losers. Charlemagne laments thus the death of his favourite nephew:

Friend Roland, I am going into France,
and when I'm in my chamber at Laon,
from many kingdoms, foreigners will come,
and they'll inquire: 'Where is the captain - count?'
I'll say to them that he is dead in Spain.
In deepest sorrow I shall rule my kingdom;
the day won't come that I shan't weep and mourn.

We headed down again through the beech-woods to Burguete. So still was it that the sweet nostalgic smell of each elderflower bush we came to, lay distinct and separate on the air. Our lodgings were in an old house with highly polished wooden corridors and oak panelling in the rooms. We found that the town brass band was being entertained in the front room and we were offered snacks and a drink. Our landlady told us that this was the last day of their four day fiesta for San Juan. The band continued on its way up the street, playing similar quick tempo tunes to those we had heard in Pamplona. The players were teenage lads and young men. The dining room of the restaurant where we ate that night, was wood panelled and rather gloomy. It had been preserved this way by the proprietor because Hemingway had liked it when he stayed there 60 years ago!

Day 14: Burguete — St. Jean Pied de Port
It was obvious that **this** was our day to cross over the Pyrenees. Knowing that we had a very stiff climb ahead of us, we slipped out of our highly polished quarters, as the church bell struck 7.0am. Above the layers of mist that carpeted the meadows and the trees, blue sky was visible. We walked up the main street of the village set on its ridge above the surrounding meadows, with water rushing down the leats on either side of it. No one stirred, only the odd dog grumbled as we passed his patch. For the last time we walked up through the beech-woods that had become so familiar to us. At Roncesvalles, backpackers were gathering, since there are several long-distance paths that pass through that spot. No one else was going our way. We were psyched up to the long climb that took us up and up through everlasting beech-woods to the bare grassy tops of Col de Leopoeder.

It was a beautiful two and a half hour ascent, which the topoguide has the grace to say was *assez raide* (quite steep). The mist lingered there and great beams of sunlight angled down through the trees. *These are the sort of cathedrals I like*, said Betty, *Who needs stained glass with light like this?* Once at the col, we came out into brilliant sunshine, looking down on the cloud and mist below. All around us we could see mountain tops only, emerging from the cloud.

We set our faces to the north and for several kilometres, had a beautiful ridge walk to the boundary between France and Spain, marked at intervals with stones. As we descended we walked down into fog, and sometime after Teobald's Cross, we met Vicki, a lone Welsh cyclist, pushing her bike up hill. She had been inspired to undertake this journey from what she had learnt about the pilgrim route in her lectures at university. Cahors, she had not liked. She confided in us that this was mostly because, when she had visited the cathedral, she found she was locked in, when the custodian had left for the night. However, after sitting down and having a good cry at the prospect of spending the night alone in the gloomy cathedral, in desperation she had managed to pull back the rusty bolts on one of the doors and escape.

It was strange to be eating our picnic up there with the warm fog swirling round us and to hear for the first time in months the call of '*bon appetit*' from two passing French backpackers. For some time we followed the road, which was called Route Napoleon, because Napoleon had used it in his disastrous retreat from Spain. It may have been disastrous for him, but if we had stuck to it that day we would certainly have reached St. Jean by nightfall. As it was we branched off to follow the red and white markers which led us off this route and then abandoned us. We turned off by a farm with free range pigs that were lazing about enjoying the sun, and soon began a precipitous descent through beech-woods. Although our guide mentioned crossing a stream, when we reached it, there were no markers and we lost time trying to discover which way we should go. In the approach to St. Jean, we were led astray by a multiplicity of marked tracks and as night fell, we had to admit we were lost. To regroup, we made ourselves a cup of tea and from our position halfway up the mountain side, we could see the town of St. Jean Pied de Port across the valley to the north. There was no way we were going to reach it that night, so we found a grassy spot beside the track to pitch our tent, and toasted the near-completion of another major stage in our journey in the warm dusk.

Useful information, addresses and bibliography

Maps: *Michelin* 1:400,000 No.442

Guides (see page 214)

Airports: Santander or Vitoria for Burgos and Biarritz\Bayonne for St.Jean Pied de Port

Train Stations at Burgos and St.Jean Pied de Port

Autobus: Bayonne to St.Jean Pied de Port. (restricted service, weekdays only)

Tourist Offices: Place Charles de Gaulle, 64220 **St.Jean Pied de Port** Tel.05 59 37 03 57

Plaza de Alonso Martínez, 7, 09003 **Burgos** Tel.(947) 20 31 25.

FRANCE . . . AGAIN

We soon reached St. Jean the following day and found ourselves a shady spot on the camp site where we noticed an old woman picking up sheep droppings from the road. We were picnicking down by the river when Madame 'Merdes des Moutons' sat down beside us to rest from her labours and chat. She explained that the sheep droppings would be used to fertilise her potatoes, a few went in with each she planted. She had to collect as many as she could while the sheep were still going out to pasture this way. Soon they would be gone, up to the mountains. They all belonged to M. le Curé, who had a lot of sheep and land. Granny Sheep Turds said that her grandfather was Spanish, but she had not travelled. Her family could not afford to travel, they had to stay put and work, but young people nowadays wanted to run about and didn't want to work. So there she was working, picking up the sheep turds to fertilise her garden, one by one, with her bare hands. She proudly opened her plastic carrier to show us the results of her labours. A powerful aroma of sheep shit came out from the near-full container. *Yes monsieur, in my day we were brought up to work*, she said and, bidding us, *Bon appetit*, she went off to get her lunch.

We were able to buy a topoguide for the next part of the G.R.65, as far as Cahors, and a Michelin 1:200,000 scale map of the area. At Ostabat, a sleepy little agricultural hamlet, the kindly old man who owned the *gîte* gave us some lovely fresh eggs, which supplemented the rather basic fare available in the tiny village shop. An old jettied timber-framed building had been restored to provide accommodation. It was very attractive, almost like a Swiss chalet; pink and red geraniums in pots and window boxes decorated the verandah. In medieval times, Ostabat was the place where four pilgrim routes met, having come down through France from Tours, Vezelay, Le Puy and Arles. Sometimes it was necessary for the various religious houses of Ostabat, now long gone, to house and feed up to 5,000 pilgrims. It is easy to see why the horde of pilgrims moving along in these numbers has been called a 'moving village'. Without the support of the church and states of Europe, no such small settlements as Ostabat could have dealt with them.

At St. Palais, we stayed at the Franciscan monastery. We all sat down to eat at the long refectory table with the three elderly monks and M. and Mme. Dubonnet; she was the cook who we had seen dashing about the garden earlier. The monks were virtually silent as they ate and took no interest in the visitors, whilst M. Dubonnet directed his urbane enquiries first to one visitor then to another. It was a wonderful meal. Mme. Dubonnet was an excellent cook who was obviously interested and ready to give away her secrets when asked by one of the guests. The home grown vegetables were used to great effect in her soup, and the flavour of herbs and fresh picked lettuce made the salad special. In particular, she was asked about her salad dressing. She used shallot and garlic, finely chopped with seasoning, lemon juice and a good olive oil. We ate this after omelette with slices of home-cured fat bacon. Wine was served with the meal, and the bottle kept coming round for refills. A lovely creamy sweet followed.

Navarrenx was almost entirely built within the 16th century fortifications, which had been constructed for the town at the order of the King of Navarre, by the foremost Italian military engineer of the time, Fabrici Siciliano. The previous defences had succumbed to the Prince of Orange, but the new Italian model successfully resisted a three month siege in 1569. Perhaps because the town was designed within the fortifications which were meant to defend it rather than dominate it, Navarrenx seemed a pleasant and compact place.

Woodland and pasture and some arable formed the landscape, with little change day after day. One tends to forget how enormous France is! In deep woodland, one day, having gone hopelessly astray, we arrived at the end of a track, where several strange towers had been built amongst the trees. The supports were constructed out of long poles and a series of wooden ladders led up to tree-houses, high up in the tops of the trees. Ropes, wires and pulleys were festooned everywhere. There must have been about a dozen of these tree-houses in various stages of decay, on this remote knoll in the woods. We puzzled over who had built these towers and for what purpose, without coming up with a satisfactory answer.

When we reached Sauvelade we found the *gîte* in an ancient abbey, closed up and abandoned. Once it had been established that we were bona fide pilgrims, the lady mayoress came in her car with her keys, and let us into a large stone-built hall, the *Salle de Réunion* (Village Hall). We were thankful that this strange community, not so much a village as a collection of renovated holiday homes of the wealthy, still retained that feeling of obligation to provide shelter for the pilgrim. This was proof, if ever needed, that these old traditions of hospitality along the route, die hard.

It came on to rain hard as we started walking along the level valley floor of the Gave de Pau. Shelter appeared, almost miraculously in this region of huge arable fields, in the form of a little workman's shack. We dived into it and started to brew up. Through the heavy rain, a tall figure with a hooded oilskin cape covering a pack, was on the point of passing by, when I hailed her and she came in out of the rain. Petra had walked all the way from Holland on her own and was going to Santiago. Her route down had been by Paris, Orleans, Tours and Cahors. She was one of that breed of lone Dutch female travellers, for whom we had come to have a great respect.

Condom had an air of solid prosperity, with streets of ample stone houses. The shops in the centre were stuffed full of preserved duck and goose and *foie gras*. Whole shops were devoted to the sale of Armagnac, but sadly none were offering free tastings. After this the walking changed, with a more open sort of rolling country. We felt that at last we had escaped the geological straight-jacket of river valleys fanning out from the Pyrenees, which had made the journey from one to another so predictable. It's a great feature of good walking, that the landscape keeps you guessing what's coming next. Another very important feature was the lovely earth paths we were following again for most of the time, which made a blissful change after so many days of tarmac. We met a lone French pilgrim, who praised the *gîte* at Romieu and another one further on, near Rocamadour on the G.R.46, which would be on our route after Cahors.

Huge fields of sunflowers, with their discs wide open and tracking the sun, dominated the landscape. The scent was slight but sweet.

As the weather turned from sunny to overcast, the discs stayed focused on the last point before the sun disappeared.

Under a plum tree, with ripe fruit, we stopped to picnic, close to the Chateau de Lacassague. A notice told us that the enormous complex of stone buildings around a wide courtyard, was the Salle des Chevaliers du Malte. Most of it was closed up, but part was an active working farm, with lovely old stone barns, now hopelessly undersize for the enormous modern farm machinery, which was all lined up at the edge of the fields — tractors, harrows, sprayers and combines. The two brothers of the farm were busy combining, and exchanged friendly greetings as they passed us. Two black slobber-dogs came and gave us a good nosing over for any spare food, and hoovered up a few of the ripe plums that had fallen on the ground. These wild plums were delicious and they made us a lovely pudding that evening. The dogs returned later and leaned on us genially, threatening to knock over our cups of tea in the process. Their attention diverted, they gambolled off, to investigate what was happening out in the field.

In Sainte Mère, we got the key for the *gîte* from a 94 year old woman. Though sharp as needles about the money, she seemed a bit vague as to where she had put the key. The *gîte* was part of the silent and derelict chateau of La Busquette. It was housed in one of the stone buildings of the farm courtyard. Originally a barn, it was now full of cast off garden furniture and ancient household equipment distributed around on an uneven stone floor. We opened up the great double doors of the barn and let the warm evening sun flood into the dark space. The dusty air was full of the smell of the cut barley, and we watched the combines working in the afterglow when the sun had set. When we could no longer see them, we could still hear their bleepers and the squeak and clatter of the machinery.

The next morning Betty felt some warning twinges in her back, which brought her up sharp every now and again, and made her nervous about setting off along the route. Although we had only completed about two thirds of the distance from St. Jean, we decided to go straight to Cahors and rest up for a few days at the Youth Hostel.

The city of Cahors is built in a great meander of the Lot. By the 14th century, the town was protected on the western loop of the river, by the fortified Pont Valentré, whose three tall defensive towers still survive. The medieval city itself, was squeezed into the eastern third of the space created by the meander, with the other two-thirds left for gardens and various religious houses. Boulevard Gambetta, the main thoroughfare of the modern town, was constructed over the filled-in defensive ditch on the western side of the medieval city.

Here we were, once again celebrating Bastille Day in France. We had a grandstand view of the superb firework display from our bedroom window. The 15th Festival of Blues followed on, and lasted over several days. It started off with Ray Charles, who we heard over the pantiled rooftops. Another night there were groups of musicians outside most of the cafes up and down Boulevard Gambetta. You could wander in the warm dusk from one to another. Long after we had slipped away to bed, the music went on. It was a great show, with everyone out there on the streets enjoying themselves.

As far away as Porto in Portugal, the wine of Cahors had been praised, and the man at the camp site at Condom had kissed bunches of fingers in praise of it. Now we gave it our seal of approval by going back each day to a *cave* close to the cathedral to get a litre each of delicious *rosé* and *rouge*. Going to and fro on my way to the *cave*, gave me several opportunities to look at the multitude of 12th and 13th century gargoyles on the north side of the cathedral. Inside, the mawkish pictures of saints and overly elaborate and disgracefully ornate altar pieces, reminded us of Vicki, the lone Welsh cyclist we had met in the Pyrenees. I was not surprised that she had sat down and cried when she found herself locked in the place.

Our next objective was to call on our old friends the Landons, to whom we had written from St. Jean, at their home near Aubusson. In order to reach them from Cahors, we would leave the pilgrim highway, the G.R.65, and head north on the G.R.46. After a few days rest Betty's back was better; now all we had to do was tear ourselves away from this delightful place.

The ascent of the valley of the river Vers was unexpectedly magical. We climbed gently, mainly on woodland paths, which sheltered us from the day's developing heat. At Cras, we emerged from our wooded shelter into the full heat of the sun, on the limestone tops. Labastide Murat was a small country town of stone built houses and somewhat improbably was the birthplace of a King of Naples, by the name of Murat, one of Napoleon's protégés.

By woody lanes between dried up pasture land, and then deep in oak woods, our path turned off on a little used track, signed to La Rouquette where we stayed. This was a big old stone farmhouse with all its barns and buildings arranged on a little plateau. Attached to the farmhouse, was a round tower, newly-built of stone. The evening meal was served *en famille*, and six other guests arrived just in time — three sisters and their husbands from Nantes. We sat around a long, highly polished table in a low beamed dining room with a huge stone fireplace. Our host regaled us with tales of his appearances as a knight in 'medieval' pageants and mock battles, at Cahors and Carcassonne, amongst other places. He showed us armour, helmets and halberds, that he had made himself. The stone tower we had seen as we arrived, was also his construction. After the meal we were taken in torch-lit procession up the stone stairs of this tower to view his handiwork.

Our route then crossed the Causses des Grammat, undulating uplands of scrub oak, sparsely populated but with occasional clearances to make fields for maize or oats. Some derelict settlements were going back to nature, with the old stone buildings choked and nearly hidden by vegetation. Where pastures had been abandoned, the steady return of the bush was evident, with little oak and pine trees springing up everywhere amongst the thinly-growing grass. It was hard, basically sheep country. It was hard walking too, because these limestone uplands were divided by quite abrupt gorges. We came eventually on to a wide top at Rocabilière, which had formerly been a group of three or four farms, quite a large settlement for these parts. It was deserted now except for three large new barns. The weather was heavy, threatening rain, and the flies, which joined us in multitudes for our picnic, forced us to move on quickly.

As we approached Couzou, there were stone walls enclosing huge fields, which merged into the woodland, already reclaiming the edges of the cleared areas. On the outskirts of the village, there were small infields where, beside the track, little garden plots grew tomatoes and beans. Though Couzou, wasn't much of a place, about 80 inhabitants, it must have been the centre of these high lands for miles around. It still sported a Hotel de la Terrasse, which is what we were relying on for our overnight accommodation. There was a heavy listless air about the place because of the heat and the flies. When the air had cooled a little towards nightfall, we wandered round the village. There was a little square with a fountain by the church and the cottages round it each had its small enclosed, flower-filled garden, with dark, near black, hollyhocks and pink geraniums. Many of the houses had square towers, built into their corners, which served as pigeon lofts. Some of the large stone barns were still in use for their original purpose and were an important feature of the economy of the village, which for all the second homes, was a working agricultural village, with the road surface covered with a layer of sheep droppings to prove it. The biggest of the barns had been built in 1903 — a really huge, stone-built structure, with a ramped causeway giving access to the upper storey.

Having plunged steeply down densely wooded paths, we climbed the other side of the gorge on to an open and featureless top. The contrast between the precipitous clefts of the gorges, with their thick vegetation, and the bare flat tops, couldn't have been greater. Our topoguide curtly informed us, *A droite: dolmen.* This would have been difficult to spot without knowing what you were looking for — the remains of a stone age burial chamber, with massive stone uprights supporting an equally massive top stone. This particular one was still half-buried in its surrounding circular mound. Its siting was impressive with huge views over the wooded slopes around. Perhaps it was the last resting place of a chieftain who controlled all this terrain.

Two English girls, in light summer clothes, passed, making us very envious of their unencumbered ease of walking. They had started from Couzou as we had, and asked if we'd been to Rocamadour before. *No*, I replied. *Well*, one of them said, *It's well worth the walk*, as if we were just out for a stroll. But so it proved to be, as we zigzagged down the canyon of the river Alzou and on the other side, climbed up the street of this extraordinary village, clinging to the near-vertical rock face. The trouble with extraordinary places is that their power to amaze dwindles in proportion to the numbers of visitors they attract. We were happy to climb the hill and leave the milling throngs behind.

At Gluges we had a delightful swim in the river Dordogne and picnicked in the shade of the poplars. The topoguide we were following finished at Turenne, so we journeyed by train to Limoges and caught the bus from there to visit our friends near Aubusson.

Though we had only visited Le Bournazeau, twice before over the years, and then only briefly, arriving there, was, in a strange way like coming home. It was a big old farmhouse, with a fan of stone steps leading up to an imposing front door. The house itself had remained unmodernised, with only the minimum of changes. There was a particularly fine, old-fashioned throne for a loo. Over two generations, the family had gathered there for holidays. We remembered calling once, when our children were little, and bathing two of them in a tin bath in front of the fire. The house had a wonderful serene presence and Mme. Landon, now as before, added her smiling welcome. She was very frail, but her great spirit showed. M. Landon managed a brief, but courteous welcome. Therese and Bernadette, their daughters, who had visited us in England as schoolgirls, were there with their husbands and children. We were really lucky to have visited when they were all there together, which happens once a year at most. We joined the whole family for lunch around the big table in the well-remembered farmhouse kitchen, with its wooden dressers and open fireplace, over which the cooking would once have been done.

In the afternoon, we walked to Les Farges down the lovely leafy lane, with hazels meeting overhead, making a tunnel of cool shade. Jean Louis was busy as ever, working on a new water supply. His face lit up when he saw us. *Ah, les pelerins sont retournés* (Ah, the pilgrims have returned), he said, as he shook us by the hand. We went into the wonderful old front room of their painstakingly-restored cottage, with its low beams and its floor of large, worn granite blocks. The open staircase had the original encased beds, which were built-in underneath it. Madeleine, older sister of Therese and Bernadette, greeted us with their youngest son Joffroi who we had last seen as a little boy, now a strapping 19 year old. Jean Louis opened a celebratory bottle of Bordeaux. Madeleine had set the table under the shady trees in the garden, and we sat down in the cool to have an *aperitif.* There was a lot of family news to catch up on. Jean Louis remarked that he could think of nothing better than good food and wine, taken in good company, which summed up the conviviality of the occasion.

The department of Creuse is heavily wooded, with rounded granite hillocks and studded with numerous lakes. From Aubusson we made our way back towards Limoges, along country lanes and paths, amidst woods of oak and beech, following another stretch of the G.R.46. It was easy country to get lost in and we did, but we were not the only ones. A French father, with his two boys on bicycles, stopped and asked, in an authoritarian way, to see our map. *Madame, votre carte, s'il vous plaît* (Madam, your map please), like a policeman asking to see our papers. He studied it and returned it pronouncing, *Votre carte est très bonne, madame, monsieur* (your map is very good), nodding to each of us in turn and setting off ahead of us. The boys, who were quite young, about 9 and 12, seemed fairly reluctant and fed up. Later, we caught up with them again at Lavaud-Hugier, where an old woman was shouting instructions at the father, at the top of her voice. Obviously confused by the multiplicity of directions, he led them off and immediately turned the wrong way, and got more instruction shouted at him. It seemed to cheer the boys up somewhat, that dad was making such a hash of finding the way, and they pedalled after him, smirking.

We detoured from the G.R.46, to camp beside Lac de Vassivière, for some serious sunning and swimming before returning to Limoges and the bus for England. The camp site was mostly occupied by families with young children, under canvas or in motorhomes or caravans. There were no other walking backpackers like us, which explains the sentence Betty overheard, as a group passed by our pitch, *Là sont les marcheurs* (There are the walkers) — a rare breed! Posters, displayed everywhere, invited us to visit *Le Monde des Insectes* (The World of the Insects) at a village nearby. Somehow this particular tourist attraction lacked even more allure than most for us, who had, on and off over the last year, been fairly well bitten and stung by the more predatory of the insect community. On both nights at Broussas, the stars put on a wonderful display. Unfortunately there was competition from laser lights, probing long fingers into the sky from the east. From somewhere over there, were also the thumps and disjointed fragments of music - no doubt another tourist attraction. Fortunately by about 3.0am, the stars were left to their firmament and shone brilliantly, not to be outdone by such frippery.

In Limoges, the train arrived in the monstrous, 1920s Gare Benedictin. The interior of its huge hall was decorated with vast, slothful relief sculptures, symbolising the different regions of France, The windows were of a vapid, cinema-like stained glass. The exterior was a pastiche of styles, which succeeded only in being vulgar. The name of the station was the only monument to the Benedictine Monastery, that was destroyed to make way for it. In fact the station doesn't do justice as an introduction to an elegant city. There is an impressive cathedral, a number of surviving timber-framed houses and an unusual garden planted with all the medieval medicinal herbs. The city is principally known for its exquisite medieval enamels and its later fine porcelain.

The coach for London moved off precisely on time and conveyed us in reasonable comfort to a 5.0am ferry. It was all horribly smooth. We hardly knew we had left France and were on the ferry. The grey-white cliffs of Dover hove into view on an overcast morning, and there we were back in the 'sceptred isle' once more, with a tug at the heart strings and then a slow sinking feeling, realising that this was it, our long walk was almost finished.

A couple from near Shrewsbury, who had travelled with us, asked what it was like to see the white cliffs, and to be back in England again, after so long. I'm afraid that neither of us could summon up a great deal of enthusiasm. After all, it was 62 weeks since we had set sail on North Sea Ferries from Hull, and we could neither of us truthfully say that we had missed England very much. We had started out with high hopes on a long walk, not knowing how we would fare, whether we could cope with it and with one another, day after day. What had started in this way, had settled into a way of life. We found we could both cope with the walking and the transitory life, and that all that we saw and experienced together, strengthened the bonds between us. We took to this travelling life like ducks to water. So that it perhaps was not too surprising that when we saw those grey cliffs and realised that this particular journey was nearly at an end, we could not feel that great joy on returning home that travellers are supposed to feel. I guess we both felt and still feel that there is unfinished business.

Useful information, addresses and bibliography

Maps: *Michelin* 1:400,000 Nos.233, 234 & 235.

Topoguide 613 Sentier de St. Jacques, Cahors-Roncevaux GR65, GR652 (from FFRP) and GR46 Cahors-Turenne, local topoguide available in Cahors

Youth Hostel: 20 Rue Frédéric Suisse, 46000 Cahors.

... ENGLAND, AFTER ALL

To help us acclimatise to England once again and to look at some of the comparisons, we planned to walk up through eastern England on our way home. We left London on the evening train towards Kings Lynn. Our objective was Downham Market, where we would stop the night and start walking from there the following day. As we glided through the barley fields of Cambridgeshire, I thought of the Cambridgeshire man we had met on Calpe station months before. You can indeed walk a long way in a long time, just as he had said. We sped on through black fen to Ely, past Littleport, scene of martyrs, and got off the train into a warm still evening. The Crown at Downham Market was every bit as nice as we remembered. We slept quiet and sound in this old timber framed coaching inn. It wasn't too bad to be back in England after all.

Table of Distances

1. Downham Market - North Runcton	15.0km
2. North Runcton - Sutton Bridge	17.0km
3. Sutton Bridge - Woodhall Spa (bus)	80.0km
4. Woodhall Spa - Horncastle	9.0km
5. Horncastle - Ruckland	16.5km
6. Ruckland - Ludford Magna	21.0km
7. Ludford Magna - Caistor	18.0km

Day 1: Downham Market — North Runcton

We had decided to devise our own route round the Wash, starting at Downham Market, in order to link up with the Viking Way in Lincolnshire. For several miles we walked on a raised spit of land between the Great Ouse and the main drain to its east, which gave us expansive views in this flat countryside. The drainage works around there were carried out by the Dutchman Vermuyden, in the 17th century. They brought into cultivation an enormous area of the rich, flat, fen-land, which characterises this part of East Anglia. It was a hot and perfect day, and we realised how lucky we were to have come back to such good weather in unpredictable England.

After a morning's peaceful walking we picnicked by the river and came away from it at a ruined church, walking eastwards by lanes, to the main A10 at Setchey. There followed a long half mile of road walking, made hideous by traffic, before turning off eastwards along lanes that brought us to North Runcton. An old man, who obviously fancied himself on his new garden buggy with three huge rubber tyres, drew up on the road in front of us and started firing questions at us. When we had satisfied his curiosity, he gave us directions to the camp site, praising its qualities and the hospitable nature of its owner. His house was a large and rather flashy new bungalow, facing out on to the common. It had two tall flag poles and a wooden sign over the gateway styling it something like, Topknobs Manor. It was fairly obvious, that his main motivation for giving us accurate directions, was to make sure that we didn't spoil his view, by camping on the common. Even with his directions we nearly missed the place. It had just one motor-home on a large grass field with mature trees, and a small shower block, but no notices announcing it to be a camp site. Mr. Yuppam, its proud owner, welcomed us with the enthusiasm of someone new to the game. He was quite flabbergasted when he heard who had directed us there and that he had praised the camp site, because it sounded like the person who had opposed his planning application. Mr. Yuppam showed us the facilities of the site, like a child with a new toy, then gave us directions to a local pub where we could eat and asked us to mention that he had sent us. He went away chuckling to himself; our news had obviously made his day.

Day 2: North Runcton — Sutton Bridge
In the morning it was misty and dewy, suggesting a hot day to come. We braced ourselves for an unavoidable two miles of road walking along the A47 to Kings Lynn. On the way to the little passenger ferry that took us across the Ouse to the start of the Sir Peter Scott Walk, we had a passing view of the fine 18th century brick houses of this prosperous port. Then we walked out along the dead straight Ouse outfall, where there were clouds of butterflies, Painted Ladies and

Tortoiseshells, on the thistles along the bank. We picnicked, watching the potato-pickers hard at work. The going was along stretches of sea bank, two to three miles long, and the next slight angle in these massive bulwarks against the sea, was always just about discernible in the haze ahead. After the potatoes, there was no more human interest for hours, while we walked along, looking down on barley to our left and salt marsh to our right, as far as the eye could see. There was no view of the sea.

Peter Scott Way

Then in the haze ahead of us, on the seaward side of our bank, various darker splodges gradually composed themselves into a recognisable herd of cattle grazing on the salt marsh. Two posts beside them resolved themselves into human form, and after a while we could decipher a group of three figures close to one of the cattle, which was lying down. All this looked like a nice family group, the farmer, his wife and daughter, out checking their herd. But then the beast tried to get up, staggered and fell back. As we came closer we saw it try again and noticed that it was a bull. Doubtless the farmer was wondering what to do for the best with this sick animal, far from any help. The heat and the afternoon haze closed around this dramatic interlude as we slogged on with little to divert us.

There was the occasional swift passage of a group of ducks, or oyster catchers. Herons rose lazily from the salt marsh and curlews got up in groups from the bank ahead of us, making their beautiful liquid calls. We angled gradually round, in long straights, to start the final turn in towards the new cut of the river Nene. Eventually, we spotted the lighthouses on either side of the river, built for no better purpose than to commemorate the new cut of the river. As we worked our way steadily towards them, we encountered several people from another world, strolling out towards us in the evening sun. This was a sure sign that a car park was not far off. After 12 miles of nothing it was a welcome sight to see one's fellow humans again.

I had thought that the eastern lighthouse, which in the 1930s had been home to Peter Scott, would contain a display in memory of the work which he had done there, to study the migratory birds, for which the Wash is internationally famous. But instead there were private notices and barbed wire everywhere. That walk did not seem a worthy memorial. No one in their right minds would choose to undertake it as a linear walk. It certainly cured me of my enthusiasm for continuing along the sea banks to Boston, much to Betty's relief.

Day 3: Sutton Bridge — Woodhall Spa
Sitting in the hot sun, we waited for the Spalding bus. Our revised plans were to get to Boston by bus and then on to somewhere to pick up the Viking Way, a long-distance footpath across the Lincolnshire Wolds, which would take us close to home. This left us time to sample some excellent fish and chips, sitting in the deep shade provided by Boston Stump. This is the rather unattractive name given to the soaring tower of Boston's magnificent parish church. We watched the Saturday afternoon wedding parties come and go, assembling for photographs on the grass outside. I marvelled once again at this lofty tower, the crowing glory of an outstanding church. A recent plaque, at last commemorates the famous Elizabethan musician, John Taverner, a former organist there.

The bus took us out through the barley fields to Woodhall Spa, set in its peaceful woods. From its sleepy centre we walked out to camp at Bainland Country Park. Though we were distinctly out of place in this gathering of the latest in motor homes and caravans, we were grateful for a reasonably priced pitch, with all the facilities.

Day 4: Woodhall Spa — Horncastle

Woodhall Spa with its quiet and beautiful woods, exuded a peaceful and relaxing atmosphere, but this was spoilt by the unnecessary number of 'private' and 'keep out' notices everywhere. Woodhall became a spa in the early 19th century, when a local farmer prospecting for coal, found instead water with health giving minerals, bromine and iodine. It was interesting to speculate just how different it would have been, if he'd found his coal. It wouldn't have been such a pretty place, certainly. There would have been pitheads, strikes and slag-heaps, instead of snobbery, private notices and golf courses. After a while, the old railway line ran side by side with the disused canal, both of them monuments to 19th century optimism. As we approached Horncastle, the canal was full of yellow water-lilies.

Day 5: Horncastle — Ruckland

Old paths with battered iron seats on them, took us around the edge of housing estates on the north side of Horncastle. Then we were out on open farm tracks, leaving West Ashby to our left, as we climbed easily and steadily on to the Wolds, the low rolling chalk uplands and cereal growing belt of Lincolnshire. A really tedious stretch followed, with several right angle zigzags, taking us round the edge of huge fields, where the verges had virtually no wild flowers and the cultivation was uniformly dull arable. You felt no sense of an on-going path, just that you were there on sufferance, on a track negotiated by a Footpaths Officer, with reluctant farmers, in order to get you from Horncastle to Fulletby. The old footpaths, which took farm workers from their homes to their place of work had long since gone. Then there was a good up and down stretch to Belchford. We passed a field of splendid vigorous hemp plants growing to around three metres, whose vivid green foliage made a welcome change from the cereals all around it. On the slopes, which were too steep for the heavy machinery of cereal cultivation, meadows with cattle and sheep added a little variety to the landscape.

Belchford had quite a focal centre, with a pub and post office next door to one another. On the way up Park Hill we found a good shady spot to have our lunch. We were just starting to tuck in heartily, when an old man, who, unbeknown to us, had followed us up from Belchford, appeared at the stile. He was a local man, on his way to visit a friend at Scamblesby and had obviously been using this path long before the Viking Way was invented. We were a captive audience and he wanted to talk. Having left school at 14, he had done all sorts of jobs, first working as a ploughboy. He wanted us to guess his age, and I erred safely on the young side. He was in fact 70 and obviously proud of his fitness. *I've just cooked myself cabbage and potatoes for my dinner*, he said with deep satisfaction, as if there could be nothing finer. *They give rain for tomorrow, so I'm going to visit my friend today instead.* Amongst the many jobs he had done, he had been a lay preacher and had taken funeral services. As a result he claimed to know all the hymns in the book by heart. For an awful minute we thought that he was going to sing them all to us. As he left us to climb effortlessly to the top of Park Hill, he unexpectedly took out a cigarette and lit up. He seemed a man of habit, and perhaps if we had not been there, he would have stopped at the style, once over it, leant on it, lit up and checked the view back over his village for the hundredth time, familiar but always satisfying.

Scamblesby has a straggle of suburban houses and bungalows, spreading out a mile and more to the south of its centre. We turned off to the right, before getting into the village proper, to climb steeply up Ramsgate Hill towards the Youth Hostel at Woody's Top. We came then to an arable plateau, which had vast fields and had been stripped more or less completely of hedges and other landscape features. Combine harvesters crawled in tiny clouds of dust over this huge dehumanised, arable desert. We had seen nothing as extreme as this in all our travels. At Maidenwell, consisting only of a farm, down a track, a pair of farm workers' cottages, a disused school and a phone box, we halted to check our route. A kid passing on a bike put us right. Pointing to the only group of trees to be seen, way over on the horizon, he said, *I think it's over there*.

The kid was right, the trees seen on the horizon were a lovely coppice of beech, beside which we found the Youth Hostel. Once arrived, there was no question that it had been worth the five mile trudge from the Viking Way. Woody's Top was a very special place, with an intimate and welcoming air. We cooked in the communal kitchen- cum-dining area and chatted to the other hostellers and the warden and partner. The sun set and the outlines of this prairie land softened. We slept with the door open. It was one of the most perfect night skies for ages, the stars having no competition from lights on Earth.

Day 6: Ruckland — Ludford Magna

William Cobbett passing through this area in the 1830s, observed that the houses were white and thatched. They were made from easily weathered chalk blocks. Virtually none of these now remain, and they have given way to characterless modern housing. A great shame. Biscathorpe lake, must be one of the best stretches of the Viking Way. There we watched the combines and following tractors and trailers on the horizon, looking for all the world like moving castles. Someone was crouching down, reaching below the water level, at the grills of the downstream end of the lake. He was after freshwater crayfish. *You can tell them by their red colour underneath*, he confided, and he picked one up to show me. While he held it up, it was reaching round with its pincers, trying to find its captor. He had a net of them, all about four inches long.

We walked on past the extraordinary little church of Biscathorpe, a 19th century Strawberry Hill Gothic gem, alone amongst the pastures. All that is left of the medieval village of Biscathorpe is a series of grassy mounds and platforms, by which we walked up to the woods beyond. The Viking Way continued on farm tracks past a lone barrow, Grim's Mound, and as we turned west down the valley towards East Wykeham, the weather began to look ominous. It was a long haul up past Girsby Top farm, on the other side of this valley and by then it had started to rain. It settled in, came steady and then heavy, as we trudged the last three miles or so into Ludford.

Day 7: Ludford Magna — Caistor

We passed the ruins of Bayon's Manor, once a grandiose Victorian mansion, which belonged to the Tennyson family. In the churchyard of the rather self-consciously pretty, village of Tealby, we briefly occupied the seat outside the church for a cuppa. As the vicar passed with his family in tow, bringing flower arrangements to his church, we got a long down-the-nose look and no reply to our 'good morning'. We thought of the old country sacristan we had met in Spain — rude and rough he may have been but he welcomed all.

At the Ramblers' Church at Walesby, we couldn't squeeze our packs through the kissing gate and realised, with some amusement, that it had not been built for our sort of long term traveller. Dog turd disposal bins on the way down from the church and into the village, added to our feeling that it was a bit over-refined. But an old countryman, a lay preacher, gave a different impression of Walesby. He hoped it was going to keep fine, because he'd got a funeral at Stainton-le-Vale. *The last rites are always much pleasanter, when performed in good weather*, he said, as he filled our water bottles.

We climbed the flank of the Wolds, to the ridge where we picnicked in warm wind and fitful sun, with a long view down to Lincoln cathedral sitting atop the limestone escarpment. Bowling along these open tops, we passed Normanby-le-Wold, reminiscing about times past and my excavations of a Saxon settlement there. Bernadette, who had been visiting us at that time, had said when we met her again in France, *C'était une belle époque* (That was a great time).

As we approached Caistor, we decided to end our long walk there. It was time to get back for the family reunion that awaited us. At the Red Lion, where the new owners were in the midst of doing the place up, we were offered the upstairs function room, into which they would put a bed after the motor cycle club had finished their meeting that evening. When our function room was free, we straight away slept, on the bed that had been made up for us on the dance floor below the disco lights. A fittingly bizarre resting place for our last night on the trail.

Useful information, addresses and bibliography

Youth Hostel: Woody's Top, Ruckland, nr. Louth Lincs.

Peter Scott Walk Booklet, Kings Lynn Tourist Office, Kings Lynn, Norfolk.

The Viking Way by Stead. Cicerone Press.

Long Distance Walkers' Handbook, 5th Edition 1994, published A & C Black.(UK footpath network)

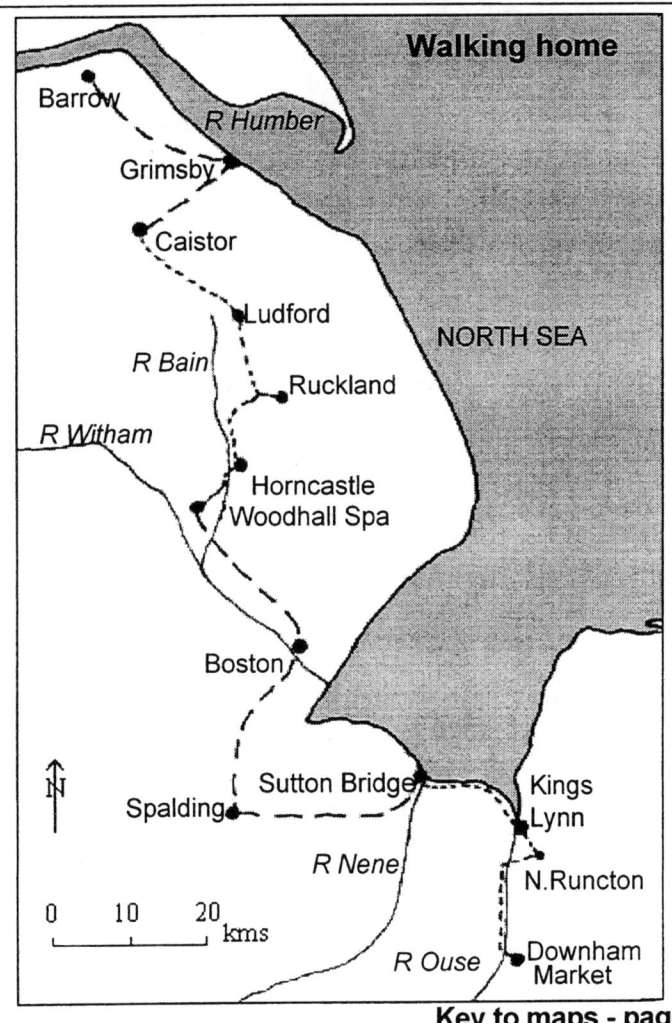

Walking home

Key to maps - page 27

Afterwords

AFTERWORDS

The grand tourist commonly returns home more conceited, more unprincipled, more dissipated, and more incapable of any serious application, either to business or study, than he could well have become in so short a time had he lived at home.

Adam Smith.

We can only assume that this was sour grapes on the part of Adam Smith. For us it was a risk at our age, but a great adventure which came off. It certainly has an unsettling effect as people had warned. But the overall feeling was one of great satisfaction in having done something for ourselves that we had long wanted to do. There are too many people who will say, that there are no more big adventures left, but the truth is that you have to make your own.

There was a growing sense for us as we travelled, of feeling at home in Europe. It was also instructive to see England from the outside. From the perspective of the BBC World Service, there was seldom a mention of England — a Bradford riot, a leadership bid, an IRA bomb, was about all. Being in Europe and feeling part of it, it was disconcerting to see the isolationist attitudes of the British government within the European Community, and the embarrassing xenophobia of the tabloid press, especially at the time of the World Cup football game against Germany. From setting off on an adventure to travel to unknown foreign parts, our perceptions changed to feeling just as much at home here as in England. This particularly applied to Spain which we feel had been given a bad press. English people are given to pronouncing on Spain, but anyone who pronounces on it today will be out of date tomorrow as it is rapidly changing.

The question we are most frequently asked is, how did you two get on together? Somehow people seem to feel that once you step outside the norm, they are permitted to ask these impertinent questions! If we hadn't got on together we wouldn't be sitting here writing these 'afterwords', because it wouldn't have worked. It is also true that we got to know one another as never before. Obviously, as in any relationship, we had to work at it. There was damage limitation on conflicts and a degree of delicate neogtiation necessary. Whilst we were travelling, there was an interesting review of a book about the esprit de corps of military groups, who trained and marched together, suggesting that part of this effect was achieved through effort in unison. Though in no way thinking of ourselves as a military unit, a similar bonding effect was undoubtedy achieved by all our tramping together.

Calpe, Alicante, March 1997

Ben & Betty Whitwell

INDEX OF PLACE NAMES

Aguas, Rio de 171
Aiglun 46-52
Alaric, Montaigne d' 100-102
Albufera, Lake 139-140
Alhambra 158-159
Alicante 144-149,221
Almeria 148,160-170,180-181
Alpilles, Canal des 72-76
Alpilles (mountains) 71,75
Alps (mountains) 26-36
Alpujarras (mountains) 158-168
Alto do Poyo 197-203
Anduze 74,81-84
Apúlia 191
Arca 197-198
Arre River 88
Arzúa 197-199
Aspremont 46-47
Aubusson 236-240
Aude River 97
Auron 39
Ayes, Col des, 30-34

Barcelona 117,128-133,217
Barrow (-on-Humber) 97
Beaucaire 76-80
Belfort 16
Belorado 217-219
Berga 114,122-123
Blainon, Col du 39
Boduen 61
Bonette, Col de 36-37
Boston 246
Bousieyas 31-37
Briançon 30-31
Brunissard 31-32
Burgos 197,213-217
Burguete 217,228-229

Cádiar 161-167
Cahors 221-237
Caistor 243,250
Calasparra 149-155
Calpe 136-148,243
Calzadilla de la Cueza 197,210-211
Cambrils 134
Camino de Santiago (see Pilgrim Routes)
Camino Francés (see Pilgrim Route)
Camoes, Luis Vaz de 184
Canigou (mountain) 108
Caramany 100-108
Caravaca 149-156
Carcassonne 87-100,237
Carluc, Priory of 65
Carrión de los Condes 197,211-212
Castel d'Areny 122-124
Castellane 47-53
Castrojeríz 197,212-213
Catalonia 111,127-131
Cathar, Sentier 106
Ceillac 31-36
Céreste 58-69
Cevennes (mountains) 74-87
Chamesol 18
Chamonix 29
Chapelle-des-Bois 17,24-25
Chasteuil 54
Château Durfort 100-103
Château Queyras 31-33
Cizur Major 217-226
Colestre River 62
Collias 74,78
Colognac 74,82

254   Europe at walking pace

Colombière, Col de 37
Condom 234-236
Corbières 100-107
Cordillera Cantabrica (mountains) 09-210
Courtefontaine 18
Couzou 237-238
Crousette, Col de 40

Deltebre 135
Dio 87-90
Dordogne River 239
Doubs River 18-24
Douro River 189
Downham Market 243
Dranse River 28-29
Duilhac 100-106
Durance River 35,63,71,76

E4 (long-distance footpath) 154
Ebro Delta 134-139
Ebro River 135
El Burgo Ranero 197,208-210
Elda 148-150
El Palmar 139
Estella 217,221-223
Esternay River 52
Err 114-116
Evian 63
Eygalières 59,71-72

Falgars, Santuari de 114,119-121
Feches-le-Châtel 17
Fenouillèdes 100,107
Fessevillers 17-19
Figuera da Foz 187
Fontaine-de-Vaucluse 58,67-69
Francoli River 134
Fromage, Col, 33-34
Frómista 197,212

Galibier, Col 30
Galicia 162,194-197,204
Gardon, Gorge de 78
Gardon (Gard) River 74-81
Garraf National Park 133
Gattières 47
Girardin, Col, 33-40
Gluges 239
Gordes 58,67
Goumois 19
GR4(long-distance footpath) 49,52-65,122
GR5 16-47,97
GR6 65-84
GR7 84-97
GR46 234-240
GR36 94-107,116
GR51 47-49
GR65 232-236
GR99 60
Granada 153-162
Grasse 47-49
Greollières 47-50
Gréoux-les-Bains 58,63,91
GR(Spain)4 117-128
GR(Spain)4.2 120
GR(Spain)7 147,148-157
GR(Spain)65 221
GR(Spain)92 133-134
Guardiola 114-120
Guillestre 31-35
Guil River 35

Haute Savoie 28
Horncastle 243-247
Hull 16,97,241
Humber River 16

Ibañete, Col de 228
Ille-sur-Têt 107-109

Jalon 140-147
Jausiers 31-37
Jumilla 149-153
Jura 16,19,28,72

Kings Lynn 244

Labastide Murat 237
Labastide Rouairoux 87-95
La Carcassé 100-105
Lac Leman 26-28
La Côtote 17-20
Lac St. Croix 59
Lac Saint Point 24
La Cure 26
Lagrasse 100-102
Lamalou-les-Bains 87-91
Lamanon 59,71
La Molina 114-118
L'Ampolla 134
Lanjaron 161-162
La Palud-sur-Verdon 46-59
La Pobla de Lillet 114-119
La Quar 114-124
La Vacquerie 87-94
Le Bief de la Chaille 17,25
León 197-208
Les Alliés 23
Les Hopitaux Neufs 24
L'Esperou 74,84
Les Plantiers 74,82-83
Les Rousses 25-26
Les Salles 58-60
Le Vigan 74-88
Limoges 239-241
Lisbo(n)a 183-189
Llobregat River 120-27
Lodève 87-89
Logroño 217-221
Longons, Refuge des 31-42
Los Arcos 217-221
Los Molinos 171-176

Lozère 83
Lubéron (mountain) 64-70
Ludford Magna 243-250

Malbuisson 17,24
Mallemort, Col 36
Manosque 58-64
Manresa 114,126-128
Mansilla de las Mulas 197,208
Maubec 59,68-70
Medieval 90,139
Melide 197-200
Mercantour, Parc National 35-38
Mérindol 59,69-70
Midi, Canal du 81-97
Minho/Miño River 192,201
Modane 29
Monbenoît 17,22
Monistrol de Montserrat 114,128
Monóvar 149-150
Mons 91
Mont Aigoual 74-84
Mont Blanc 20-29
Montgenèvre 30-31
Montlaur 100-101
Mont Louis 112-116
Montserrat (mountains) 127-128
Mont Thabor 30
Moratalla 149-156
Moulines, Col des 41
Moussac 74-80
Moustière 59
Mouthe 17-25
Mozarabic 147
Mulhacén (mountain) 164
Murcia 148,221

Nájera 217-221
Narbonne 101
Navacelles 87-88
Navarrenx 233
Nazaré 186

Nene River 246
Nice 16-18,40-47,76
Nîmes 78-79
Nore, Pic de 87-101
North Runcton 243-244
Nyon 17,26-28

O Cebreiro 203-204
Olargues 87-93,
Oliva 145-153
Oppedette 58,65
Orgiva 161-163
Ostabat 232
Ouse River 243-244

Padrón 193-194
Palas de Rei 197-201
Pal, Collado del 119
Pampaneira 161-164
Pamplona 217,225-229
Pedreguer 140
Peñiscola 137
Peñon de Ifach 141-145
Perpignan 100-116
Peyrepertuse, Château de 105-106
Pilgrim Route(s) 148,196-231
Pinoso 148-152
Poble Nou 136,-37
Ponferrada 197,206-207
Pontarlier 1723
Pontevedra 193
Pont du Gard 78
Pont St. Nicholas 74-79
Porto 185-190,236
Portomarín 197-202
Póvoa de Varzim 190
Praia de Vieira 187
Pre-Alps (mountains) 46,53
Puente la Reina 217-224
Puigcerdà 114-117
Puigreig 114-127
Pyrenees (mountains) 16,68,87,96-127,185,203,225-236

Queribus, Château 105

Redondela 192
Régua 189-190
Remoulins 74-78
Rhône River 46,71-76
Riez 58-61
Rocamadour 234
Roncesvalles 217-229
Rougon 47,54
Rousillon 58-67
Roustrel 58-66
Roya 31-40
Ruckland 243-249

Sagas 114-126
Sagunto 138,153
Sahagún 197,210
Sainte Mère 235
San Miguel, Collado 120,121
Santiago (de Compostela) 180-228
Sant du Doubs 20
Santo Domingo 217-219
Sant Vicenç de Castellet 114,128
Sao Jacinto 188-189
Sao Martinho do Porto 185
Sarria 197-203
Sauvelade 233
Sénanque, Abbaye de 67
Sierra Nevada (mountains) 156161
Sir Peter Scott Walk 244
Sorbas 171-176
Sorgue River 68
Soule Cernay 18
St. Andreaux 58-61
St. Auban 47-52
St. Croix 58-61
St. Dalmas de Selvage 37
St. Etienne de Grès 74-75
St. Etienne de Tinée 31-38

Index   257

St. Hippolyte 17-18
St. Jeannet 47-48
St. Jean Pied de Port 217-236
St. Juan de Ortega 217-220
St. Martin des Brômes 58-62
St. Palais 233
St. Paul de Fenouillet 100-107
St. Paul-sur-Ubaye 31-36
St. Pons de Thomières 87-94
St. Rémy de Provence 59-75
St. Sauveur de Tinée 31-43
Sunseed Desert Project 148,170-180
Sutton Bridge 243-246

Tarascon 74-78
Tarragona 117,133-134
Tavernes de la Valdigne 140
Tejo River 183
Têt River 109-115
Thonon-les-Bains 28,63
Tocha 188
Tourette 48-49
Trevélez 161-166
Triacastelo 197,203
Tui 192-194
Turenne 239
Turia River 139

Ugíjar 161-168

Valença 192
Valencia 138-149,217,
Valloire 30
Vallonet, Col 36

Valmeinier 30
Vandoncourt 17,18
Vanoise Massif 29
Vars, Col de 35
Vars-les-Claux 35
Vars River 35,47
Vassivière, Lac de 240
Vaucluse, Plateau de 66-68
Vega de Valcarce 197-205
Vegay 50-51
Vence 48
Verdon, Canyon de 55
Verdon, Gorge de 46,59
Verdon River 53-63
Verdouble River 105
Vers River 236
Vézénobres 74-81
Viana do Castello 192
Victoriano, Collado de 150
Vieux Chateleu 17-22
Vignols 41-42
Viking Way 243-246
Vilada 114-122
Villafranca del Bierzo 197-221
Villard St. Pancrace 31-32
Villeneuve Minevois 88-97
Villers Blamont 18
Villers-le-Lac 17-21
Vis River 87

Woodhall Spa 243-247

Zeebrugge 16
Zubiri 217-226

Third Age Press

The independent publishing company inspired by thirdagers

The Third Age is the period of life after full-time, gainful employment and family responsibility. Nowadays, it may last for thirty years or more and should be a time of fulfilment and continuing personal development . . . a time of regeneration.

Third Age Press exists to provide materials to encourage that regeneration. We hope that our publications will also give pleasure and lead the users into many rewarding pursuits.

Dianne Norton
Managing Editor

Third Age Press books are available from good bookshops or Third Age Press, 6 Parkside Gardens, London SW19 5EY

All prices include UK P & P. Please add 20% for other countries. Sterling cheques payable to *Third Age Press*, please.

... the first series published by Third Age Press. It is specifically designed to stimulate reflection ... to see the lines that connect your life not only to the past, but to the present and future as well. We hope it will encourage you to record, in some fashion, a picture of a unique individual.

by Eric Midwinter

A Voyage of Rediscovery: a guide to writing your life story

A Voyage of Rediscovery is a 'sea chart' to guide your reminiscence. It offers 'triggers' to set your memory to full steam ahead (although backwards might be more appropriate) & provides practical advice about the business of writing or recording your story.

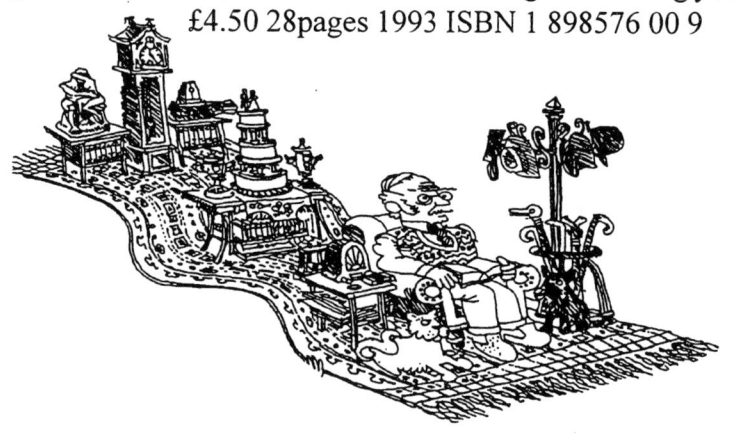

£4.50 28pages 1993 ISBN 1 898576 00 9

perspectives

.. offers a comprehensive publishing service for people wanting to produce a memoir for sale or one beautiful heirloom book for their family. Marketing is up to you (should you wish to distribute to a wider public). Every project is individually priced and given expert, personal attention. Write to Third Age Press for details.

On the Tip of Your Tongue: your memory in later life
by Dr H B Gibson

... a book written particularly for older people about memory. Dr Gibson (a mere octogenarian himself) explores memory's history and examines what an 'ordinary' person can expect of their memory. He reveals the truth behind myths about memory and demonstrates how you can manage your large stock of memories and your life. Wittily illustrated by Rufus Segar.

£7.00 160pages 1995 ISBN 1 898576 05X

> ... Unlike much of the self-improvement literature I have come across, Gibson's book seems to me to be immensely practical and reassuring.
>
> Colin Ward, New Statesman

Special offer
Buy any **two** of the following books ~
On the tip of your tongue ~A little of what you fancy ~ Consider the alternatives ~ Changes and challenges
and get 20% off the total price

A Little of What You Fancy Does You Good: your health in later life
by Dr H B Gibson
illustrated by Rufus Segar

'Managing an older body is like running a very old car ~ as the years go by you get to know its tricks and how to get the best out of it, so that you may keep it running sweetly for years and years' . . . so says Dr H B Gibson in his new book . . . a sensible and practical book which respects your intelligence and above all appreciates the need to enjoy later life. It explains the whys, hows and wherefores of exercise, diet and sex ~ discusses 'You and your doctor' and deals with some of the pitfalls and disabilities of later life. But the overall message is positive and Rufus Segar's illustrations once again bring whimsy and insight to a very readable text. £8.50 256 pages Illustrated by Rufus Segar 1997 ISBN 1 898576

So it's great to be grey; and this new book . . . could become the essential manual for every grown-up, whether they admit to feeling old or not.
Vintage Times

. . . a broad-ranging book . . . reassuring and cheering.
Saga Magazine

Consider the alternatives ~ healthy strategies for later life

Dr Caroline Nash

Acupuncture, Bach Flower Remedies, Chiropractics... it's not as simple as ABC but this book offers a clear and unbiased explanation of the nature and uses of alternative therapies... what you can expect from complementary medicine... and why yoga, tai chi, pets, music and humour can contribute to your personal strategy for a healthy old age. Dr Nash, from a wealth of experience, looks particularly at conditions that affect people in later life and explores a wide range of possible treatments. The book has two other contributors.
Dr Michael Lloyd, psychologist and pain management specialist believes that choosing one's own mental and physical responses to pain is a central element of pain management since chronic pain is a mind/body phenomena.

Conventional medicine has an important role to play but if you are dissatisfied with your health care or just want to try something different, as pensioner *Tony Carter* points out, this book will help you take control of your own health.

ISBN 1 898576 114   Price   1998
£10.00

Changes and challenges in later life ~ learning from experience

Older people share with those of all ages the desire for fulfilment - a need to transform surviving into thriving. This book brings together experts from Britain's major caring organisations to share their wealth of experience and practical advice on situations of later life.

Contents

Learning from Experience	Claire Rayner
Making the Most of Change	Mervyn Kohler
Who Cares?	Jill Pitkeathley
Neighbours	Archana Srivastava & Yvonne Craig
The Right Retirement Home	Rudi Reeves
Care Homes, Residents and Relatives	Jenny Stiles
Mistreatment and Neglect	Frank Glendenning
Legal Rights and Remedies	Barbara Beaton
A Good Ending	Gillian Dalley

Yvonne Craig (ed), illustrated by Maggie Guillon. 1997 160 pp. £10.00.

And now . . . for something completely different!

No Thanks to Lloyd George
The forgotten story ~ how the old age pension was won

A new edition to celebrate the 90th anniversary of the Old Age Pension Act

by Dave Goodman ~ Foreword by Jack Jones

1998   99pp.   £3.60   ISBN 1 898576 12 2